A HISTORY

OF

LOVE AND HATE

IN

21 STATUES

A HISTORY

OF

LOVE AND HATE

IN

21 STATUES

PETER HUGHES

Aurum

First published in the UK in 2021 by Aurum
An imprint of The Quarto Group

The Old Brewery, 6 Blundell Street
London N7 9BH, United Kingdom
T (0)20 7700 6700
www.QuartoKnows.com/Aurum

British Library Cataloguing-in-Publication Data
A catalogue record for this book is available from the British Library.

ISBN: 978-0-7112-6612-4
E-book ISBN: 978-0-7112-6614-8
Audio book ISBN: 978-0-7112-6615-5

Printed and bound by CPI Group (UK) Ltd, Croydon, CR0 4YY
1 3 5 7 9 10 8 6 4 2

For Sara,
with all my love

When the light dove parts the air in free flight and feels the air's resistance, it might come to think that it would do much better still in space devoid of air.

IMMANUEL KANT
Critique of Pure Reason

CONTENTS

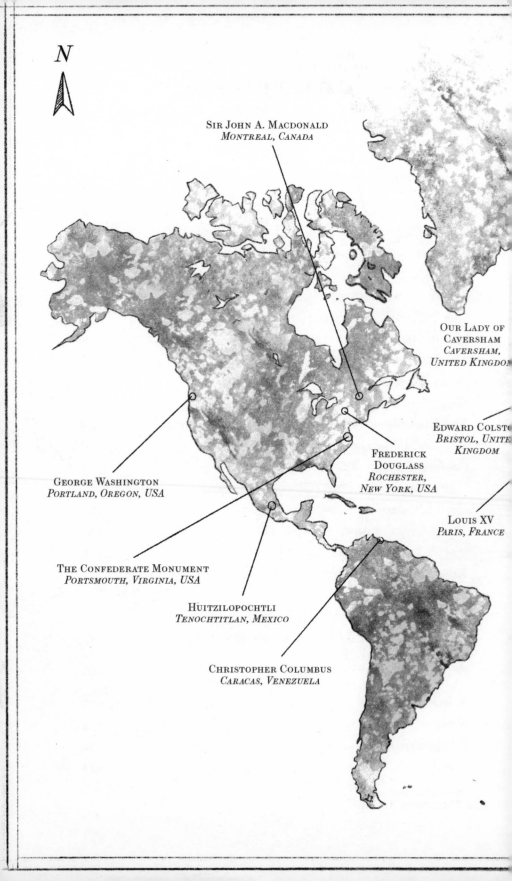

N

SIR JOHN A. MACDONALD
MONTREAL, CANADA

OUR LADY OF
CAVERSHAM
*CAVERSHAM,
UNITED KINGDOM*

EDWARD COLSTON
*BRISTOL, UNITED
KINGDOM*

FREDERICK
DOUGLASS
*ROCHESTER,
NEW YORK, USA*

GEORGE WASHINGTON
PORTLAND, OREGON, USA

LOUIS XV
PARIS, FRANCE

THE CONFEDERATE MONUMENT
PORTSMOUTH, VIRGINIA, USA

HUITZILOPOCHTLI
TENOCHTITLAN, MEXICO

CHRISTOPHER COLUMBUS
CARACAS, VENEZUELA

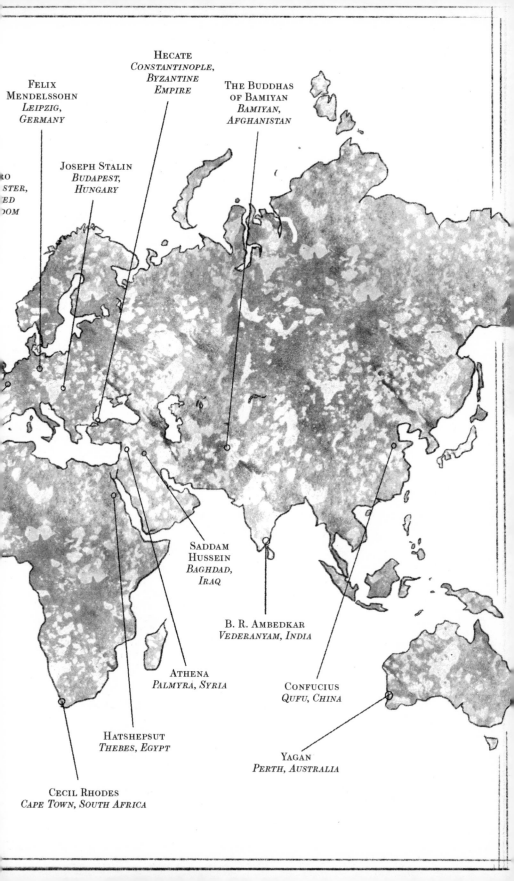

FELIX
MENDELSSOHN
*LEIPZIG,
GERMANY*

HECATE
*CONSTANTINOPLE,
BYZANTINE
EMPIRE*

THE BUDDHAS
OF BAMIYAN
*BAMIYAN,
AFGHANISTAN*

JOSEPH STALIN
*BUDAPEST,
HUNGARY*

RO
STER,
ED
OOM

SADDAM
HUSSEIN
*BAGHDAD,
IRAQ*

B. R. AMBEDKAR
VEDERANYAM, INDIA

ATHENA
PALMYRA, SYRIA

CONFUCIUS
QUFU, CHINA

HATSHEPSUT
THEBES, EGYPT

YAGAN
PERTH, AUSTRALIA

CECIL RHODES
CAPE TOWN, SOUTH AFRICA

INTRODUCTION

Lone and Level Sands

On 22 May 1538, a large crowd gathered in the sunshine as an extraordinary procession made its way through Smithfield in London. The site had witnessed many executions of heretics and dissidents, including the disembowelling of the Scottish knight, William Wallace and the beheading of Wat Tyler, one of the leaders of the Peasants' Revolt. But never before had it seen such a strange double execution as that about to take place.

A month earlier, Thomas Cromwell, chief minister to King Henry VIII, ordered the removal of a large wooden statue from a remote Welsh church. He did so in support of the king's wish to annul his marriage to Catherine of Aragon and to hasten the break with Rome and the Papacy that this would entail. Relentless in his destruction of Catholic 'idolatry', Cromwell arranged for the statue of Saint Derfel Gadarn (Derfel the Mighty) to be transported to London.

In Welsh folklore, Derfel was one of seven warriors who survived the fateful Battle of Camlan, at which the legendary King Arthur is said to have died. Perhaps haunted by the experience, Derfel entered the monastic life and died in 660. By 1538, the saint's statue at his church at Llandderfel had become a focus for pilgrimages and this was sufficient reason for Cromwell to order its removal.

At the same time as Derfel Gadarn's statue was making its way from the Welsh mountains to London, John Forest, a Franciscan friar and confessor to Catherine of Aragon, was sentenced to death for his refusal to acknowledge King Henry as head of the Church in England.

On 22 May, friar and statue had a gruesome meeting.

It began, according to an account by Father Thaddeus[1], with the statue being carried 'by eight men, and three executioners holding it tight with ropes, in the manner of a criminal condemned to death'. The statue was thrown onto a pile of wood above which the chained figure of John Forest was suspended in a cage.

Hugh Latimer, the bishop of Worcester, gave a sermon urging the condemned man to recant. When he refused, the bonfire was lit. The vast crowd watched as the statue and Friar Forest turned to ash, fulfilling an ancient prophecy that claimed the 'holy image of Derfel Gadarn would set a forest on fire'. The life of a man and the statue that symbolised his identity and values, were consumed in the same fire.

Almost 500 years after the burning of John Forest and Derfel Gadarn, the poet Percy Bysshe Shelley and his friend, the banker Horace Smith, wrote competing sonnets based on a passage from the Greek historian Diodorus Siculus. In his *Bibliotheca Historica*, Diodorus described three statues discovered in the tomb of an Egyptian king, one of which bore an inscription, 'I am Ozymandias, king of kings; if any would know how great I am, and where I lie, let him surpass any of my works.'[2] Ozymandias is the Greek name for Ramesses II, one of the greatest of Egyptian pharaohs. Diodorus describes his statue as 'the greatest in all Egypt, the measure of his foot exceeding seven cubits'.[3]

Of the two sonnets written about this great ruler, Smith's is forgotten, while Shelley's is one of the most famous poems in the English language:

> *I met a traveller from an antique land*
> *Who said: Two vast and trunkless legs of stone*
> *Stand in the desert. Near them, on the sand,*
> *Half sunk, a shattered visage lies, whose frown,*

And wrinkled lip, and sneer of cold command,
Tell that its sculptor well those passions read
Which yet survive, stamped on these lifeless things,
The hand that mocked them and the heart that fed:
And on the pedestal these words appear:
'My name is Ozymandias, king of kings:
Look on my works, ye Mighty, and despair!'
Nothing beside remains. Round the decay
Of that colossal wreck, boundless and bare
The lone and level sands stretch far away.

The vanity of the 'king of kings', his command to his enemies to 'despair' at the scale of his power, contrast with the 'lone and level sands' that 'stretch far away'. This return of power to the dust from which it rose is the spectre behind every throne and Ramesses II dedicated his life to defying that dust. He erected so many statues and shrines to magnify his glory, that his builders ran out of stone. Undaunted, he ordered them to destroy the temples, monuments and statues of his predecessors and requisition the stone for his own use. It culminated in four enormous 21-metre-high statues of himself at the entrance to the Temple at Abu Simbel in the far south of Egypt. Inevitably, his labours were in vain. By the time 'an antique traveller' came across the remnants of his greatness, all that remained were 'two vast and trunkless legs of stone'.

When serving the grandiose fantasies of tyrants like Ramesses II, Joseph Stalin or Saddam Hussein, statues 'dominate, impress and intimidate'.[4] When their function is more benign, statues define and sustain our identity through time. They tell us who we are and who we are not. They are our beliefs, values and memories sculpted in marble, stone and metal. However, throughout history, where the very idea of 'our identity' is contested, statues have become a stimulus for grievance and hostility. The stories in this book are stories of the collision of identities, which are unable or unwilling to reason and compromise. The result is a rapid descent into intolerance and violence. Where we are unable to share or forgive events in the past, we are less likely to live to share a future. 'It is possible,' wrote Czesław Miłosz, 'that there is no other memory than the memory of wounds'[5] and no society can survive the endless excavation of past injustice. Collapse is inevitable, fuelled by a retreat into identity groups whose self-love and cohesion are predicated on punishing those they accuse of harm and oppression. The destruction of statues is a marker of this collapse.

Yet, for much of our lives, we give little thought to the statues that surround us. As the historian David Olusoga claimed, 'statues for the most part don't matter. We walk past them every day, they're grey, and they're boring.'[6] They stand as harmless historical relics. 'Most of them,' he concluded, 'are benign and they're benign to me but I can accept that some of them are not benign to other people.' However, Olusoga's 'grey' and 'boring' statues have a sting in the tail. Whenever social cohesion fractures, they leap out from the background of our lives. Whether we protect or destroy them, they become the stone and steel on which we carve our warring identities.

Today, even as the facts bear witness to the progressive tolerance shown by liberal democracies, mobs gnaw at the imperfect foundations that keep our societies standing. We are like the travellers in Charles Baudelaire's poem, *The Voyage*, who set out to relieve the monotony of their lives only to find, at each destination, an 'oasis of horror in a desert of ennui'. The travellers end their voyage longing to die, to plunge 'into the depths of the Unknown to find something *New*'.[7] This bleak vision describes the psychological consequences when we cannot accept the failure of reality to bend to our hopes and expectations. Faced with this frustration, narcissists grow impatient with the slow pace of change. They imagine, unlike Baudelaire's travellers, they can eliminate the horror and injustice of this life without having to enter the next one. Full of revolutionary fervour, they are blind to the lessons of history. They dream of toppling statues, erasing hierarchies and eliminating injustice. The ruinous outcome is everywhere the same.

This problem is, at its core, the problem of the Other, of how we accommodate difference when, as the writer Ryszard Kapuściński observed, 'all civilisations have a tendency towards narcissism.'[8] When that narcissism becomes tyrannical, the Other will be the one for whom we have contempt and from whom we have nothing to learn. When our hunger for domination and moral certainty overrides our curiosity, we exhaust ourselves in purges and punishments, which often begin with the destruction of statues. In an extraordinary passage at the end of *Crime and Punishment*, Dostoevsky's protagonist Raskolnikov, having confessed to the murder of an elderly pawnbroker, describes a 'feverish and delirious' dream in which 'microscopic beings … spirits endowed with intelligence and will' enter human bodies and possess them. Entire communities are driven to madness. Everyone believes they hold the truth. People no longer understand each other. Violence and killings occur everywhere, and no one knows why. Somewhere in the world a chosen few survive. It's their destiny 'to renew and purify the earth, but no one anywhere had seen these people, nor heard their words and voices'.[9]

Are we, today, living inside this terrifying dream? As we fragment into multiple, uncomprehending identities, have we surrendered to an irrationalism that will consume us all? The stories of destroyed statues, recurring throughout history, often with very similar underlying narratives, are not about the death of reason. They show that reason was never as alive as we believed it to be, that bubbling under the surface of our lives is a compulsion to transgress, to shatter into pieces what should be preserved and built upon. We will see, in the course of this book, that these acts of transgression, in their festivity and violence, are one of the ways in which we express our thirst for transcendence, our hunger for the sacred.

Perhaps there are some statues that few, if any, would want to destroy because they are symbols of the deepest feelings that bind us to Others. Kapuściński believed Europeans first made contact with Others on trade routes. Then came centuries of 'conquest, slaughter and plunder' followed by attempts at understanding, which led to where we are now, the remarkable, and unprecedented discovery, that the 'monstrous Other so unlike us is a *human being too.*'[10] Statues that connect us to this common humanity, detached from allegiance to a specific identity group, affirm the universality of human experience, often through the experience of suffering and grief.

In a cemetery in the Belgian village of Vladslo, two granite statues, a man and a woman, kneel on granite plinths. The man stares straight ahead, his arms folded tightly around his chest. The woman bows her head, her hands placed like her husband's, her grip more fragile. Stretching out ahead of them are the graves of more than 25,000 German soldiers killed during the Great War. One of the soldiers was Peter Kollwitz, the couple's son. In 1903, when Peter was seven, his mother, the artist Käthe Kollwitz, used him as a model for her etching *Woman with Dead Child.* The prophetic scene is a reinterpretation of the Christian pietà in which Mary cradles her dead son. The grief is raw and indescribable. When war broke out eleven years later, Peter enlisted in the German army. He left home in August. By October, he was dead. Overwhelmed with grief, his mother wrote: 'There is a wound in our lives which will never heal.'[11]

To make sense of her suffering, Käthe Kollwitz made *The Grieving Parents* as a memorial not just to her son, but to the dead sons of all parents. As Käthe and her husband Karl look out at the devastation, it is their inner collapse that holds our attention, not the names of the dead laid out before them. This is what a wound that never heals looks like: two people, kneeling over an abyss, staring into nothingness, arms wrapped around their hearts to stop them from falling.

The pain of *The Grieving Parents* is our pain. That they survived their grief may, in part, be because Käthe was able to externalise it in granite. The two statues stand both as symbols of remembrance and a refusal to let the past die without a witness.

The preservation of memory is a function of every statue. But the past changes depending on who looks at it. Collective memory cages us in competing identities. The stories we tell ourselves about who we are and who we are not, create partisans who struggle for dominance. If statues remind us of these struggles, would we be better to stop memorialising the past with all its violence and injustice? The poet Matthew Arnold wrote that 'we forget because we must',[12] but forgetfulness, and the forgiveness it implies, are beyond most of us. We are proud in victory and bitter in defeat. It might be better if we destroyed every statue that those with whom we disagree may, at some point in the future wish to tear down. And when they are gone, it might be better that we never built new ones but that is not going to happen. Identities go too deep, and memory is too long. The sociologist Gary Younge was naive to argue that 'all statues should be taken down,' including those of 'freedom fighters, trade unionists, human rights champions and revolutionaries'.[13] If we took this course, our collective wounds would deepen in the purge. A return to Year Zero is rarely a prescription for cultural harmony.

An alternative might be to stop creating statues of 'Great Men and Women' and replace them with works of public art, such as *Grieving Parents*. But, when identity trumps reason, nothing is free from the potential to cause offence. In 2020, museums in the US and UK cancelled a retrospective of Philip Guston's work until his 'powerful message of social and racial justice' can be 'more clearly interpreted'.[14] A similar fate befell an exhibition of charcoal drawings highlighting police violence against black and Latino men. Despite its message of racial justice, The Museum of Contemporary Art Cleveland cancelled the exhibition after a 'troubling community response'.[15]

In the current febrile cultural climate, the destruction of statues and the erasure of names is justified by the iconoclasts for any offence, regardless of intent or context. The words and actions of historical figures are investigated for any perceived defects of character or lapses in judgement. Of course, no one can withstand such scrutiny, as activists discovered when, in 2020, a petition was launched to rename The David Hume Tower, a building at the University of Edinburgh. The reason given was that Hume, one of the leading figures of the Scottish Enlightenment, 'championed white supremacy'. It was suggested that the tower be renamed The Julius Nyerere Tower, in honour of the Tanzanian politician who studied at the university. However, this idea was soon abandoned when the petitioner realised her error: not only was Nyerere 'homophobic', he was also a Maoist. During his dictatorial tenure as president of Tanzania between 1964 and 1985, he forcibly moved eleven million Africans into villages, often against their will. According to one account, many 'people were ill-treated, harassed, punished in the name of TANU under socialism and those who questioned it were told, 'This is Nyerere's order.'[16] The effect was to disrupt food production and decimate the Tanzanian economy.

Regardless of whether they should stand or fall, statues act as lightning rods for love and hate. Through the values and ideals they embody, they stand as visible symbols of meaning and structure, attracting or repelling our affections. At the beginning of *The Twilight of the Idols*, Nietzsche reminds us that 'if we possess our *why* of life, we can put up with almost any *how*'.[17] This discovery of meaning creates a space of primal safety. It gives the ego power and purpose. The absence of this psychological safety is catastrophic for the self. It leaves it exposed and vulnerable to collapse. More than a decade before she filled her coat pockets with stones and walked to her death in the River Ouse, Virginia Woolf described this terrifying struggle for identity and the constant threat of disintegration: 'Beneath it is all

8

dark, it is all spreading, it is unfathomably deep; but now and again we rise to the surface and that is what you see us by.'[18]

The fear of being pulled back under the surface is what drives the self to crave security. This is a raw struggle for psychological survival, which we experience as a flight from the unknown. In classical Freudian terms, it is the struggle of the Ego to preserve itself against the primal forces of the Id. When it succeeds, it does so by making the world familiar, habitable. In the same way as the self is forged out of the undifferentiated mass of the Id, statues rise out of formless matter. In both cases, the identity we create needs an Other against which it can measure itself and through which it can understand itself. The stability of our societies is predicated on the necessity that these differences between individuals and groups be managed peacefully. It is when this peace breaks down, when we believe our identity is under threat, that we fight to preserve the symbols of our identity group and destroy the symbols of those who stand in opposition to us.

Inevitably, we justify the destruction that ensues as an act of self-defence. The wave of iconoclasm that followed the murder of George Floyd showed that many of those who destroy statues believe they are doing so in the service of an idealised obligation to the poor and oppressed. This is a pattern that repeats itself throughout history and the violence that follows is justified as a legitimate assault on the privilege of those seen as oppressors. This view of the world entails a sharp division into polarised identity groups, which mutually reinforce each other. Where one group tears down a Confederate monument, another forms a protective screen around the statue of Winston Churchill. Fuelled by cavernous, online echo chambers, the ideal of a shared narrative collapses. We lose any tolerance of difference, which is the glue that binds us. Whether their faces bear a 'sneer of cold command', the tyrannical stare of Stalin or the resolute eyes of Frederick Douglass, the statues we erect, defend and destroy, mark out and deepen these divisions.

As we descend into spirals of hate, which become increasingly difficult to unravel, we mock the ideal to love our enemies, which I understand simply as respecting the humanity of those with whom we disagree, especially when we find ourselves in conflict with them. One of the finest expressions of this ideal can be found in the Gospel of Luke (6: 27–32). Jesus says, 'Love your enemies, do good to those who hate you, bless those who curse you, pray for those who abuse you ... If you love those who love you, what credit is that to you? For even sinners love those who love them.' We fall short of this ideal to love our enemies in two ways: on the one hand, we accept the ideal but find ourselves continually succumbing to the temptation to hate; on the other, we refuse to accept that we have an equal obligation to all people and we justify this refusal in the belief that there are those who deserve our love and those who do not.

We may feel anger at those who insult our feelings and denigrate our values but, beneath the anger, lies distress that our identity is under attack. In his seminal work, *Prisoners of Hate*, the psychologist Aaron T. Beck wrote that people 'generally believe that their anger is their first response to an offense ... Upon reflection and introspection, however, they can almost recognise that their initial response is a distressed feeling rather than anger.'[19] It has become commonplace, especially among young activists, to seek safe spaces as protection against distress. This is a mistake. Distress is a necessary part of the human condition. With typical incisiveness, Nietzsche writes that to 'trace something unknown back to something known is alleviating, soothing, gratifying, and gives moreover a feeling of power. Danger, anxiety, disquiet attend the unknown – the first instinct is to *eliminate* these distressing states.'[20] If we seek to follow this instinct, we will do so by calling out those we hold responsible for our discomfort and demonise them. This may begin with the destruction of statues, but it ends in the killing of people.

HATSHEPSUT

BUILT: *c.*1460 BCE

DESTROYED: Unknown

The men arrived bearing stone chisels, wooden mallets, axes and the brute force of their limbs. They hacked at the face of the statue, severing the *uraeus* cobra from the brow of the dead king's head. As it fell, they tore at the beard and ceremonial *nemes* or headdress before chiselling off its nose. Finally, they cut off the head of the greatest female ruler of the ancient world. Her name was Hatshepsut, pharaoh of Egypt.

The desecration of the memory of Hatshepsut begins with two stories: the military triumphs of her father, Thutmose I and the mythical battle between Osiris and Set.

In 1492 BCE, the second year of his reign, Thutmose I led an army against the kingdom of Kush, which lay to the south of Egypt. Whether he feared its power or sought its gold, the assault was an extraordinary success. Thutmose I ransacked Kerma, the Kushite capital, and marked his triumph with an inscription on a large rock outside the city, claiming that 'there is not a single one of them left (and) their entrails drench the valleys'.[1] He took the body of the defeated king aboard his ship where he hung it from the bow and watched it rot as he sailed home in triumph. In a second inscription, on a quartz rock that rose up from the banks of the Nile, he mentioned the presence of his daughter Hatshepsut at the scene of the battle. It was more than merely marking his triumph. He was preparing the ground for a dynasty.

However, Hatshepsut's path to the throne of Egypt was difficult because of her sex. Her father had many children, one of whom was a younger half-brother who, after Thutmose I's death, inherited the throne and reigned as Thutmose II. Despite believing she had a stronger claim to the throne since her mother was their father's chief consort, Hatshepsut knew it was pointless to protest. Instead, she married Thutmose II. His military victories mirrored those of his father but, after a relatively short reign, he died.

Thutmose II had a young son, who was Hatshepsut's stepson. He was perhaps as young as two years old when anointed as his father's successor and Hatshepsut took advantage of her stepson's infancy to act as his regent. It was a precarious position. Thutmose I had other sons, brothers of Hatshepsut's dead husband, who believed they had a stronger claim to the throne. The main problem she faced was her identity as a woman. Ancient Egypt was a patriarchy and the myth of Osiris gave divine justification for kingship being passed through the male line.

The god-king Osiris was killed by his malevolent brother, Set. Jealous of his brother's power, Set tricked Osiris into stepping into a wooden chest. Once his brother was inside, Set slammed the lid shut and hid the chest by the banks of the Nile, intending to return later to dispose of the body. When Isis, the wife of Osiris, heard of her husband's death, she went in search of him and found the chest before Set had returned. She opened it, removed her husband's corpse and hid it. Before she was able to perform the rituals necessary to ensure his safe transition to the afterlife, Set found the body and tore it into fourteen pieces, which he scattered throughout Egypt. Transforming herself into a falcon, Isis flew throughout the kingdom, refusing to rest or eat until she had found them all. One by one, she gathered thirteen of the pieces and put them back together. The missing piece was the phallus of Osiris, which had been eaten by a fish. Undaunted, Isis fashioned a phallus out of wood, attached it to Osiris's body and conceived a god-child named Horus. Having secured his future among the living through his son, Osiris then returned to the Underworld. Fearful that Set would kill the child, Isis hid him among the reeds and when he grew up, Horus sought revenge. After a long struggle, he triumphed over Set and took his father's place as god-king of Egypt.

In the *Papyrus of Ani*, an Egyptian funerary text, Osiris says, 'I have knit myself together; I have made myself whole, and complete; I have renewed my youth; I am Osiris, the lord of eternity.'[2] He is a symbol of spiritual self-regeneration, yet the transformation of the dismembered remains of Osiris into a living spirit depended on the preservation of his body. Only when Isis reconstituted all the parts of his body could Osiris become fertile. For the same reasons, the preservation of the mortal remains of pharaohs through mummification is a prerequisite to the eternal life of the spirit. In the myth, while Osiris symbolises the life of the spirit, Horus is the embodiment of the avenging hero. But father and son are inseparable. They are the two elements of a single, mythical identity: without the preservation of the body, the spirit cannot live; without the father, the son cannot fulfil his heroic destiny; without the son, the father cannot regenerate his spirit.

For Hatshepsut, the myth of Osiris represented a problem because it affirmed that the right to rule passed from father to son. But Hatshepsut was determined, perhaps from a combination of self-preservation and personal ambition, to rule in her own right. Thutmose III was a small child. Time was on her side. But before she could take power, she first had to protect the right of her stepson to be king. If he was usurped by one of her father's brothers, then she would be marginalised. And this is where the myth of Osiris helped her, because it taught that a brother who inherits the throne is destined, like Set, for an ill-fated reign. This gave Thutmose III a legitimacy that a brother could not possess.

As soon as Thutmose III's position was secure, Hatshepsut began consolidating her power. She had one advantage over her stepson. He was the son of Thutmose II by a low-ranking woman, while Hatshepsut had a more auspicious birth. The Egyptians believed that a future king was conceived when the creator-god Amun-Ra took over the body and soul of the king as he had intercourse and in narratives inscribed on the stone walls of her temples, Hatshepsut retold the story of her divine origins to consolidate her power. In one telling, Ahmes, her mother, 'awoke because of the fragrance of the god …The majesty of the god did all he wanted with regard to her. She placed his body upon hers. She kissed him.'³

Realising her vulnerability as a woman, Hatshepsut needed the male elite of Egyptian society on her side. In exchange for their support, she funded enormous statues and extravagant tombs in their honour, bestowing patronage at every opportunity. But the main parts of her strategy to become king were to undertake an extensive programme of monument construction and to begin the process of transforming herself into a man.

She constructed two large obelisks, which showed her wearing the double-plumed headdress as God's Wife of Amun-Ra and placed these strategically on the banks of the Nile. All who sailed by would witness her divine right to exercise royal power, even if, as yet, she did not call herself a king. She did not wait long, however, before making her move. As early as Year 3 of Thutmose III's reign in 1477 BCE, Hatshepsut marked the Nile and every major urban centre with statues and monuments paying tribute to her kingship and superimposed her image on monuments designed to honour her stepson.

There was a precedent for this. When Nefrusobek, the last ruler of the Twelfth Dynasty, completed her dead father's pyramid temple at Hawara, she gave prominence to her name in the carvings at the expense of her husband and brother. Likewise, Hatshepsut affirmed her connection to her father Thutmose I above those of her half-brother and husband, Thutmose II. To emphasise this dynastic link to her father, she gave herself the title, King's Eldest Daughter.

Growing in confidence, Hatshepsut built a magnificent shrine in the Sinai mountains. In Thebes she transformed the temple of Amun-Ra into a shrine of extraordinary grandeur, where she affirmed her divine origins as daughter of the god. On the base of an obelisk, her stonemasons inscribed, 'I have done this with a loving heart for my father Amun ... The people who shall see the monument in future years and speak of what I have done ... will say, "How like her it is to be loyal to her father!" ... For I am his daughter in very truth, who glorifies him and who knows what he has ordained.'4

Yet, it was against the backdrop of the sheer cliffs at Deir el-Bahri, near the royal mausoleum complex of the Valley of the Kings on the west bank of the Nile at Thebes, that she built one of the most magnificent temples of the ancient world. Known as Djeser-Djeseru or the Holy of Holies, it was built as her funerary temple and featured shrines to the gods Amun-Ra, Hathor and Anubis. She decorated it with real and mythical scenes from her life, ranging from her divine birth to the expedition to the Land of Punt, to the south of Egypt, from which her ships returned laden with gold, ivory, incense and all manner of riches.

As Thutmose III grew older, Hatshepsut had to acknowledge his role as a male heir. In statues and reliefs, she represented him standing alongside her, a move calculated to elevate his status without diminishing her own. Her self-representation also changed over the course of her reign. At the beginning, when she was a young woman and her nephew still a child, she depicted herself as female, but she knew, if she wanted real power, this would have to change. As early as Year 2 of her stepson's reign, (1478 BCE), she erected reliefs in the Semna Temple in Nubia, which showed her as a woman but with masculine features, and many of her early statues depict her as Osiris. Over time, images of Hatshepsut became more masculine. In reliefs inside the Red Chapel, the architectural masterpiece of her reign and the centrepiece of the Karnak Temple of Amun, Hatshepsut is portrayed as a man. As the process of masculinisation gathered pace, she appeared in a male body with a beard, *nemes, shendyt* and the musculature of a man.

Hatshepsut also appropriated titles to bolster this transformation. When Thutmose III was about ten years old, Hatshepsut achieved her ambition and was crowned king. After her coronation, she adopted the regal name *Maatkare,* a throne name given to male kings. She also took the title *Khenemetenamun Hatshepsut,* which means 'at one with Amun', thus binding her to the essence of a male god. She was even ambiguous in her use of pronouns, sometimes using *she,* at other times referring to herself as *he.*

When Hatshepsut died in 1458 BCE, her stepson at first honoured the memory of his stepmother and even completed unfinished monuments in her honour. While he reassigned some of Hatshepsut's statues and monuments to himself and dismantled the Red Chapel, such acts of destruction were rare. This changed more than twenty years after Hatshepsut's death when Thutmose III began a campaign of destruction to erase all reference to her as king of Egypt. He did not disturb statues and monuments that referred to her as queen or mother. His sole aim was to erase Hatshepsut as a king, not as a woman, a wife or a mother. Thousands of statues were destroyed. Inside her funerary temple at Djeser-Djeseru, every one of them was reduced to dust.

The change was driven by his desire to secure the succession for his son, Prince Amenhotep. In practice this meant creating a clean line of succession from his grandfather Thutmose I, through his father Thutmose II, then to him and eventually to his own son. There was no room for a woman in this patriarchal line. In his determination to secure the throne for Amenhotep, Thutmose III was obliterating more than the right of Hatshepsut to be remembered as a king; he sought to reassert an ideology that denied all women the right to rule.

The decapitated head of Hatshepsut described at the beginning of this chapter once stood in Thebes. It now rests in the Brooklyn Museum in New York. Originally, the head was attached to the body of Horus, who avenged the death of his father Osiris. The damage to its facial features might appear to be the result of time, weather and chance, yet those who ruined the face and head of this statue did so deliberately and methodically. In Egypt, statues were believed to house the souls of the dead. The Egyptologist Edward Bleiberg wrote that the ancient Egyptians believed statues 'could be activated to host a supernatural power. This power could be either divine or the soul of a deceased human who had become divine at death … There is scarcely any difference in the ancient mind, in this context, between images created by sculptors and the living bodies of the gods.'[5]

This explains why the damage done to Egyptian statues targeted specific body parts. If the statue represented an offering to the gods, they destroyed the right hand to prevent the offering being made; if the intention was to represent the receipt of an offering, the left hand would be cut off. The removal of the *uraeus* cobra from the brow of Hatshepsut removed protection. But the destruction of the *nemes* and beard obliterated symbols of kingship. The destruction of the nose was, perhaps, of greatest significance. For Hatshepsut, the ability to enter the afterlife with her nose intact was essential to her spiritual survival. By removing her ability to breathe, Hatshepsut would be unable to make the transition to the afterlife.

This primal significance of breath is fundamental to many myths, religions and philosophies. In Genesis, God 'formed man of the dust of the ground and breathed into his nostrils the breath of life; and man became a living soul' (2:7). The pre-Socratic philosopher Anaximander saw *pneuma* as the primal element out of which all life emerged, while Hinduism identified 'vital breath' with the soul or *atman*.

It should not be surprising, therefore, that we should be afraid of being unable to breathe. Taphophobia, the fear of being buried alive and of suffocating in our own coffin, exists in every human culture. It led the Victorians, the arch-taphophobics, to design Safety Coffins, complete with air tubes and strings connecting the body to a bell or flag aboveground, which could be rung or waved in the event that the deceased person came back to life.

In a speech shortly before his death from cancer, the journalist Christopher Hitchens, when asked how he was feeling, observed that he was dying and that 'we are all only one breath away from the end'. It is this proximity of breathing to death that makes the struggle for breath so difficult to witness. The phrase 'I can't breathe' was instrumental in turning the murder of George Floyd into a global movement. Floyd's death and the chiselling away of the nose of Hatshepsut, have immense symbolic power because breathing is a biological necessity laced with psychological and spiritual meaning. The Vietnamese Buddhist monk Thich That Hanh claimed 'conscious breathing is my anchor' and the *hamsa* breathing technique involves focusing on the space between breaths, the space after one state and before another, the space between sleep and waking, night and day, life and death.

In relationships, an unhappy partner will claim he or she 'can't breathe', that they are being 'suffocated'. When, however, relationships are stable and loving, breathing binds couples together. A study[6] conducted at the University of Colorado found that an empathetic touch by a loving partner alleviated mild pain. The touch anchored the couple in a state of 'interpersonal synchronisation' where 'their heart and respiratory rates sync', allowing the pain to ease. When touch was prohibited by the experimenters, it severed the synchronisation between couples and they breathed to their own rhythms. Sharing experiences such as singing, making love, or walking in the countryside, all create an 'interpersonal synchronisation' that binds us, one to the other.

The philosopher Georges Bataille described this process where the isolated self extends itself towards another as a 'rhythmic restlessness ... movements of heat or light moving from one person to another, or from you to another person, or from another to you'.[7] There is a sacred quality to it because it threatens the Ego with absorption into the Id, where the self is dissolved through contact with the divine. This, for example, is the essence of Saul's conversion on the road to Damascus.

When human beings enter into close proximity with the sacred, survival is uncertain. Like Saul, we want to survive contact with the divine and live to preach our gospels. Yet the beauty and savagery of love is that it transgresses the isolated boundaries of the self, extends us towards the Other and threatens us with dissolution. At some point in our lives, most of us will have felt deep love for a person, an ideal or a god, and it can break us when the object of our love is taken away, denigrated or destroyed. The same love that drives us to acts of selfless compassion and generosity, can also drive us to acts of hate and violence against those who wound what we love. When we build and destroy statues, we are acting out this love and hate in symbolic acts of veneration and vengeance.

The ruined nose and face of the statue of Hatshepsut may rest in a museum in the United States, but for ancient Egyptians, statues embodied the soul of the dead and served as boundaries between the sacred and the profane. To erase traces of her kingship, her statues and monuments had to be defiled and have their faces mutilated. The erasure of her rule from history and the prevention of her soul from entering the afterlife were only part of the reason behind the destruction. In a wider assault on the right of women to rule, Thutmose III sought to prevent the emergence of another female king in the future.

Hatshepsut's reign was economically and militarily successful. Victory on the battlefield funded an unprecedented building programme. Her statues, monuments and temples were prodigious in quantity and breathtaking in scale. They were also a battleground over her identity. Statues rose and fell in defence and defiance of her rule. They portrayed a woman compelled to pose as a man in order to become the greatest female ruler of the ancient world. She was the first female king to adopt the title of pharaoh and was buried near the Valley of Kings at her death in 1458 BCE. It was believed, after the burial of her mummified body, that she was transformed into the god-king Osiris.

NERO

BUILT: *c.*50

DESTROYED: *c.*61

Almost 1,900 years after the armies of the Celtic Queen Boudica sacked the great Temple of Claudius in Camulodunum (Colchester), a local schoolboy, Arthur Godbold, made a remarkable discovery. In 1907, as Arthur played on the banks of the River Alde a few kilometres north of Colchester, he noticed something strange sunk in the river-bed. He scrambled down to get a closer look, and when he pulled it out of the mud, he found himself holding a severed bronze head, part of the ruined statue of a man who would later be identified as the Emperor Nero.

The statue had probably stood in the Temple of Claudius and was found embedded in mud on what would have been the boundary between the tribal lands of the Iceni and Trinovantes. The manner of its destruction was particularly violent. The backward tilt of the head was reminiscent of equestrian poses and suggested Nero may have been sculpted on horseback. Marks on the back of the head indicated that it had been subjected to a sustained attack with a sharp implement. At the front, the line of the neck was jagged from the force used to tear it off the emperor's shoulders. In a forensic analysis of what they call 'the decapitation strategy', Miles Russell and Harry Manley from Bournemouth University noted the 'extreme level of violence employed … It is likely that the statue had been toppled and was lying on its right side as the assailant(s) struck multiple blows to the lower neck in an attempt to detach the head.'[1] The decapitated bronze head suffered multiple blows from an axe or mattock, which was a fraction over 4cm long and 7mm wide.

The battle that preceded the decapitation was fought by an alliance of British tribes led by Queen Boudica, whose hatred of the Romans was deeply personal. Her husband Prasutagus, king of the Iceni, had divided his estate between three people: his two daughters and Nero. He did this hoping that his family would be protected in the event of his death. However, as soon as he died, the Roman procurator refused to honour his bequests and when Boudica protested, she was flogged and her daughters raped. The Roman centurions who destroyed Prasutagus's household and abused his family no doubt believed that the hate Boudica felt for Rome would be tempered by her fear of the consequences of revolt. Perhaps they remembered the popular Roman maxim, 'Let them hate if only they fear.' Yet Nero was about to find out that Boudica's hate would not be cowed by fear.

Before her first battles with the Romans, Boudica drove round the massed British tribes in her chariot, yelling, 'I am fighting as an ordinary person for my lost freedom, my bruised body, and my out-raged daughters. Nowadays Roman rapacity does not even spare our bodies. Old people are killed, virgins raped. But the gods will grant us the vengeance we deserve.'[2]

The Roman historian Cassius Dio describes Boudica as being 'of greater intelligence than often belongs to women'. Physically she was very tall and 'in appearance most terrifying'.[3] Her glance was 'fierce; and her voice 'harsh'. He also records a much longer speech in which Boudica began by reminding the Britons they had been taxed into slavery by the Romans: 'Have we not been robbed entirely of most of our greatest possessions and do we not pay taxes on the rest?'

We can imagine the power of her oratory, fuelled by her intelli-gence and rage, as she rode amongst the ranks of warriors, praising the subjugated tribes for their resolve to crush the hated Romans. 'Do not at all fear the Romans,' Boudica told them, before mocking Nero, 'for though he has the name of a man, he is in fact, a woman as one can tell from his singing, his lyre playing and his grooming.'[4]

This assault on Nero's vanity was shared by other Roman histori-ans. Suetonius Tranquillus concludes in *The Twelve Caesars* that Nero's narcissism and craving for popular approval led to an insatiable thirst for recognition for his acting, singing and musicianship. The emperor even went so far as to believe he equalled the god Apollo as a singer and he murdered an actor called Paris whom he considered a rival.

During the first revolt, Boudica's armies achieved notable victories. These came, however, at an enormous human cost. As many as 80,000 Roman soldiers and citizens lost their lives. The cities of Londinium, Verulamium (St Albans) and Camulodunum were burned and looted. The slaughter was indiscriminate. Tacitus recounts the brutality of 'the natives' who 'could not wait to cut throats, hang, burn and crucify – as though avenging, in advance, the retribution that was on its way'.[5]

Retribution came in the form of Suetonius Paulinus, governor of Britain. Hampered by overconfidence, Boudica chose to fight at a place picked by Paulinus. She even asked her warriors to bring their families to witness the Romans' defeat. However, despite being outnumbered, the Roman army won a decisive victory. Boudica fled the battlefield and committed suicide to avoid capture. In a gruesome symmetry, the Romans killed 80,000 Britons, a number that mirrored Boudica's slaughter of the Romans during the first part of the revolt.

Boudica fought against the injustice of an occupying army, the treatment of her dead husband and the violent assaults on herself and her daughters. But for all her fury and brilliance, her efforts ended in defeat as both sides unleashed a spectacle of unrestrained cruelty.

Hate and anger, unmoored from reason, are impossible to control and in his essay *On Anger*, the Stoic philosopher Seneca asked 'what is more loving to others than man? What more hostile than anger? Man is born for mutual help; anger for mutual destruction ... For human life is founded on kindness and concord, and is bound into an alliance for common help, not by terror, but by mutual love.'[6]

Despite Seneca's optimism about the primacy of co-operation in human nature, one of the tragedies of 'mutual love' is that it can be at its most intense when nurtured in the womb of hate. By asserting the primacy of group identity over the individual, we bind ourselves to our group, seek out enemies, strip them of all nuance and create a caricature we define as the opposite of what we stand for. Inevitably, we meet them on the battlefield and when we do, we exploit the differences we have engineered to mobilise our forces. This engine room of love and hate prepares us to fight and die for a cause we believe in.

The ferocity of the decapitation of the statue of Nero and the fact that the severed head was carried a few miles from its original site suggests it may have been given to the gods as a sacrificial offering. Such rituals served both as an act of gratitude for success in battle and as a means to ensure the gods delivered future victories. That the gods failed to repay the sacrifice with victory would not have surprised the philosopher Seneca. He would have been as contemptuous of the natives' superstitions as he was appalled at the bloodbath that inevitably followed the collapse of reason.

The relationship between Nero and Seneca can help us understand the slaughter on both sides of the battle between Boudica and the Romans. When Nero was still a child, Agrippina, his mother and the wife of Claudius, enabled Seneca to become Nero's tutor. In 54 CE, at the age of sixteen, Nero became emperor after Agrippina poisoned Claudius. At his funeral, Nero delivered a eulogy written by Seneca. It was a difficult speech to write because Nero had to acknowledge the brutality of Claudius towards senators, many of whom he had murdered, while paying homage to his status as a dead emperor. Seneca misjudged the mood. While Tacitus acknowledged 'the speech, composed by Seneca, was highly polished – a good example of his pleasant talent',[7] he also records that people laughed when Nero spoke about Claudius's 'foresight and wisdom', not least because he hadn't foreseen his own death at the hands of his wife.

As one of the greatest Stoic philosophers, Seneca's role in Nero's life was to teach him the value of reason and moderation in judgement, and of not allowing his soul to be consumed by passions such as anger or hate. Ultimately, this proved to be an impossible task.

Nero's reign began with little indication of the horror that was to follow. He lowered taxes, gave financial gifts to citizens and senators and gave grain to praetorian cohorts of the imperial guard. When asked to condemn a criminal, Suetonius records Nero as saying, 'Ah, how I wish that I had never learned to write!' He even refused a vote of thanks from the Senate, declaring, 'Wait, until I deserve them!'[8]

Such temperate governance did not last. Violence and cruelty soon seeped through the cracks in his personality. Early in his reign, Nero invited his stepbrother Britannicus to a lavish feast at which the guests included senators, Nero's wife Octavia and his mother, Agrippina. When Nero offered Britannicus a hot drink, his step-brother accepted graciously but asked his food taster to drink it first. When he felt no ill-effects, Britannicus put the cup to his lips only to find it too hot to drink. He asked for some cold water to be added. It was. Along with poison. When Britannicus had a seizure, Nero claimed it was simply the latest effect of a long-standing condition. Within a few weeks Britannicus was dead, a victim of Nero's calculated cunning.

In the years that followed, Nero killed his mother, whom he once described as 'the best in the world' and subjected his wife, Octavia, to a brutal execution. After accusing her of adultery, he sent her into exile. However, Octavia was far more popular than Poppaea, her rival for Nero's affections. Sensing he was in a difficult position, Nero reinstated Octavia as his wife. The crowds took to the streets in celebration of the emperor's change of heart, overturned statues of Poppaea and showered flowers on those of Octavia. Fearful for her life, Poppaea convinced Nero to stick to his original course. Unwilling to lose the mistress he adored, the emperor ordered Octavia to be executed. The Roman historian Tacitus records that, after Octavia was suffocated in a hot vapour bath, 'an even crueller atrocity followed. Her head was cut off and taken to Rome for Poppaea to see.' Poppaea's triumph, however, was short-lived. She, too, suffered the anger of Nero and died, pregnant with his child, after he kicked her in the stomach.

Perhaps foreseeing the path the young emperor would take, Seneca wrote an essay 'On Mercy', dedicated to Nero. Written shortly after the assassination of Britannicus, Seneca reminds Nero of the vulnerability of power by telling him that 'you are nailed to your pinnacle'.[9] The pleasures to be taken from this precarious position, are those of restraint, judgement and mercy. There is no place for anger and rashness among kings, who must wear 'the peculiar marks of a lofty spirit'.[10] He urges Nero to be merciful to others as a means to be merciful to himself.

For the first decade of Nero's reign, Seneca served as a force of restraint on the emperor. Like two sides of the Stoic coin, the philosopher embodied reason while the emperor succumbed to passion. Where Seneca urged mercy and tranquillity of mind, Nero allowed himself to be overwhelmed by fear, anger, lust and hate.[11]

An error often made about the beliefs of Seneca and the Stoics is the confusion of self-control and indifference. Seneca believed human nature to be essentially loving and kind. Hate and cruelty were deviations from this norm, a loss of our true identity, which unleash chaos in the world. For Seneca, when love becomes a slave to unregulated emotion, it severs reciprocity, as the self seeks to receive love without giving anything in return. When the self realises the futility of this endeavour and senses the impossibility of a meaningful connection to other people, it gets mired in grandiosity, resentment and fear. In Nero's case, to elevate his own status as an actor and performer, he tore down the statues of previous winners of competitions and threw them into latrines. When a fire, allegedly started by Nero, destroyed much of Rome, the emperor plundered Italy. His previous excesses having proved insufficient to satiate his hunger for adoration, he built a palace called The Golden House and placed a 37-metre-tall statue of himself at the entrance.

When reason loses its primacy over passion, as it did with Nero, there is no point at which we can say we have enough power, enough wealth, enough love, nor are we able to take responsibility for the circumstances in which we find ourselves. In frustration, we lash out at those we blame for our frailties and misfortunes. Of course, we can follow Seneca and take another path. Even in the face of great suffering, we can refuse to let it usurp our reason and ruin the tranquillity of our mind. When we do this, as Seneca discovered, it gives us the wisdom to meet suffering with love and equanimity. As a young man, Seneca spent time in exile on the island of Corsica from where he wrote to his mother, urging her not to worry or grieve for him, claiming that 'to be afflicted with endless sorrow at the loss of someone very dear is foolish self-indulgence'.[12] That final loss of 'someone dear' came in 65 CE when Nero sentenced Seneca to death.

Three years earlier, and by then an ageing and tired man, Seneca sought to retire to the country, but Nero refused his tutor's request. He had become frustrated with the philosopher and his talk of reason, self-discipline and maintaining the balance of one's mind. The emperor, a stranger to restraint, had grown increasingly unpopular and, following a plot to overthrow him in which Seneca was implicated, Nero ordered his old tutor to commit suicide. When, a Roman officer, Gavius Silvanus, interrupted Seneca and Paulina, his wife, as they ate their evening meal to inform the philosopher that he must take his own life, Seneca replied with characteristic stoicism, 'After murdering his mother and brother, it only remained for him to kill his teacher and tutor.'[13]

He may have been prepared to lose his own life, but Seneca feared what might happen to Paulina after his death. She, in turn, had no desire to live without her husband. They each took a knife and made a single cut to their arms. Seneca was old and the blood did not flow freely, so he made more cuts behind his ankles and knees. In terrible pain, he still did not shed sufficient blood to die. Able to bear his own suffering better than witnessing his wife's agony, he asked her to retire to another room while his doctor gave him hemlock, the poison that killed Socrates. Weak and with death close, Seneca was carried to a vapour-bath, where he suffocated. Nero, who had no grudge against Paulina, ordered his soldiers to save her life. This they did by stemming the flow of blood and bandaging her wounds. She lived for a few years, in poor health, before her eventual death.

With Seneca dead, Nero's life spiralled even further out of control. Haunted by death, he oscillated between terrifying fatalism and defiant optimism. One night, he dreamed the statues that adorned the Theatre of Pompey came alive. They walked towards him and encircled him to prevent his escape, before the doors of a mausoleum opened and a voice from within called, 'Enter Nero!'

Accepting the fate that now seemed inevitable, he asked his friends to dig his grave. As they worked, Nero, still consumed by grandiose self-love, lamented, 'Dead! And so great an artist!' When the end came, it was short and brutal. With the help of his secretary Epaphroditus, Nero stabbed himself in the neck. Before he died, he begged his companions to ensure no one cut off his head so he could be buried with his body intact. With that command, Nero may have avoided the fate of his statue in the Temple of Claudius near Colchester, but they both suffered a savage assault.

We can imagine a Stoic ideal where the place of statues is debated and their fate decided in tranquil committee rooms. After the wave of iconoclasm that swept the United Kingdom in the summer of 2020, Sadiq Khan, the mayor of London, attempted to do this. He formed the Landmark Commission, composed of leaders from the arts, architecture, community engagement and business. The commission's aim is to increase public understanding of the reasoning behind statues, memorials and street names. While the intention was

not to remove statues, Khan previously said, 'I suspect the committee may take down slavers' statues.' Regardless of the remit of the
commission or its future decisions, such rational decision-making
is an attempt to defuse the clash of ideas, values and identities that
statues ignite.

Yet, amid all the statues toppled in protests about imperialism
and colonialism, one unusual symbol of the British Empire was left
untouched. In 1902, five years before Arthur Godbold discovered
the severed head of Nero, a large bronze statue of Boudica was
erected on Westminster Pier, overlooking the Houses of Parliament
in London. It portrays the Iceni queen standing in a war chariot fitted
with scythed blades on each wheel, her daughters by her side. Two
horses rear up as they gallop, and an inscription on the base, taken
from William Cowper's famous poem *Boadicea: An Ode*, reads:

REGIONS CAESAR NEVER KNEW
THY POSTERITY SHALL SWAY

But what regions did Boudica conquer that made her greater than
Caesar? This claim about the relative breadth of her power and influence seems historically inaccurate until we understand that the statue
was meant to be installed during the reign of Queen Victoria. Indeed,
the sculptor, Thomas Thornycroft, used horses from the royal stables
as models for the horses pulling the chariot and the face of Boudica
resembles that of a young Queen Victoria. It is, then, to Victoria's
reign, not that of the queen of the Iceni, that the word 'posterity'
refers. The statue connects two queens and serves as a symbol of
British imperial power.

The empires represented by Boudica and Nero have both vanished,
as all empires must. Perhaps the statue of Boudica avoided the fury of
the mob only because few people remember who she was and almost
none know of the link between the statue and the British Empire.

On the other side of the Houses of Parliament, protestors attacked a statue of Winston Churchill and sprayed 'was a racist' beneath his name. The statue was boarded up to protect it from further damage. Perhaps the protestors imagined brave new worlds emerging out of the ashes of destroyed statues. If they did, they are naive. In tutoring Nero, Seneca taught us about the limits of our power. He understood that we will not control the forces our anger sets free. If love is to triumph over hate and anger, it will do so when we turn the focus inward and learn to manage ourselves before we tear at the heart of our democracies. If the protestors had read Seneca, they would have left the statue of Winston Churchill untouched and walked the short distance to the British Museum. There, the head of Nero, a symbol of Boudica's victory, is on display. Much as modern iconoclasts imagine their actions mark the beginning of a new order, and not a descent into chaos, the triumphant Britons believed that offering the severed head of Nero to their gods would bring an end to Roman occupation. They were wrong. Roman rule persisted for another 350 years and when the Britons looked to the skies as the Romans took revenge, their gods were silent.

ATHENA

BUILT: *c.*123

DESTROYED: *c.*385 and 2016

Twice, they came out of the desert.

The first time, according to the classicist Catherine Nixey, 'Palmyra must have been expecting them ... bands of bearded, black-robed zealots ... Their attacks were primitive, thuggish and very effective. These men moved in packs – later in swarms of as many as five hundred – and when they descended, utter destruction followed ... Great stone columns that had stood for centuries collapsed in an afternoon; statues that had stood for half a millennium had their faces mutilated in a moment.'[1]

More than 1,600 years later, they came out of the desert a second time. The same men, the same black robes, the same certainties, the same fury. Again, Palmyra must have been expecting them. As with the earlier attacks by fourth-century Christians, the ancient city stood powerless before their advance and in May 2016, ISIS captured Palmyra, by now a UNESCO World Heritage Site, from the Syrian regime of Bashar al-Assad. Within a week, they had released a video of the execution of twenty-five prisoners. Kneeling before the Temple of Baalshamin, the captives, some of them crying, listened as a religious leader read a prepared statement. When he fell silent, they were shot in the head or had their throats cut.

For ISIS and the Christians that came before them, the killing of people and the destruction of statues were inseparable. Both groups shared a hatred of paganism. Early Christians believed statues housed demons. ISIS believed statues of false gods were an affront to Allah. Indeed, the prohibition of figurative art is central to Islamic teaching. ISIS also believed the Palmyra statues housed the values of a cultural heritage that Allah commanded them to destroy.

In a strange historical coincidence, both groups mutilated the same statue of the Greek goddess Athena. Based on an original made by the Greek sculptor Phidias in the fifth century BCE, the statue of Athena would have been about 2.5 metres high. Carved out of Pentelic marble, she stood in the Temple of Al-Lat in Palmyra, built in the second century when the city was one of the great cultural and trading centres of the ancient world. A vast colonnade, more than a mile in length, stretched through Palmyra, with smaller pillared avenues breaking off it like tributaries connecting the major temples and structures. Its power was such that, in the middle of the third century CE, it took on the might of the Roman Empire. After Sapor, the king of Persia captured Emperor Valerian, the imperial position was rescued by Odaenathus, the Roman-appointed ruler of Palmyra, who remained loyal to Valerian's son and successor Gallienus. When Odaenathus himself was murdered in 267, probably by members of his own family, his wife Zenobia came to power. Sharing none of her late husband's loyalty to Rome and sensing its weakness, she set about expanding the Palmyrene empire. By 270 her armies had conquered modern-day Syria, Anatolia and Egypt. Imagining herself invincible, she gave her son the Roman imperial title Caesar in 271, an act of defiance that sparked a predictable Roman response. In 272, the armies of Emperor Aurelian laid siege to Palmyra and Zenobia knew she was defeated. Historical sources are undecided on what happened next, but it is likely she was captured and taken back to Rome where she was paraded in Aurelian's victory procession and then probably lived out her days as the wife of a senator.

More than a hundred years later, when Palmyra was past the peak of its power, the Christian zealots came, burst into the Temple of Al-Lat and unleashed their fury on the tall, imposing statue of the goddess Athena. They hacked at the folds of her robe, gouged out her right eye, sliced off her nose, and when she fell to the ground, they hacked at her body, cutting off her left arm, leaving her, face down, where she remained until she was discovered by a team of Polish archaeologists in 1975. Parts of her body were scattered throughout the temple, while others, such as her left shoulder and arm, were never recovered.

Between 1975 and the emergence of the second band of zealots to come out of the desert, Athena stood on a restored plinth in the Palmyra museum. As ISIS advanced on the city, Abu Laith al-Saudi, one of their commanders, warned that the statue of Athena would be 'pulverised'. This time the world witnessed the assault on Palmyra, as ISIS fanatics rampaged through the city. They destroyed Athena's surviving right arm and beheaded her, leaving behind a headless, limbless torso.

Two groups of religious fanatics, at different historical moments, beheaded and desecrated the same statue. Incapable of doubting their own beliefs, they carried the same hate in their hearts. To be merciful and forgiving requires us to see the world from the point of view of another person. This leads to understanding and when we understand other people, we humanise them, we look for common ground and a way to build bridges. When, on the other hand, we need to be absolutely certain we are right, that our beliefs are the only true ones, then it becomes impossible to find a common humanity with people who do not share those beliefs. As our world-view narrows and our frame of reference shrinks, we become desperate to justify our increasingly fragile identity. The result is violence and bloodshed.

It is one of the ironies of the statue of Athena, that she was the goddess of love and war, but took no pleasure in either. For her, love was calm, measured and platonic. In conflict, she shared none of her half-brother Ares' delight in the heat of battle. She simply wasn't born for unruly passion. She remained a virgin and the Parthenon, her temple on the Acropolis in Athens, is named after *parthenos*, the Greek word for a virgin. Athena sacrificed passion in favour of law and stability and she came into the world ready to fight for justice, even if her birth was preceded by a crime.

Athena's father, Zeus, the king of the gods, fell in love with Metis, the Titan goddess of wisdom and cunning. She resisted his advances, so he chased her, transforming himself into a bull, a bear, a lion and an eagle. Despairing at being unable to catch her, he became a serpent, wrapped himself around her and she conceived his child. However, when Zeus heard a prophecy that Metis would bear him two children, a girl followed by a boy, and the boy would overthrow him, Zeus decided to kill her. Fearing for her life, Metis transformed herself into a fly. Zeus responded by becoming a lizard and swallowed her.

That was not the end of Metis or the child she carried in her womb. Months after he swallowed her, Zeus felt a searing pain in his head. Unable to bear the torment any longer, he asked Hephaestus, the god of craftsmen, blacksmiths and fire, to free him from his agony. Hephaestus raised his axe and split the head of Zeus in two. A woman, fully clothed and armed, emerged. The armour symbolised war and an owl that flew down and perched on her shoulder shortly after she was born, represented wisdom. This goddess's name was Athena and it is in the concluding play of *The Oresteia*, a trilogy of Greek tragedies written by Aeschylus, that we witness her wisdom, her understanding of the dangers of irrational hate and her impulse to seek peaceful settlements.

The Oresteia begins with the victorious return of King Agamemnon after the victory of the Greeks in the Trojan War. During his absence, his wife Clytemnestra, along with her lover, Aegisthus, plots to kill him and when Agamemnon takes a bath, Clytemnestra plunges an axe into his heart. Haunted by the murder of her husband, Clytemnestra has a nightmare that she gives birth to a son who draws blood when he suckles at her breast. Fearing this is a prophecy that she, too, will be killed, Clytemnestra makes an offering to the gods. It is too late. Orestes, the son she bore with Agamemnon and exiled after she killed her husband, returns to the palace to take revenge for the murder of his father. Disguised as a traveller, he gains access to the palace by pretending to bring news of Orestes' death. Once inside, he reveals himself to his mother and kills her.

Far from bringing the cycle of violence and retribution to an end, the matricide escalates the horror. Orestes is pursed by the Furies and takes refuge in the Temple of Apollo. Born from the blood of Ouranos, the sky god who was castrated by his son Cronos, the Furies were three chthonic deities, cronish women who pursued and murdered mortals, especially those guilty of matricide or patricide. Dressed in black robes with a nest of serpents entwined in their hair, not even the gods could prevent them from exacting revenge.

In *The Eumenides*, the final play in *The Oresteia* trilogy, these avenging spirits pursue Orestes into the Temple of Apollo. Unable to protect Orestes from his inevitable fate, Apollo does what he can to delay the Furies by casting a spell that puts them to sleep. This gives Orestes time to escape to Athens. After he flees, the ghost of Clytemnestra comes to the temple, breaks Apollo's spell and awakens the Furies. They fly from the temple, following the scent of blood that stains every step of Orestes' journey to Athens. Determined to kill him as punishment for his matricide, the black-robed Furies catch up with Orestes and surround him. In desperation, he calls for Athena 'queen of this land, to come and rescue me ... She is a god who hears men far away. So may she set me free from what is at my back.'[2]

Athena responds to Orestes' pleas and summons twelve Athenian citizens to serve as jurors to decide whether Orestes should live or die. The process of reasoned argument and judgement is set against the insatiable desire of the Furies, 'the sad daughters of the night', to exact revenge. 'We are the Angry Ones ... We shall let loose indiscriminate death,'[3] they chant.

Even as they agree, reluctantly, to participate in the trial of Orestes, one of the Furies says, 'if I do not win this case, I shall come back to this land and it will feel my weight'.[4] This threat hangs over the proceedings and when the jurors are split evenly, it is down to Athena to free Orestes or let the Furies tear him to pieces. She sides with Orestes.

The Furies condemn Orestes and forgive Clytemnestra because they see matricide as a greater crime than parricide, but for Athena all killing is equal. Unlike the marauders who destroyed her statue at Palmyra, she uses patriarchal descent as a justification for mercy, not violence. Reason, freed from the emotional biases that enslave it to the passions and align it with cruelty, is the tool she employs to ensure fairness in the dispensation of justice. Her judgement, however, will only stand if the Furies accept it. To assuage their anger, Athena offers them the opportunity to serve peaceful ends as protectors of justice and the city of Athens. 'Do good,' she tells them, 'receive good, and be honoured as the good are honoured. Share our country, the beloved of god.'[5] Again the Furies resist, unable to contain their rage at having their right to exact vengeance taken away. In a final plea, Athena offers them a 'place free from grief and pain. Take it for yours.' Softened by the power of Athena's reasoning, the chorus of Furies call for an end to 'passion for revenge and bloodshed for bloodshed' and leaves the citizens of Athens with this hope: 'Let them render grace for grace. Let love be their common will.'[6] With this, the Furies become known as the Eumenides or the Kind Ones.

Athena's greatness was her skill in persuasion rather than coercion. She understood that the Furies were beyond the power of a god to use force to dampen their thirst for revenge. If there was to be an end, or at least a suspension, of the cycle of violence and retribution, it had to be built on rational foundations, on understanding, empathy and argument. Yet, the transformation of Furies into Eumenides, vengeance into the rule of law, is fragile. The impulse to take revenge against those who attack values, beliefs or people we love, can be overwhelming. It is the reason why, after Cain killed his brother

Abel in the Book of Genesis, God put a mark on Cain, to ensure
that anyone who recognised him would not kill him. God protected
Cain because he knew that if revenge was taken against Cain or his
descendants, they, in turn, would exact their own revenge and the
cycle of violence would be passed down through the generations.

We are all, even Athena, capable of losing control of our emotions
and lashing out at those who offend us. When Tiresias saw her bath-
ing naked, she was so enraged that she blinded him. Only when his
mother, the nymph Chariclo, pleaded with her, did Athena's anger
subside. Unable to reverse the spell that blinded him, she gave him
the power of clairvoyance in recompense for taking away his sight.

Individual acts of rage and retribution, common to mortals and
gods, are unlikely to tear apart the fabric of the world. When the
passions cool, we make amends and rekindle the ties that bind us.
But when those passions are fuelled by an ideology, the impulse to
take revenge becomes insatiable, even when that revenge is against
an imaginary enemy, such as a witch.

The most brutal witch-hunt in the history of England happened
during the Civil War when Matthew Hopkins and his accomplice
John Stearne began questioning women suspected of witchcraft.
Questions soon became trials and trials became killings. In his study
of what he calls 'a seventeenth-century English tragedy', the historian
Malcolm Gaskill describes the psychology behind the persecution,
'In the confines of a moral world now made strange by time, the
unspoken fears and transgressive fantasies of an entire parish might
converge on a single individual: her life-force become a death-force,
her emblems in nature no longer the sunrise and the harvest but the
chill of winter and the midnight moon.'[7]

That moral world is not strange to us. The black-robed zealots
who twice came out of the desert to mutilate the statue of Athena did
so in the belief the statue was a living thing. For the early Christians,
it housed demonic spirits. For ISIS, it was alive as a blasphemous

symbol of beliefs they sought to obliterate. The witch was, according to Gaskill, 'plebeian fear made flesh' and, for the black-robed iconoclasts, Athena was the same fear sculpted into marble. When people believe in a moral world where their identity is threatened on all sides by demonic forces, then the compulsion to respond with violence is irresistible. The eyes of reason may watch in horror as events unfold, but those eyes, precisely because they are naive in their belief in the power of facts and evidence to neutralise ideological fantasies, will repeat the same mistake: they won't see how dark the horror can become until the darkest of nights descends upon them.

Such a descent into barbarism in the early Christian Church is described by Edward Gibbon in *The History of the Decline and Fall of the Roman Empire*. He writes how 'the primitive church ... delivered over, without hesitation, to eternal torture, the far greater part of the human species'. Reason is no match for the force of such sanctified violence and the Church 'unanimously affirmed that those who, since the birth or the death of Christ, had obstinately persisted in the worship of daemons, neither deserved nor could expect a pardon from the irritated justice of the Deity'.[8]

Realising the psychological consequences of these beliefs, Gibbon quotes the early Church Father Tertullian. Writing almost 200 years before the first destruction of the statue of Athena in Palmyra, Tertullian gloated at the fate of unbelievers. 'How shall I admire, how laugh, how rejoice, how exult, when I behold so many proud monarchs, and fancied gods, groaning in the lowest abyss of darkness ... so many sage philosophers blushing in the red hot flames with their deluded scholars.'[9]

ISIS, too, was fond of spectacles. Public executions and beheadings were commonplace. It was not, however, sufficient to commit acts of murder. What mattered was turning them into a propaganda tool. The beheadings of the aid workers Alan Henning, David Haines and Peter Kassig were filmed and circulated on social media, as were the executions of military captives such as the Jordanian pilot Muath al-Kasasbeh. Like the fourth-century Christians who came out of the desert before them, ISIS wanted revenge. For them, it was revenge against the 'Crusaders' for their occupation of Muslim lands and revenge against unbelievers for the very fact of their unbelief. As such, it was an endless war, winnable only in the imagination of fantasists after a final, apocalyptic battle between the forces of Good and Evil. For ISIS, executions of people and the destruction of statues were merely means to mark the passage to the End Times. An article in *Dabiq*, the magazine of ISIS, titled 'The Law of Allah and the Laws of Men' and published in July 2015, stated, 'If you are truthful in your claim that you are upon the religion of Islam and are followers of the Messenger, then demolish all these idols and flatten them to the ground.'[10]

This apocalyptic fury, fuelled by an insatiable appetite for revenge against their enemies, explains the ferocity of the attacks on the statue of Athena. A woman, a pagan goddess and a symbol of reason stood little chance when fanatics arrived to demonstrate their purity before God and claim their place in the afterlife. Like the Furies, all fanatics are fuelled by real or imagined injustices. To remedy the bottomless pit of wrongs done against them, they unleashed violence and terror, which they then blame on its victims. But that psychological path is as exhausting and dehumanising for them as it is for their victims. Athena understood this, which is why she offered the Furies 'a place free from grief and pain'. She sacrificed passionate love and vengeful hate in order to stand against all forms of fanaticism. In doing so, she asked us to be mindful of our intolerance and to sacrifice our own instincts for scapegoating others. Headless and limbless, what is left of her stands as a symbol of wounded mercy, the brittle barrier that stands between us and the return of civilisation into the desert sands from which it emerged.

THE BUDDHAS
OF BAMIYAN

BUILT: *c.*507 and 554

DESTROYED: March 2001

I n 1886, when asked by the *Illustrated London News* to describe the Buddhas of Bamiyan, the war artist William Simpson imagined 'a general meeting of all the colossal statues of the world'.[1] That gathering included the Colossi of Memnon, four statues of Ramesses II and two bronze Japanese Buddhas from Kotuku-in and Todai-ji temples. Also present were the goddess Athena from the Parthenon and the statue of Zeus at Olympia, both made by the Greek sculptor Phidias. Last in line came the Colossus of Rhodes, the tallest statue of the ancient world. Simpson concluded that every one of these magnificent statues would be dwarfed by the Buddhas, alongside which 'what pygmies most of them would then seem!'

Before they were destroyed by the Taliban in 2001, the Buddhas stood looming over the lush Bamiyan valley in Afghanistan for almost 1,500 years. Set 800 metres apart and rising to a height of 53 metres and 35 metres respectively, they were the largest Buddha carvings in the world. For centuries, they stood like sentinels watching travellers, merchants and missionaries make their way along the ancient Silk Road. They witnessed friendship, prayer, trade, love and hate.

In 1221, Genghis Khan laid siege to the town of Bamiyan. The Persian historian Ata-Malik Juvayni, writing more than thirty years after the siege, described what happened after an arrow struck Khan's favourite grandson and killed him:

The Mongols made the greater haste to capture the town, and when it was taken Genghis gave orders that every living creature, from mankind down to the brute beasts, should be killed; that no prisoner should be taken; that not even the child in its mother's womb should be spared; and that henceforth no living creature should dwell therein.[2]

In 1335, more 100 years after the death of Genghis Khan, the Berber legal scholar Ibn Battuta gave a haunting account of how Genghis had 'massacred the inhabitants of Bamiyan and destroyed it from top to bottom, with the exception of the minaret of its Friday mosque'.[3] The massacre was so brutal that Bamiyan became known as the City of Sorrows and the City of Screams. Yet, perhaps from awe or the strong Buddhist influence at the Mongol court, Genghis Khan left the Buddhas standing.

Six hundred years before the arrival of the Mongols, the Chinese monk Xuanzang left us the oldest surviving account of the Buddhas of Bamiyan. Xuanzang travelled across the treacherous 'snowy mountains' of the Hindu Kush before arriving in 629 in the Buddhist kingdom of Bamiyan, where he found a vibrant community of 'several tens of monasteries with several thousand monks'. Carved into the mountains, he marvelled at 'a stone statue of the standing Buddha. It is 140–50 feet high, of a dazzling gold colour and resplendent with ornamentation of precious substances. To the east of it is a monastery built by an earlier king of the country. East of this is a standing image of Shakyamuni Buddha, more than 100 feet high, made of brass, the pieces of which have been cast separately and then assembled to make up the statue.'[4]

A recent analysis conducted by the University of Munich confirmed Xuanzang's description. Erwin Emmerling, the leader of the research team, claimed 'the Buddhas had an intensely colourful appearance' with clay garments painted red, pink, orange, blue and white.[5] These resplendent Buddhas contrast with the unadorned, austere sandstone giants that succumbed to rockets, tank shells and dynamite in March 2001, their destruction sanctioned by Mullah

Omar, then leader of the Taliban. Encouraged by Osama bin Laden and al-Qaeda, he laid waste 'the gods of the infidels'.

Unlike the volcanic rage that tore down statues of Confucius, Nero or Edward Colston, the destruction of the Buddhas of Bamiyan was slow and systematic. After a barrage of tank and artillery shells failed to destroy them, the Taliban conscripted local people to help, forcing them to carry explosives on their backs. If they refused or were unable to bear the weight, they were killed. Mirza Hussein, a member of the Hazara Shi'ite minority who were persecuted by the Taliban, recalled 'one of the men had a bad leg and couldn't carry the explosives any more. The Taliban shot him on the spot and gave the body to another prisoner to dispose of.'[6]

Overseen by Chechen and Arab fighters, this small army of conscripts slid down ropes attached to the statues and cut holes into the Buddhas. They carefully placed explosives in the holes, a task they repeated many times. Anti-tank mines were placed between the feet of the Buddhas and, after twenty-five days gruelling labour, it was time for the destruction to begin. Detonators located in a nearby mosque were activated and the Bamiyan Buddhas vanished in a cloud of dust. The Taliban cheered, danced and fired shots into the sky. Nine cows were killed, breaking the fragile line that separates celebration from slaughter.

Years later, Mirza, a conscript consumed with remorse at his unwilling part in the destruction, recalled the event: 'I regretted it at that time, I regret it now and I will always regret it. But I could not resist, I didn't have a choice because they would have killed me.' Dadali, another conscript, said his 'heart bleeds'[7] every time he walks past the hole in the mountain where the Buddhas stood.

In a 2017 report, UNESCO sought to reclaim Bamiyan as 'a place of collective identity and memory'.[8] The French philosopher Maurice Halbwachs, who died in Buchenwald concentration camp in 1945, developed the idea of collective memory, which he regarded as the means to define and sustain group cohesion. 'No memory is possible,' Halbwachs wrote, 'outside frameworks used by people living in society to determine and retrieve their recollections.'[9] He argued that history is the province of semantic memory, or the memory of facts, while collective memory is closely aligned with episodic memory, or the memory of lived experience. When collective memory disintegrates, the identity group no longer has a shared experience of the past and ceases to exist in any meaningful sense.

It is a matter of psychological and historical fact that neither collective memory nor collective identity, can ever be universal and the conflicting identities to which we attach ourselves demonstrate the uneasy peace that binds us together. Who we believe we are, who we consider to be our friends and those we define as enemies, all frame our historical memory. Even when we can agree on basic historical facts, we are likely to disagree on their interpretation. This reveals memory for what it is: a dance of discordant fragments, each piece fighting to bind itself to a self-serving picture that makes sense of our past, our present and our future. There is an abyss in UNESCO's hope that Bamiyan might be reclaimed as a place that transcends the partisan construction of memory. It is the same abyss into which ruined statues fall.

Yet, there was hope that the Buddhas of Bamiyan might have remained standing. To the Taliban, the statues were idolatrous, but in September 2000 Mullah Omar said they 'will not be destroyed but protected.'[10] This did not mark a shift in his theology. Rather, he saw them as a means to generate income from international visitors. A few months later, despite the revulsion expressed by most of the Muslim world and a visit by eleven Islamic leaders to Herat to plea for the statues to be preserved, Omar sanctioned their destruction. He declared, in an edict, the 'statues have been and remain shrines of unbelievers and these unbelievers continue to worship and respect them. God Almighty is the only real shrine and all fake idols must be destroyed'.[11]

What changed his mind?

Some believed it was his adherence to an intolerant version of Islam. For others, it was political opportunism, an act of defiance designed to bolster his status as a radical Islamic leader. The truth, perhaps, is in his disgust at what he saw as the world's hypocrisy in seeking to preserve two statues as thousands of Afghans starved. While this moral posturing ignores the fact that it was the Taliban's own brutality that excluded them from the community of nations, it was a view shared by some in the West. Two weeks before the statues were blown up, The Economist featured an article claiming that 'the world seems to care more about the destruction of two stone statues, which – let's be honest – hardly anyone had heard of until ten days ago, than about 100,000 refugees who have been starving and freezing to death near Herat, a few hundred miles away from them'.[12]

Another force in driving Omar's change of heart was bin Laden. If Omar faced internally towards the people of Afghanistan, al-Qaeda faced outward. They cared nothing for Afghanistan or its people. Their focus was vengeance against the United States and since they were at that time largely unknown, they needed a spectacle to serve as a provocation and a statement of intent. The destruction of the Bamiyan Buddhas provided both. A few months later, human beings took the place of statues in the rubble of the Twin Towers.

Two Buddhas. Two Towers. The same meaning.

Writing about the significance of the spectacle, (in this case, of the scaffold), the philosopher Michel Foucault wrote that a 'successful public execution justified justice, in that it published the truth of the crime in the body of the man to be executed.'[13] That body may be an American banker falling from the 110th floor of a building or an ancient Buddha carved into a mountain. Flesh or stone, the message is the same: 'It is,' wrote Foucault, 'the theatre of hell, the cries of the condemned man, his struggles, his blasphemies, that already signify his irremediable destiny.'[14]

In the public executions of the seventeenth and eighteenth centuries, the assembled crowds heard the cries of the condemned man. In Bamiyan, the statues were silent. It was we, the audience watching in distant lands, whose cries mattered most to the Taliban and al-Qaeda. In both cases, the ultimate witness was God. For the blasphemer or the regicide hung, drawn and quartered on the scaffold, his punishment before God was both evidence of guilt and an opportunity for repentance. For bin Laden, the Buddhas blown into fragments were a symbolic punishment of America before Allah for what he saw as its crimes against the Muslim world. After al-Qaeda attacked New York, he exulted 'the pieces of the bodies of infidels were flying like dust particles'.[15] His description could be applied, unchanged, to the Bamiyan Buddhas.

How easily we move from the desecration of stone, marble and steel to the desecration of the human body. We break them both in public displays of dominance, where we assert our values in the language of cruelty.

In 2015 in Raqqa, a bearded cleric read out a list of charges against three captured Syrian soldiers, after which the mob beat the men to death before tying them to motorbikes and dragging their corpses through the streets to the accompanying cheers of the crowd.

A few months later, in the town of Umm el-Marra, close to the northern Syrian city of Aleppo, soldiers loyal to the regime of Bashar al-Assad, took their revenge. After killing an ISIS fighter in battle, they tied his body to the back of a pick-up truck and dragged it through the streets. The breaking apart of bodies, living or sculpted, is as old as our species. Such acts are intended for an audience and gain their meaning through being witnessed.

As for the Buddhas of Bamiyan, for 1,500 years they watched as the slow procession of humanity passed before their feet, caught as we all are in the Wheel of Time, living, dying, returning to dust. 'When merchants coming and going,' wrote Xuanzang, 'happen to witness visions of heavenly deities, whether as good omens or as predictions of disaster, they worship the deities to pray for blessedness.'[16]

While prayers for the sanctification of our souls may be a human universal, the absence of facial features on the Buddhas is symbolic of many forms such prayers take. The Buddhas were carved with flat faces, leaving a smooth surface onto which a wooden mask was fixed until time caused it to rot and crash to the ground. The bare, exposed stone reminds us of the truth of all statues, which stand as canvases onto which we write our identity. We venerate the faces we love. We desecrate the faces we hate.

A few weeks before William Simpson imagined the Buddhas of Bamiyan as the mightiest guests in a gathering of all the great statues of the world, President Grover Cleveland spoke at the dedication of the Statue of Liberty in New York (at 46 metres, excluding the base, it was much smaller than the larger of the two Buddhas). The president stated that the statue's 'stream of light shall pierce the darkness of ignorance and man's oppression until Liberty enlightens the world'.

Statues embody our values, ideals and a vision of political, religious, scientific and cultural achievement. If Grover Cleveland is right to link statues to enlightenment, it is as witnesses of a biased, partisan enlightenment, the vindication of the collective memory of an identity group. Yet the featureless faces of the Bamiyan Buddhas are more subtle witnesses, reminding us of the vanity of these identities, all of which are masks that crumble in the millstone of time. In the end the Buddhas stood for nothing other than their own transience. When they were blown to pieces, the world lamented a cultural loss. Yet, the *Lokottaravada* Buddhists, who built the statues would have understood that loss as already having happened. This counter-intuitive idea comes from the belief that our sense of self and the apparent reality of the world outside us, are an illusion, anchored in the belief that the world is composed only of *sunyata* or emptiness. The literal translation of *lokottara* is 'transcendental' or 'beyond the world of the senses' and for Lokottaravada Buddhists even the physical birth, life and death of the Buddha was an illusion. According to the Buddhist writer and teacher Sangharakshita, who died in 2018, the *Lokottaravadins* believed the body of the Buddha 'was transcendental from the time of His apparent birth to the time of His apparent death (and) the *Lokottaravadins* were, logically speaking, compelled to regard the Buddha's Enlightenment as having taken place long before His present birth'.[17]

For their creators, the Bamiyan Buddhas, despite their breathtaking scale, were simply the illusion of an illusion: they represented a Buddha who himself lived, died and was reborn many times in a transcendental body that existed beyond the world of the senses.

There is great irony in the destruction of the two Buddhas. For all the shooting, cheering and shedding of bovine blood that accompanied their ruin, there was no cause for celebration. What was destroyed was, inevitably, going to fall and, according to the *Lokottaravadins*, had already fallen many times. The statues were patient prophets of their own destruction. Impermanence is at the heart of Buddhist doctrine and empty spaces in a sandstone cliff were always going to be the fate of the Buddhas of Bamiyan. The message of the statues was a simple one: nothing endures, not even our greatest creations.

There is a moral dimension to this view of the world, captured beautifully by the Chan Buddhist patriarch Sengcan, who lived around the time of the construction of the smaller of the two Bamiyan Buddhas. 'The Great Way,' he wrote, 'is not difficult for those who have no preferences. When love and hate are both absent everything becomes clear and undisguised. Make the smallest distinction, however, and heaven and earth are set infinitely apart. If you wish to see the truth then hold no opinion for or against. The struggle for what one likes or dislikes is a disease of the mind.'[18]

When people destroy statues, they succumb to this disease. Consumed by intolerance, the destruction of a statue is an attack on an idea, a set of values and an identity, which the assailants have decided must be crushed and obliterated from the historical record. When bin Laden urged Mullah Omar to destroy the Bamiyan Buddhas, his motivations were ideological and represented what he called 'a clash of civilisations'. Yet, to a sixth-century *Lokottaravadin* monk, the Taliban destroyed nothing because there was nothing to destroy. The Bamiyan Buddhas embodied the 'Great Way' described by Sengcan and were immune to love and hate.

There's no denying the difficulty in following the path advocated by Sengcan. It feels inhuman to 'hold no opinion for or against,' to be in such control of our minds that we do not react when provoked. For Islamists like Mullah Omar or bin Laden, their identities were built in opposition to what they hated. America, the West, Christianity, Shia Muslims, moderate Muslims, unveiled women, the list was endless. The more distinctions they made between who they were and who they opposed, the more 'heaven and earth are set infinitely apart'. These divisions and the hate that fuels them are seductive. By seeing other people only as representatives of the groups to which they belong, we sacrifice their individuality to an abstraction. Submerged in groups, they become easier to hate. When our psychology is emaciated in this way, love becomes a pale reflection of itself. Rather than extending love towards those with whom we disagree, we reserve it only for those who are like us, who believe what we believe, love what we love, hate what we hate.

Sengcan is not, however, asking us to develop a more expansive love. He is asking us to abandon the illusion of love and hate and see, 'clear and undisguised', the true nature of the world. The Bamiyan Buddhas make the same provocation: how much living and dying do we need to witness before we see the emptiness that is the essence of all things? By surrendering to this emptiness, we let go of the illusion that our identities and the beliefs that forge them stand on solid ground. It is the ultimate expression of humility that allows us to find a connection to each other that is deeper than love. It releases a profound compassion for the suffering we all share, regardless of the gods we worship. To the Buddhists who built them, it never mattered whether we looked up at statues or at the empty spaces where they once stood. The archaeologist and Jesuit priest, Peter Levi, who travelled to Bamiyan, observed that, 'No statue that has had its face removed can express justice or law or illumination or mercy,' before adding, 'but there is a disturbing presence about these two giants that does express something.'[19] He was right: they express Nothing. It is in these two, vast empty spaces where the Buddhas once stood that we feel the presence of an absence, the memory of the giants around whose vanished feet travellers would walk, repeating the circular motion that marks the passing away of all things. Like the 'colossal wreck' of Shelley's Ozymandias, the Buddhas of Bamiyan are witnesses to our vain hunger for permanence and a broken canvas on which we carve our love and our hate.

HECATE

BUILT: Unknown

DESTROYED: *c.*840

John the Grammarian, Patriarch of Constantinople, looked up as three men climbed slowly, their ladders pressed against the stone column. When they reached the bronze, three-headed figure at the top, they set about its destruction. Using mattocks and smaller tools, they each hacked at a head. Balancing uneasily on the wooden rungs, they went about their work with relish. Below them, the patriarch chanted incantations, his voice growing stronger as the first head broke off and fell. Shortly after, the second head smashed as it struck the ground. By now exhausted, they hacked at the last remaining bronze head. The neck began to break off, but it wouldn't fall. When it slumped forward and swung to one side, barely attached to the statue's shoulders, the patriarch fell silent and called the men down. Their work was done. The only surviving image of the destruction is found in A *Synopsis of History*, compiled in the eleventh century by the Greek historian John Skylitzes.

A short time after the destruction of the statue, barbarians attacked Constantinople. The historical record is unclear as to who precisely they were but it may have been the first incursion into the Byzantine Empire by warriors from Rus' Khaganate. It is likely they originated in Scandinavia and traded in the Crimea and modern-day Krasnodar Krai in Russia. Whoever the barbarians were, their attack ended in defeat. Two of their chiefs were killed in battle while a third, badly wounded, escaped.

The attack happened around 840, the statue was of the Greek goddess Hecate and the attempted triple beheading takes us to the heart of the story of one of the longest iconoclastic periods in history. That story begins with the Roman Emperor Constantine the Great and the foundation of one of the most important cities of the ancient world.

In 330, Constantine made Byzantium the capital of the Roman Empire. To give the city the grandeur required of an immortal capital, he imported statues, relics and icons, stripping distant temples, palaces and sanctuaries of their statues and ornaments. His armies transported them to Constantinople, the city that had now taken his name. More than a hundred years after the emperor's death, the Greek historian Zosimus observed that Constantine's aim was to make the city 'a residence worthy of an emperor'.[1] Sozomen, a fifth-century lawyer and church historian, described the 'brazen images, skilfully wrought, which were carried to the city, named after the emperor, and placed there as objects of embellishment, where they may still be seen in public places, as in the streets, the Hippodrome and the palaces. Amongst them was the statue of Apollo ... the statues of the muses from Helicon, the tripods from Delphos, and the much-extolled Pan.'[2] It is likely that the statue of Hecate was also among them. She stood in the Hippodrome, the city's chariot-racing arena, whose gates were guarded by a statue of four horses, a masterpiece by the Greek sculptor Lysippus.

The emperors who succeeded Constantine continued to bring statues and ornaments to Constantinople, albeit in fewer numbers. The Benedictine monk and historian Paul the Deacon, writing in the eighth century, recalled what happened when, in 663, Emperor Constans II became the first emperor in 200 years to set foot in Rome: 'Remaining at Rome twelve days, he pulled down everything that in ancient times had been made of metal for the ornament of the city, to such an extent that he even stripped off the roof of the church of the blessed Mary ... and he took away from there the bronze tiles and sent them with all the other ornaments to Constantinople.'[3]

Even at the height of its power, the city was the target of invaders. In 717, Emperor Leo III defeated an army of 80,000 Muslims who laid siege to Constantinople. Yet even this great victory offered little more than temporary relief and it was only a matter of time before the next attack. But victories on the battlefield and the city's growing wealth and power convinced the people that God was on their side. That changed in 726, nine years into Leo III's reign, when a long-dormant volcano erupted. Lava and stones, some as large as hills, were hurled miles into the air. The earth shook as they crashed to the ground and the Aegean Sea clogged with volcanic debris. For many days, the sky darkened. To a people steeped in superstition, the devastation meant only one thing: God was angry. But why?

In an age when natural events were filled with supernatural meaning, the volcanic eruption could only indicate malevolent forces at work. In searching for reasons why these forces should turn against the empire and what could be done to pacify them, Leo and the leaders of the Church returned to a debate that was already raging in the Byzantine Empire. It centred on the role of icons (sacred images or paintings, usually depicting Jesus, the Virgin Mary or the saints). To ordinary people, such images were a source of great comfort. Facing constant anxiety about the collapse of their civilisation, either through invasion by the Islamic armies of the Umayyad caliphate or as a result of other divinely ordained disasters, ordinary people prayed to their icons to protect them. Through them they also found a direct connection to God. Some early Christians believed the relic of a saint contained the actual presence of the saint. This belief that the faithful had direct access to the saints through their relics was now transferred onto icons. Stories abounded of their power. A text written in the early sixth century tells how a linen cloth that bore the image of Jesus Christ was found in a well in Kamouliani in Syria. Despite having been in the stagnant water for some time, the cloth was dry and the image untainted. Emperor Justinian I even had the miraculous cloth paraded periodically through the city.

Over centuries, the idea spread that the person represented in an icon was actually present in it. Arculf, on his pilgrimage to the Holy Land in the late seventh century was told the story of a soldier about to go into battle. Seeking an auspicious departure, the soldier knelt before an image of St George and asked 'to be delivered from all dangers'. He spoke to the image as though St George 'were present in person'.[4] This story mirrors a much earlier account by Gregory of Nyssa of the effects of the relics of St Theodore: 'Those who behold them embrace them as though the very body were living and flowering ... then they shed tears for his piety and suffering and they address to the martyr their prayers of intercession as though he were present and whole.'[5]

Whilst the idea of the presence of a saint in his relics was widely accepted, the expansion of this presence into icons created a deep schism within the Church. In 692, the Quinisext Council sought to distinguish between acceptable and unacceptable images. There was concern that impressions filtered through the bodily senses might corrupt the soul and the council ordered 'that henceforth there shall in no way be made pictures, whether they are in paintings, or in what way so ever, which attract the eye and corrupt the mind'.[6] Many Church leaders were appalled that icons were even being used as godparents during baptisms and, with the remnants of the erupting volcano still burning, Leo III made his move. He attributed the volcanic eruption to God's displeasure at the worship of icons. There was now no going back and the first wave of iconoclasm (literally 'the smashing of icons') began in earnest in 730. Leo personally destroyed *Christ Chalkites*, an image of Christ that marked the entrance to the Great Palace of Constantinople.

These actions provoked riots as the people resisted, but the destruction of icons continued under Leo's son Constantine V, who succeeded him in 741. A reaction by those who defended icon worship, led by Constantine's brother-in-law Artabasdos, who briefly deposed him, was rapidly and brutally crushed. As punishment, Constantine publicly blinded Artabasdos and his two sons. He also captured Anastasios, the patriarch who crowned the usurper, beat and stripped him before making him ride backwards on a donkey while the baying mob jeered him.

Buoyed by his triumph, Constantine accelerated the destruction of icons and in 754 he convened a synod at Hieria. Dominated by iconoclast clergy, the synod was unequivocal in its condemnation of icon veneration. How could a painting, they argued, be an appropriate object of worship when it contained only the human side of Jesus and excluded the divine? And if those who worshipped icons believed the divine aspect of Jesus was present in a work of art, then they were mingling what cannot be mingled, the divine and the human.[7]

This argument takes us to the heart of Byzantine iconoclasm, and it set the priests against the people. Ordinary people had little interest or ability to engage in complex theological debates about the dual nature of Christ. They drew comfort from the belief that icons gave them direct access to the divine and they were in no mood to relinquish them. For the ecclesiastical authorities, however, this was not only theologically incorrect but threatened their position as intercessors between the sacred and the profane. For them, the divine and the human were irredeemably separated and came together only in the Eucharist.

Yet, for many, the removal of any sacred presence from the icon stripped it of meaning. Even today, when we stand in front of a painting, it is not enough simply to admire the technical skill of the artist. It is the beating heart of the artist or the traces of the people in the paintings that moves us. In van Gogh's *Wheatfield with Crows*, it's the spectre of the artist, shortly before his suicide, that gives the painting its power. In Rembrandt's *The Return of the Prodigal Son*, the tenderness of the father and the repentance of the son mark the canvas with the presence of extraordinary grief and compassion.

Without this presence paintings are cold, clinical and hold our attention for a few bewildered seconds as we pass by, unmoved. The importance of the artist to the meaning of the work of art has been challenged by the deconstructive work of Jacques Derrida, for whom art, literature and the products of culture are merely a play of signs defined by the absence of any subject to make that play meaningful. Behind a letter, a word or a face are other letters, other words, other faces. We never find an author, an artist or a god in a work of art. A work of art is disconnected from any notion of the 'real world' and has no meaning outside itself.

This intellectualisation of art as a playful dissemination of signs would have made no sense to the Byzantines. For them, realism and emotional significance were the determinants of the value of a work of art. It confronted them with something greater than themselves and acted as a stimulus to their deepest emotional needs. It was protective, healing and redemptive. It was, as the contemporary performance artist Marina Abramovic said of her own work, 'like Lourdes'.[8]

It was this sacred quality of Byzantine icons that gave them a powerful hold over the imagination of the people. No amount of ecclesiastical power or theological nuance could loosen this grip. There is a story of a monk and icon painter called Lazaros who was ordered to stop painting by Theophilos, the last of the iconoclast emperors. When Lazaros refused, the emperor threw him into prison. On his release, the monk still refused to stop painting. As punishment, his hands were branded with red-hot irons. Despite his injuries, which nearly killed him, Lazaros continued to paint. Another story, in the *Treatise Against Demons* by Anastasios of Sinai, tells of a painting of St Theodore that hung on the walls of a church outside Damascus. When a Muslim invader thrust his hand through the portrait, the painting bled. At that very moment, twenty-nine Muslim soldiers collapsed and died.

The miraculous properties of paintings have also been claimed for statues. The idea that statues can bleed, weep and even drink milk, is common across many religious traditions and is believed by the faithful to this day. In 1998, a statue of the Virgin Mary was taken from the Bosnian town of Medjugorje to a small church in Mora, Spain, where it cried tears of blood. In 1995, after a statue of the Hindu god Ganesh began drinking milk, similar incidents were reported in Hindu temples around the world.

For the people of the Byzantine Empire, to be present before an icon was to be present before the sacred. This was no theoretical position; it was a matter of faith. Statues were universally believed to be animated, bewitched. As such, they shattered the boundary between sacred and profane, divine and human. In this animistic view of devotional art, it was entirely reasonable to believe that the plundered pagan statues that decorated Constantinople housed demons. While ecclesiastical leaders had often sought the destruction of these statues, they were usually left untouched. This was largely out of fear that the sinister soul encased in bronze, marble or gold might be unleashed. And there were plenty of stories to suggest this was the case. In 602, a calligrapher passing the temple dedicated to the Greek goddess Tyche in Alexandria, heard a strange noise coming from within. As he peered inside, he stared in disbelief as all the statues came down from their pedestals and told him of the assassination of the Emperor Maurice in Constantinople that very day. Shocked, the calligrapher passed the message on and, even though he was not believed, nine days later the assassination was confirmed.

Brief Historical Expositions, an eighth-century guide to Constantinople, contains many stories about the power of statues that reflect the beliefs of ordinary people. One of the stories tells of the removal of the antique statue of Phidaleia, the wife of King Byzas, the mythical founder of the city. The place where the statue stood began to tremble and when the tremor became an earthquake, it required the intervention of St Sabas to bring the earthquake to an end. Another story is a cautionary tale, set in about 460 during the reign of Leo I, that tells of Ardaburius, the Master of Soldiers, who destroyed a statue of Aelius Herodianus. When the statue crashed to the ground, Ardaburius found 133 talents of gold on the pedestal. Convinced of the virtue of his actions, he gave the gold to the emperor, who, instead of rewarding him, put Ardaburius to death. This tale of a statue exacting retribution for its own destruction served as a reminder of the demons housed within statues and as a warning of what might happen if they were attacked.

The Second (and last) period of Byzantine iconoclasm began in 814 and ended in 842. The triple beheading of the statue of Hecate, sanctioned by John the Grammarian, was one of the last iconoclastic acts. Hecate was the Greek goddess of thresholds and crossroads, which explains her three heads, all facing in different directions. She was also the goddess of magic and witchcraft. In destroying the statue, John believed the demons it unleashed would protect the city against the invading barbarians. Subsequent events proved him correct. In a cruel symmetry, the death of the two defeated barbarian chiefs mirrored the two severed heads of Hecate. The fate of the third, fleeing the battle, wounded and defeated, reflected the third head of Hecate that, despite the hacking and hammering of the patriarch's men, refused to fall to the ground.

In 842, the Emperor Theophilos died of dysentery. His wife Theodora came to power as regent for their two-year-old son and her ascension marked the end of the last iconoclastic period. After he refused to resign his position, John the Grammarian was deposed, sent into exile and never returned to Constantinople. An image, believed to be that of John, can be found in the *Khludov Psalter*, a manuscript compiled shortly after the end of the Second Iconoclasm. It shows Jesus being speared by Roman soldiers during the crucifixion. John the Grammarian stands in the foreground, destroying an icon of Jesus. The image includes the text of Psalm 68, the first verse of which reads, 'Let God arise, let his enemies be scattered; let them also that hate him flee before him.' In another image from the same book, the iconophile Patriarch Nikephoros tramples John the

Grammarian underfoot. On the left of the painting sits the text of Psalm 52: 'God shall likewise destroy thee forever, he shall take thee away, and pluck thee out of thy dwelling place, and root thee out of the land of the living.'

John the Grammarian may have lost his power, but statues did not and the Byzantine belief in the magical properties of statues persists, albeit in secular clothing. We may no longer believe that destroying statues unleashes spirits or demons, but there is no doubt that the destruction of statues is viewed as having an effect beyond the heady pleasures of transgression. For John, beheading Hecate offered protection against invasion; for protestors who topple statues in modern cities, they are attacking the institutions, ideals and values that the statue represents. The difference between them is that John's demons were literal, while ours are metaphorical. In both cases, the statues are infused with a meaning beyond their aesthetic value. If this meaning were absent, the destruction would lose all purpose. We only ever destroy statues because we believe they are metaphorically possessed with the spirit, the presence, of that which we hate. It is not the stone or metal we destroy: it is what the statue represents. As Byzantine scholar Anne Karahan wrote, the iconoclast controversy was about the 'distribution of power, aspirations of riches and, last but not least, ideology'.[9]

This struggle for power and ideological supremacy is a constant in the history of statue destruction. The attacks on statues in the wake of the killing of George Floyd were attacks on the principles and institutions of liberal democracy that the protestors blamed for a multitude of evils, from racism to gender discrimination. Many observers feared the mob violence would not mark the beginning of a new social order but simply a descent into chaos. They watched as protestors toppled statues in the name of an ill-defined ideal of social justice without ever thinking how that justice might be built.

But what if collapse was the aim, even an unconscious one, regardless of the consequences? Michel Foucault, the French philosopher, took the view that 'popular justice would best be served by throwing open every prison and shutting down every court ... and then let the popular "need for retaliation" run its course'.[10] He hoped, as did many of the protestors, that this exercise of 'power without inhibitions' might lead to new mechanisms of justice.

It is, of course, easier to retaliate against real or imagined enemies than it is to engage in dialogue. It is also easier to accuse and destroy than it is to forgive and build. One of the reasons pagan statues were allowed to stand in Constantinople was because of the fear of the demons their destruction might unleash. Earlier in this chapter, we saw how people believed the removal of the statue of Phidaleia caused an earthquake. Given such terrifying consequences, it is not surprising they believed it was safer to allow pagan statues to remain standing.

This ancient fear of what forces might be set in motion by the destruction of statues is, at the very least, a reasonable one and modern iconoclasts have unleashed demons of their own: hate, intolerance and mutual incomprehension. But once they are in motion, mobs justify their attacks as acts of self-defence and when they tell the story of the statues they destroyed, they will say they did it out of love.

OUR LADY OF CAVERSHAM

BUILT: 1106

DESTROYED: 14 September 1538

L ike demons, they came in the night. Bands of men moving from one sacred site to another, bringing ruin in their wake. On 14 September 1538, Henry VIII's enforcers, led by Dr John London arrived at the gates of the church in Caversham. As well as a shrine to the Virgin Mary, the church housed many relics. Allegedly, these included two knives, one that killed Henry VI in 1471 in the Tower of London, and another that killed King Edward, known as Edward the Martyr, as he stood at the gates of Corfe Castle in 978.

Three days after his arrival in Caversham, John London wrote to Thomas Cromwell, Henry's chief minister, informing him that the statue of the Virgin Mary had been placed 'in a chest fast locked and nailed up'.[1] He promised to send it to Cromwell by the next barge to London and described, in forensic detail, the destruction of the shrine at Caversham. First, his men 'pulled down the image of Our Lady at Caversham whereunto was great pilgrimage. It is plated over with silver.' Then they 'pulled down the place she stood in with the lights, shrouds, crutches, images of wax &c about the chapel, and defaced the same thoroughly.' It was not enough to send the statue of the Virgin Mary to Cromwell, for the chief minister to destroy it at his pleasure. The shrine and the chapel that housed it had to be utterly ruined, as if one act of depravity opened the gates to another, until nothing was spared.

In a separate letter written to Cromwell's secretary, Thomas Wriothesely, London wrote that 'a relic as great as any' had been taken from the church, 'an angel with one wing that brought to Caversham the spear's head that pierced our Saviour's side upon the Cross'.[2] He also found a fragment of the noose that hanged Judas and other lesser relics. When the destruction was over, John London secured the doors of the church to preserve the lead from the roof for the king. Like scavengers around a carcass, there was to be no waste.

The destruction of the shrine brought to an end at least 500 years of pilgrimage and devotion. The earliest record of Our Lady of Caversham dates from 1106 when Duke Robert of Normandy, on his return from the First Crusade, offered a relic to the shrine. Over the centuries, the Caversham shrine became the object of many pilgrimages, one of the last being a visit from Queen Catherine of Aragon on 17 July 1532. She prayed to Our Lady of Caversham and sought the Virgin Mary's guidance in the Great Matter of her divorce from Henry VIII. Catherine's refusal to free the king to marry his mistress, Anne Boleyn, led to the Reformation in England and the dissolution of the monasteries, of which Our Lady at Caversham was one of many victims. When the statue of the Virgin Mary finally arrived in London, it was burned by Cromwell along with other significant statues, including Our Lady of Walsingham and Our Lady of Ipswich.

By the time of the attack on the shrine at Caversham in the late summer of 1538, Anne Boleyn had been dead for more than two years. After she failed to give Henry the son and heir he craved, Cromwell built a legal case against her. She was found guilty of adultery, incest and conspiring against the king. After her conviction, she denied the charges against her, but was careful to note that she had failed to show Henry the 'humility which his goodness to me merited'.

Intelligent and headstrong, Anne had made enemies. Cardinal Wolsey called her the 'midnight crow'[3] while the Spanish ambassador Chapuys Eustache delighted in the fate of 'the English Messalina'. When Chapuys heard that Anne blamed him for her fall from grace, he was 'flattered by the compliment, for she would have cast me to the dogs!'[4] Henry himself said 'she hath a stout heart' for which he was happy to make her pay with her life.

On 19 May 1536, she stepped onto the scaffold at the Tower of London. After paying the executioner and delivering a prepared speech, her voice calm and resolute, Anne's head was cut off. As it fell into the straw, her name was already being erased from royal places, where her initials were being replaced with those of Henry's new mistress, Jane Seymour. Henry never mentioned Anne's name again. Lord Thomas Howard, Anne Boleyn's uncle, observed that it was Henry's nature 'never to hold in affection any person he had cast from him that formerly he had loved'.[5]

Two women. The Virgin Mary and Anne Boleyn, a Catholic icon and a queen. Both were destroyed by a king whose transformation from a tall, handsome, athletic youth into a tyrant was, by the time of Anne's death, complete. The story of the burning of Our Lady of Caversham and the beheading of Anne Boleyn, is the story of this descent into tyranny. In a pattern we see throughout this book, the destruction of statues is symbolic of this escalation of intolerance.

Some historians[6] have laid the blame for the change in Henry's character and physical appearance after the early 1530s on his biology. They speculate he may have been syphilitic, suffering from Cushing's disease or the effects of falling unconscious for two hours after a jousting accident. There is also speculation that Henry may have been the victim of McLeod syndrome, a rare genetic disorder that typically manifests in middle age. While symptoms range from movement disorders to seizures, it also causes sudden behavioural changes, increased impulsiveness and psychosis.

What is not in doubt is the magnitude of the physical changes that occurred in the king. Between 1514 and 1536, his waist increased a mere two inches. By 1541, he had put a further seventeen inches on his waist, which now measured more than fifty inches. Leg ulcers left him in constant pain and the treatments given to him, which included an application of worms and wine, worsened the condition they were meant to cure. By the end of his reign, Henry had to be winched up and down stairs on a special engine and he used the Tudor equivalent of a wheelchair.

The psychological and behavioural changes in Henry were even more marked. With age, Henry's moods became erratic, his narcissism increased and his paranoia deepened. Such changes are, of course, typical of what happens when power loses control of itself, when kings became tyrants. The temptation of tyranny, of excessive order maintained by unjust force, is often too compelling to resist. And because a king grows tyrannical in small, incremental steps, it is hard to see what he is becoming until it is too late.

In the popular imagination, Henry's love for Anne drove him to seek a divorce from Catherine of Aragon. But there was another factor that weighed heavier in Henry's mind than love. He blamed the absence of a male heir on the fact that Catherine was betrothed first to his brother Arthur, who died a year after their marriage. In taking his dead brother's wife, Henry feared that he had displeased God, who in Leviticus (20:21) tells Moses that 'if a man shall take his brother's wife, it is an unclean thing: he hath uncovered his brother's nakedness: they shall bear their sin; they shall die childless'.

This biblical judgement on his marriage haunted Henry and put urgency into his pursuit of Anne. They met after she had spent nine years in Europe, seven of them in France. When Anne returned, now a sophisticated young woman, Henry became obsessed with her. She resisted his advances, which, as she correctly calculated, amplified them. He wrote to her, 'I wolde you were in my arms or I in yours for I think it long syns I kyst you.'[7] Like an infatuated schoolboy, he signed off a letter by separating his initials with the French phrase, *autre ne cherche* ('I look for no other'), whilst placing her initials in a heart.

Henry, who spent money voraciously regardless of the resources at his disposal, lavished gifts on his mistress. He gave Anne emeralds, rubies, nineteen diamonds to place in her hair and endless garments made of velvet, satin and the finest linens. As his passion for Anne increased, Henry grew furious at his inability to divorce his wife. He demanded that Cardinal Wolsey persuade Pope Clement VI to grant him a divorce from Catherine. When Wolsey failed to deliver, he was stripped of his office and died in 1530 on his way from Yorkshire to London to face charges of treason.

The fall of Wolsey emboldened Henry. His belief in his own infallibility grew, even as many citizens sided with Catherine. Some showed their displeasure openly. A man spotted the king riding alone through the forests of Woodstock and shouted at him, 'Back your wife!' Elizabeth Barton, a mystic nun, claimed to have taken the form of a spirit that followed Henry and Anne on their visit to Calais in October 1532. She witnessed an angel prevent Henry from receiving the host during Holy Communion, suggesting his excommunication. More ominously, in the summer of 1533, two women, one of them pregnant, were stripped, their ears hacked off and nailed to a post, for daring to shout that Catherine was the true queen of England.

Thomas Cromwell fuelled Henry's descent into tyranny by reinforcing his vanity and his divine right to determine his own future, regardless of the wishes of the Pope. Cromwell promised to make Henry 'the richest king that ever was in England'[8] and Stephen Gardiner, Bishop of Winchester, described Henry as one who 'excelled in God's sight among all other human creatures'.[9] Pamphlets were produced in ever-increasing numbers, extolling this idealised image of King Henry and he became the first monarch whose image was displayed in the homes of his people. In 1534, following a number of lesser statutes, the Act of Supremacy made Henry Supreme Head of the Church. In the same year, after the passing of the Treason Act, a clergyman, loyal to Rome, complained bitterly that 'the Devil reigneth over us now'.[10]

Where power becomes tyrannical, the centre, as the poet W.B. Yeats observed, cannot hold. Divisions are magnified as fear compels people to cower and take sides. Co-existence becomes impossible as religious and political views are no longer seen as subjects for debate but as zero-sum games where the stakes are measured in blood. Shortly before the destruction of the statue of the Virgin Mary at Caversham, Lord Lisle, the governor of Calais, took to sleeping in his armour in case sectarian violence should erupt while he slept.

In such circumstances, pleas for tolerance fall on deaf ears. As Henry's mood darkened, Thomas More, his Lord Chancellor, who was later executed because of his refusal to accept the Oath of Succession, which recognised the king's heirs by Anne Boleyn as legitimate, prayed to God 'that some of us, as high as we seem to sit upon the mountains, treading heretics under our feet like ants, live not in the day that we gladly would wish to be at a league and composition with them, to let them have their churches quietly to themselves, so that they would be content to let us have ours quietly to ourselves'.[11]

More's plea for tolerance fell, as he knew it would, on deaf ears. He understood the ruin unchecked power imposes on minds already weakened by status and vanity. It was probably this, rather than genetics, illness or injury, that lay at the root of Henry's descent into tyranny. His behaviour led Francis I, king of France, to describe Henry as 'the most strange man in the world ... so pertinacious and fiercely proud that it is almost impossible to bear with him'.

As Henry broke one tradition, one rule, one behavioural convention after another, he grew increasingly intolerant of anyone who questioned him. Fear spread through those who might have restrained him, and Cardinal Pole observed that 'here is all the difficulty in a prince. Who will tell him his fault? And if one such be found, where is the prince that will hear him?'[12] Even as his weight and leg ulcers made him a grotesque parody of the handsome youth he once was, Henry grew increasingly unable to find any fault in himself. According to Philippa Gregory 'Henry shrank from any realistic view of himself, and demanded that there should be no contradiction to his view of himself as the eternally golden, eternally young, potent Prince.'[13]

Henry may have torn a kingdom apart for love, but it wasn't his love of Anne Boleyn. Henry's primary love was himself. But with Henry mired in delusion, how can we explain that love?

We may find the answer in a brilliant passage, written long after the death of Henry VIII and Anne Boleyn. In *The Gay Science*, Friedrich Nietzsche wrote about a distorted form of love where the 'lover desires unconditional power over the soul and body of the beloved; he alone wants to be loved and desires to live and rule in the other soul as supreme and supremely desirable'.[14] Nietzsche's belief that the lover desires to receive love more than to give it, to triumph over all rivals and exert complete power over the body and soul of the beloved, is the definition of tyrannical egoism. A love driven by the compulsion to possess can only spiral endlessly into greater depths of depravity, as the impossibility and tedium of possession become apparent.

When Anne became his wife, Henry tired of her. When he took mistresses, he treated her with contempt, warning her to 'shut her eyes and endure as her betters had done'.[15] When she failed to provide him with an heir, he killed her. Those who imagine that he never spoke her name again out of grief or remorse are mistaken. His silence was born of indifference.

After the final break with Rome and Henry's accession to supreme power in Church and State, there was no longer any mediation between king and God. For any man, this is a precarious plinth on which to stand. The result is an apocalyptic nightmare, eloquently captured by Henry Howard, Earl of Surrey:

> I saw a royal throne whereas that Justice should have sit;
> Instead of whom I saw, with fierce and cruel mood,
> Where wrong was sat, that bloody beast, that drunk the guiltless blood.[16]

The spilling of 'guiltless blood' is how the tyrant makes himself known. Henry executed more than 70,000 people during his reign, or 3 per cent of the population. That is today's equivalent of 200 million executions spread across the world. With every execution, Henry felt the paradox of being powerful and powerless at the same time. While he could spill blood, he could not erase all his enemies from the face of the earth, nor could he possess the love of those who refused to give it.

Henry's fate, as is the fate of all tyrants, was a toxic brew of narcissism, fantasy, paranoia and isolation. The more power Henry took for himself, the more he saw dissent in every shadow, which compelled a physical and emotional retreat into himself. Trusting no one, he deceived himself and allowed himself to be deceived by flatterers and sycophants, the enablers of tyranny. The depth of his paranoia was such that 'if I thought my cap knew my counsel, I would cast it into the fire and burn it'.[17] In his palaces at Hampton Court, York Place and Greenwich, he built private lodgings accessible only by covered galleries or private watergates, allowing him to move about unseen. Loving and living in a world of his own making, there was no one willing or able to restore Henry's connection to himself or to the reality of the church and state over which he could never exercise complete control.

The destruction of Our Lady of Caversham and the burning of the statue of the Virgin Mary may have been symbolic of Henry's power and authority over the Church. It did not, however, give him power over the minds of those bereft at the destruction of the symbols of their faith. He may have had the power to execute Anne Boleyn, but he was powerless to stop her mocking his poetry and his sexual inadequacies. The refusal of the tyrant to accept any limits to his power is what fuels the increasing depravity of the tyranny he creates. Even if Henry had beheaded his last subject, burned the last idolatrous statue, it would not have been enough. In attempting to possess what cannot be possessed, govern what cannot be governed, the 'bloody beast', insatiable in his appetite for destruction, laid waste to everything he touched.

In routing his enemies or those he wanted to be rid of, Henry gave the appearance of due process. Confessions mattered, however ruthlessly they were extracted, and trials, whose outcomes were known in advance, took place to create the illusion of justice and order. Invariably, when an accusation was made, guilt was assumed and then 'proven'.

Corruption of this magnitude is viral. It creates the stage for vindictiveness and the settling of scores. When Henry tired of Anne Boleyn and sought evidence of her infidelity, Lady Jane Parker, wife of Anne Boleyn's brother, stepped forward and obliged him. She accused her husband George Boleyn, who was Anne's brother, of having sexual relations with his sister. If she expected Henry to remember her loyalty, he didn't. When, in 1542, she herself was accused of ena- bling an affair between Catherine Howard, Henry's fifth wife, and Thomas Culpeper, a friend of the king, she was arrested and put in the Tower of London, where she underwent a psychological collapse and was pronounced insane. Despite her condition, she was found guilty of high treason and executed on the same day as the queen.

Henry, in a typical expression of the tyrant's belief in his own victimhood, regretted 'his ill-luck in meeting such ill-conditioned wives, and blaming the Council for the last mischief'.[18] As for Thomas Culpeper, he was sentenced to be hanged, disembowelled while still alive and then quartered for his betrayal of the king. After pleas from his family, Henry granted Culpeper a gentleman's death by decapitation.

Another man, Francis Dereham, was given the same sentence as Culpeper. However, he was of low birth and did not receive the king's mercy. Accused of having sexual intercourse with Catherine before she married Henry and of promising to marry her after the king's death, Dereham suffered the horrors of the original sentence. And when it was Queen Catherine's turn to be taken to the Tower of London to await her execution, her barge was covered, so she did not see Culpeper and Dereham's heads stuck on pikes on Tower Bridge. Even Thomas Cromwell, Henry's chief minister who engineered the break with Rome to enable the king to marry Anne Boleyn, was accused of treason and beheaded in 1540.

As this spectacle of violence escalated, the majority, out of fear for their lives, did not protest. They fell silent and when cornered and compelled to speak, it was often to admit guilt for crimes they did not commit. The novelist George Eliot may have been right to suggest that every 'yoked creature' has 'its private opinions',[19] but few will express them publicly. When a man like John London, Henry's enforcer, bursts through our door and assaults the values and ideals that hold our lives together, there is not one of us who knows whether we will acquiesce or resist, or how much pain our conscience can withstand before it breaks.

HUITZILOPOCHTLI

BUILT: *c.*1487

DESTROYED: 1521

The path towards disaster began in 1517 when a Spanish expedition made contact with the Maya for the first time in the Yucatán. Despite suffering the loss of more than twenty men in battle, Francisco Hernández de Cordóba, the leader of the expedition, returned with many gold pieces. These represented payments made to the Maya by an unknown civilisation based in an unexplored territory called Mexico.

When news of the gold reached Diego Velázquez, the Spanish governor of Cuba, it set in motion a fateful train of events. Velázquez had lived in the Caribbean for twenty-five years and now he had a scent of the glory that the long-fabled gold would bring him and the Spanish Crown. He chose Hernán Cortés to lead an expedition to find its source. A compulsive gambler, Cortés seized the opportunity now given to him by Velázquez. He took eleven ships, a brigantine and 500 men and travelled inland.

Eventually, Cortés's force arrived at an island in the middle of Lake Texcoco, on which stood the great centre of Aztec¹ civilisation. Bernal Díaz del Castillo, one of the soldiers, described the amazement felt by his fellows as they saw the magnificent cities of this civilisation for the first time: 'we were astounded ... These great towns and *cues* and buildings rising from the water, all made of stone, seemed like an enchanted vision ... It was all so wonderful that I did not know how to describe this first glimpse of things never heard of, seen, or dreamed of before.'²

Most impressive of all was the Templo Mayor, or the Great Temple, set in the centre of Tenochtitlan, the Aztec capital. A vast pyramid with two parallel staircases of 113 steps leading to a stone platform at the top, Cortés described it as 'higher than the cathedral of Seville'. On the stone platform stood two sanctuaries, one containing a statue of the rain god Tlaloc and the other a statue of Huitzilopochtli, the sun god and god of war, the principal deity of the Aztecs. The arrival of the tiny force of Spaniards caught the Aztec emperor Moctezuma off balance and, together with his indigenous allies, Cortés took Tenochtitlan after a three-month siege. Eighteen years after this catastrophic defeat of the Aztecs, a remarkable trial took place that threw the fate of the statue of Huitzilopochtli into question.

In 1539, Pochtecatl Tlaylotla, a native leader, was charged with idolatry and brought before the Spanish inquisitor, Bishop Juan de Zumárraga. Tlaylotla claimed that the statue survived the Spanish conquest of Tenochtitlan. He claimed to have removed it himself, along with the statues of four other gods, to prevent the Spanish from destroying them.

The inquisitor listened incredulously. Stories told by conquistadors described a statue far too big to be carried out of the temple by a single man. One description claimed that the statue of Huitzilopochtli was twelve feet tall and made of stone. Peter Martyr d'Anghiera, a chronicler of the Indies, compared the statue of Huitzilopochtli to the Colossus of Rhodes and described it as being made of marble and as tall as three men. Bernal Díaz del Castillo gave a vivid description of the cult statue of the Aztec war god: 'it had a very broad face and monstrous and terrible eyes, and the whole of his body was covered with precious stones'.[3] Another account, from the Dominican friar Diego Durán, portrayed it as a 'wooden statue carved in the image of a man seated upon a blue wooden bench ... garbed and adorned, the idol always stood upon a tall altar'.[4]

In his second letter to the king of Spain in 1520, Cortés himself wrote of 'three rooms within this great temple for the principal idols, which are of remarkable size and stature and decorated with many designs and sculptures, both in stone and in wood ... The figures of the idols in which these people believe are very much larger than the body of a big man. They are made of dough from all the seeds and vegetables which they eat, ground and mixed together, and bound with the blood of human hearts which those priests tear out while still beating.'[5] If the statue was, in fact, a 'dough' idol, it would have been known as a *tzoalli* and made out of amaranth flour mixed with syrup or honey, which Cortés mistook for human blood. Regardless of its size, the inquisitor knew the accused man could not have salvaged the statue of Huitzilopochtli. He was certain of this because the large cult statue that stood in the shrine at the summit of the Templo Mayor had been destroyed. The inquisitor was looking for something else. He demanded that Pochtecatl Tlaylotla make a drawing of what he had taken. The inquisitor watched as the native leader drafted a picture of five wrapped bundles to represent the removal of the statues. The inquisitor smiled. He had found what he was looking for. What the Bishop Juan de Zumárraga had wanted to know was the fate of a number of mysterious wrapped and bundled idols, which had allegedly been saved from destruction. Now he had his answer.

Pochtecatl Tlaylotla did not spirit a statue made of wood, stone, marble or 'dough' out of the Templo Mayor. He took what the Aztecs called a 'sacred bundle'. These contained the objects and ritual paraphernalia associated with the gods. Held together by a fabric wrapper, they were easily carried from one place to another. In the drawing Tlaylotla made for the inquisitor and in drawings depicting the long migration of the Aztecs from their mythical homeland to Tenochtitlan, Huitzilopochtli is represented as sacred bundle.

An ancient myth tells the story of how the god, wrapped in just such a bundle and speaking through priests, had guided his people on a 200-year march in search of a lake where they were to build a great city. Huitzilopochtli told them they would know when they had arrived at the lake because they would see an eagle with a serpent in its beak, perched on a cactus. After a long and arduous journey, they finally stood before a vast lake and beheld what the god had prophesied. It was there they built Tenochtitlan.

As soon as the sacred bundle was unwrapped it released more than the objects it contained: it freed the sacred power, or *teotl*, of the god. This power was 'the secret and invisible content of the bundles' but despite its power, the *teotl* of a god was incapable of acting directly in the world. It needed an intermediary, a priest-shaman to give it form and interpret its desires. Besides, direct contact with the sacred was fatal, so bundles and statues of the gods enabled the Aztecs to speak to their deities without fear of destruction.

Sacrifice, as we shall see, played an important role in containing this sacred power, yet, in the colonial imagination, Huitzilopochtli stands as an archetype of a diabolical culture of sacrifice and cruelty. Stories spread of a barbarous people who indulged in ritualised slaughter on a breathtaking scale, such as the sacrifice of more than 80,000 victims during the coronation of the Aztec emperor Ahuitzotl in 1486. A seventeenth-century compendium claimed the main religious ritual of the Aztecs was to sacrifice thousands of victims 'to their Devil-god Vitzilopuchtli ... whose flesh likewise afterwards they did eat in a solemn banquet'.[6]

Bernal Díaz wrote how he saw captive Spanish soldiers carried up the steps of the Templo Mayor and then the Aztecs forced them to 'dance before the god Huitzilopochtli ... placed them on their backs on some stones ... and, with large flint knives they sawed open their chests, and drew out their palpitating hearts and offered them to their gods ...they kicked the bodies down the steps and Indian butchers, who were waiting below, cut off the arms and legs and flayed the faces and prepared them afterwards as a kind of glove leather with the beards still on ... and the stomachs and guts they threw to the tigers, lions and snakes'.[7]

The conquistadors saw these sacrificial rituals as acts of senseless violence, serving no purpose beyond delight in cruelty. This view confirmed their beliefs about pagan barbarism and justified their invasion. What these interpretations miss, however, is how the Aztecs viewed sacrifice. To them, sacrifice was the only means at their disposal to *contain* catastrophic violence. Where the con- quistadors saw cruelty and chaos, the Aztecs saw *protection against* unrestrained violence.

The survival of their civilisation was dependent on appeasing the gods. At any moment fire, storms, plagues, or invasion by armies more powerful than their own, could overwhelm and destroy them. The very rhythms of light and dark, sun and moon, might collapse. An eclipse was a portent of destruction that required sacrifice to sustain order. Blood and the excised hearts of sacrificial victims were believed to give Huitzilopochtli sufficient energy to prevent the sun from crashing to earth on its journey from dawn to dusk and to rise again after its descent into the underworld at night.

The sacred is a term that can be understood as referring to immense, terrifying forces that dominate and threaten the human quest for order. The Aztecs feared direct contact with the sacred, the collision of the divine and the human, because their civilisation could not withstand it. In the history of religion, we find many examples where direct, unmediated contact with the sacred is ruinous. In *The Idea of the Holy*, the German theologian Rudolf Otto described the experience of the mystic in direct contact with the divine as 'the feeling of one's own abasement, of being but "dust and ashes" and nothingness ... and so makes for the annihilation of the self'.[8]

One step removed from direct contact with the sacred, Aztec statues, idols and sacred bundles that spoke through an intermediary were a means of preserving order in the face of the overwhelming forces that threatened to destroy it. Collapse was inevitable if they were unable to appease their gods by mediating contact with the sacred through ritual. Ritualised sacrifice was the source of the great misunderstanding between the conquistadors and the Aztecs. To the

Spanish invaders, human sacrifice was uncontained or contagious violence; to the Aztecs, it was the means to *contain* the sacred power of contagious violence. What the conquistadors saw as chaos, the Aztecs regarded as their only defence *against* chaos. Essentially, seen through Aztec eyes, human sacrifice was a mechanism of restraint.

Aztec cruelty was ritualised and even war had rules. Before the arrival of the conquistadors, its aim was not gratuitous destruction, but dominance. In the Flower Wars, which dated from the mid-fifteenth century, conflicts between the Aztecs, their allies and enemies such as the Tlaxcala were fought to demonstrate skill in combat and to capture prisoners, whose sacrifice was necessary to contain the sacred power of contagious violence. The Aztecs were appalled that Spanish soldiers attacked pre-emptively and at night, killed at a distance using guns and canons and, above all, fought with the aim of killing rather than capturing the enemy.

The lack of military restraint on the part of the Spanish soldiers and their indigenous allies overwhelmed the Aztecs. When Spanish losses mounted and their men were sacrificed, the cruelty of the conquistadors escalated as the cycle of violence got out of control. Cortés's men discovered reserves of hate and violence they would have considered impossible before their expedition into Mexico. The Mexican historian Jose Luis Martinez said of Cortés, 'little by little he became tougher and he ended up being … a very tough and cruel man'.[9] The destruction of the Aztecs is a timeless tale of contained violence becoming a contagion, of fighting men transformed into genocidal killers.

Such descent into barbarism is by no means the preserve of colonial powers and Cortés was ultimately victorious because of the willing support of his indigenous allies who saw an opportunity to free themselves from the dominance of the Aztecs. The Tlaxcalteca and Tetzcoca, who fought alongside Cortés, outnumbered their Spanish allies by a factor of 200:1 and it was this combined indigenous and Spanish force, with a superiority over their opponents of as much as 5:1, that led to the defeat of the Aztec armies. Given this numerical dominance and the opportunity to exact retribution, the descent into contagious violence was entirely predictable. Men who had previously fought Flower Wars now engaged in ruthless, genocidal combat.

The historian Matthew Restall wrote, 'Condemning all conquistadors as bad is as facile as claiming all indigenous people are good; turning one entire ethnoracial group into perpetrators and another into victims is itself a kind of racism that no amount of moral indignation can redeem'.[10] While the Spanish soldiers 'let the genie of total warfare out of the bottle,' their indigenous allies eagerly accepted the power the Spanish genie unleashed. As atrocities mounted, combatants grew numb to the hell into which they were falling. At the beginning of the war, there is no doubt that Cortés wished to conquer Tenochtitlan and preserve its riches for the Spanish Crown and his own glory. After the fall of the city, as indigenous warriors marauded through the streets, killing indiscriminately, Pedro de Maluenda, a commissary working with Cortés noted, 'There is no house left to be burned and destroyed.'[11] With brutal clarity, Rodrìguez de Escobar observed that 'in order to win the city, it was necessary to destroy it'.[12]

Rudolf Otto used the biblical idea of the 'wrath of Yahweh' to express what it means to face the sacred directly and to lose oneself in its contagion. He describes it as 'like a hidden force of nature,' like stored-up electricity discharging itself upon anyone who comes too near. It is 'incalculable' and 'arbitrary'.[13]

The Wrath of God also forms part of the title of Werner Herzog's 1972 film about Lope de Aguirre, the Spanish conquistador who went in search of El Dorado, the mythical land of gold. The film, set forty years after the conquest of the Aztecs, opens with the conquistadors descending a steep mountain, barely visible through the mist. Their mission is to find El Dorado and claim its riches for the Spanish crown. Aguirre grows impatient with the limited ambitions of Don Pedro de Ursúa, the leader of the expedition. After supplies are lost and some of his men are killed, Ursúa decides the risks are too great, so he orders the conquistadors to abandon the search. Furious at what he sees as Ursúa's lack of ambition, Aguirre revolts, puts him on trial and hangs him from a tree.

Confined on a single raft, the conquistadors die, some from malnutrition, others killed by tribesmen who fire arrows from the riverbank. The Dominican friar, Brother Gaspar de Carvajal writes in his diary, 'I am sure Aguirre is leading us into destruction. I almost feel he does it deliberately.' Caravajal is right, but there is little calculation in Aguirre's behaviour. He is driven by forces he cannot control that ultimately overwhelm him. 'My men,' Aguirre says with contempt, 'measure riches in gold. It is more. It is power and fame. I despise them for it.' The film ends with Aguirre, the sole survivor, drifting to his inevitable death, his raft overrun by rats and monkeys, as he screams, 'I am the Wrath of God!'

There are many parallels between Cortés and Aguirre. The ostensible reason for both expeditions was the search for riches. Aguirre went looking for El Dorado, while Cortés told the Aztecs he 'suffered from a disease of the heart which is only cured by gold'.[14] While Cortés survived and Aguirre did not, they were both consumed by their ambition, which, in turn, consumed the world around them. 'Greed for power, like love,' wrote the poet Gaspar de Villagrá, 'will permit no rival.'[15] War and eroticism, hate and love, taken to their sacred extremes, consume everything.

Driven by a greed for power and glory, both Cortés and Aguirre made direct contact with the sacred, and it ruined them: Aguirre drifted to a lonely death; Cortés survived the war with the Aztecs, but he was a husk of the man who first arrived in Mexico. After the glory of attempting to do what Villagrá called 'things which it seems are reserved for God alone', the conqueror of the Aztecs lived an empty life, and in 1535 he arrived at a desolate beach in Baja. Like Don Quixote 'tilting at windmills', Cortés waved his sword at nothing and 'loudly' commanded his notary to write that 'the very illustrious Lord don Fernando Cortés ... discovered this land [and] I have come with my ships and fleet to conquer and settle it!'[16] This lifeless beach was his empire. There was to be no return to the glorious intensity of battle and victory. Cortés was left alone to fight himself.

Today, there is a red plaque on the whitewashed wall at the Church of Jesus Nazareno in Mexico City. It stands, austere and apologetic, to the left of the altar, out of the line of sight. Some distance from the plaque, encased in an unknown location in the stone walls of the church, are human remains. After arriving in Mexico from Seville in 1556, the remains were moved between several locations before Lucas Alamán, a government minister, hid them under a beam at the adjacent Hospital de Jesus. Facing demands that they be destroyed, he told the world they had been sent to the deceased's ancestors in Italy. Secretly, Alamán transferred the remains to the church and signed a burial act to ensure they survived a second time. When they were finally identified on 28 November 1946, some called for them to be cast into the sea. They survived. The red plaque is devoid of sentiment. It simply reads:

Hernán Cortés
1485–1547

A short walk from the plaque is the spot where Cortés, the Spanish conquistador, met the Aztec Emperor Moctezuma II on 8 November 1519. It was the first meeting in human history between the representatives of two civilisations who had no prior knowledge of each other's existence. Predictably, each side misinterpreted the other. Although the encounter ended cordially, within a year Moctezuma was dead and the two sides were engaged in a war that became a contagion. 'We are left,' Matthew Restall wrote about the final, devastating battle for Tenochtitlan, 'with the uncomfortable suspicion that, in the heat of the moment, that is all there was: the heat of the moment.'[17] It is fitting and mournful, therefore, that the defeat of the Aztecs, the loss of their culture and the destruction of the statues of their gods, is remembered by their descendants with a lament:

Do not fall down, for whoever falls
Falls forever.[18]

CONFUCIUS

BUILT: *c.*1730

DESTROYED: 29 November 1966

O n 29 November 1966, Chairman Mao received a telegram from Qufu, the birthplace and burial site of Confucius:

One hundred thousand members of the revolutionary masses would like to report a thrilling development to you: we have rebelled! We have rebelled! … We have levelled Confucius's grave; we have smashed the stelae extolling the virtues of the feudal emperors and kings, and we have obliterated the statues in the Confucius temple![1]

Local mobs and Red Guards, driven by the ideals of China's Cultural Revolution, came to Qufu to 'annihilate the Kong family business', which meant destroying anything connected to Confucius (known in China as Kong Fuzi or 'Master Kong'), his family or his disciples. They began the desecration of the Three Kong sites (the temple, the mansion and the cemetery) by smashing stelae and decapitating statues of the sage's family and disciples. They were, however, careful to leave the statue of Confucius himself untouched. This was done not out of fear or the remnants of piety. On the contrary, they had a special fate in store for it. On 29 November, they toppled the statue, placed a dunce's cap on its head and paraded it through the streets. Followers of Confucianism were made to walk alongside the statue, allowing the mob to ridicule and harass them.

When the procession reached the cemetery, a fire burned under a nearby bridge. Relics and artefacts were cast into the flames. Finally, the statue of Confucius was taken from the back of the truck and thrown into the fire. Jubilant mobs and Red Guards cheered. The desecration, however, was far from over.

Armed with picks and shovels, Mao's supporters were tasked with digging up the remains of 'the First Kongs and the Last Kongs', which referred to Confucius, the two generations that followed him and the most recent three generations of his lineage. The latter were Kong Lingyi, a seventy-sixth generation descendent of Confucius, who died in 1919, and his father and grandfather.

The mob went about its work with the fervour of zealots. Corpses were pulled out of smashed stone coffins. Precious stones, jewels and relics they discovered inside the coffins were stolen and sold. Perhaps the greatest riches, however, were found in the psychological satisfaction gained from humiliating the enemies of the revolution. On 30 November, the corpses of two women and two men were hanged from a tree. They were left on display for a week before being burned. A witness later described 'a strong memory of two odours: one was that of disinfectant, the kind you get in a hospital. It was as though they were going to operate in the open air. Then there was the stench of the corpses. It made you want to vomit.'

This proximity of violence and festivity is a constant when mobs destroy statues. In such toxic situations, when the individual's identity is submerged into the collective, there are no limits to the horror that ensues.[2] A graphic, official account of the desecration of the 'Kong family business' celebrated the vengeance of the mob against the corpse of Kong Lingyi: 'The poor and middle-lower peasants split open the coffin and dismembered the corpse. They burnt that dead dog till he was nothing but ash. In righteous anger they shouted, "See what you've been reduced to, you cur!"[3] The masses have done an excellent thing!' In addition to the desecration of corpses and statues, more than 100,000 ancient texts had been destroyed along with almost 7,000 cultural artefacts. The Maoists also authorised the Qufu Branch of the People's Bank of China to buy the gold looted from the tombs.

The Cultural Revolution began as an attempt by Mao to tighten his control over the Chinese Communist Party by turning the people against his enemies within it. On 1 June 1966, a headline appeared in the *People's Daily* urging the people to 'Sweep Away All Monsters And Demons!' Mao saw students, including those still at school, as his most reliable allies. Impressionable, resentful of their lack of power and eager to make their mark on the world, they were easy targets for ideological conformity. Those at the most elite schools, colleges and universities were particularly useful allies, since the idea of being at the vanguard of a revolution inflated their inherited sense of superiority. In *Spider Eaters*, a memoir of her activism during the Cultural Revolution, Rae Yang, a privileged fifteen-year-old student at one of Beijing's elite Middle Schools, observed that of fifty students in her class, only two girls were from workers' families. She boasted that students 'who failed to get into the four top schools were definitely inferior'.[4]

When students heard the call to protect 'Mao Zedong Thought', the response was immediate and brutal. Teachers were forced to wear dunce's hats and placards stating their alleged crimes. They were beaten and paraded through the streets. Students at Tsinghua University Middle School took turns to whip the principal and vice-principal. Privileged girls, easily mobilised in defence of the poor and oppressed, were the first to kill. After a series of escalating humiliations, students beat the vice-principal of a girls' school in Beijing with nail-spiked clubs, before dumping her body in a garbage cart. Students threw bricks at one of the teachers at Rae Yang's school until blood poured down his face. In another incident at the same school, senior students beat an art teacher to death.

A student from Zhengding eloquently described the process of denunciation that preceded the violence: 'The method was, first, to declare yourself a defender of Marxism-Leninism and Mao Zedong Thought; second to pose a series of accusatory questions about your target; and third, to expose it as yet another example of counter-revolutionary infiltration of the Party.'[5] Children were encouraged to denounce their parents and when Rae Yang believed her grandmother's home had been looted by Red Guards, her horror was quickly replaced by ideological justification: 'She is a capitalist. I am a Red Guard. I have nothing to do with her!'[6]

In Maoist China, the mobilisation of future-focused students made the past a necessary target. The writers Chia Chi Yen and Kao described this forced break with the past as a 'mystical wildfire' that turned 'heaven and earth completely on their heads, bringing turmoil everywhere, unleashing destruction like high winds and great waves, bringing great disturbances and agitation'.[7] It began in 1966, in the early months of the Cultural Revolution, when the communist military leader Lin Biao urged the Red Guards to 'smash those persons who are travelling the capitalist road ... and to forcibly destroy the Four Olds', by which he meant Old Ideas, Old Customs, Old Habits and Old Culture. A day later, posters appeared in Beijing that ended with the slogan, 'We want to rebel against the old world!'

The cult spared nothing, not even the smallest detail. In a Beijing silk store, paintings representing 'old ideas' were destroyed and replaced with fifty pictures of Chairman Mao. A few days earlier, a restaurant bearing a sign that bore the characters for classical Confucian 'virtue' (德) was smashed to pieces and replaced with one that read 'Peking Roast Duck Store'. The Red Guards then proceeded to trash every room in the restaurant, tear down traditional Chinese landscape paintings and replace them with pictures of Mao. Over 30,000 homes in Beijing were ransacked and almost treble that number in Shanghai. In Nanjing, the painter Liu Haisu had his home raided twenty-four times and in Beijing, the Red Guards obliterated ancient street names. This eradication of the former world spread quickly. In Zhengding an old woman with bound feet was made to stand in the sun for hours with a degrading sign around her neck. Libraries were trashed and book burnings became commonplace. Statues, historical monuments, churches and pagodas were ruined and graves desecrated.

As the searching of homes intensified, families hid or destroyed letters, books, paintings, mementos – anything that might incriminate them. Anyone suspected of harbouring old ideas or valuing old culture was made to walk through the streets to be harassed, humiliated and spat upon, all while wearing a placard detailing their alleged crimes.

In 'Struggle Sessions', those suspected of being 'class enemies' were hauled before a crowd, again weighed down with a placard, where they were expected to denounce themselves, their friends and families, while begging forgiveness for their crimes. Wu Qing, a lecturer at Beijing University whose parents were also intellectuals, remembers how her 'parents were forced to kneel on the ground for over three hours ... [The Red Guards] searched our home and took everything away. They were like robbers and took away whatever they wanted.'[8] Later, the stolen goods were displayed at Minzu University in an 'Exhibition of the Bourgeois Life of Wu Wenzao and Xie Bingxin'. Wu Qing described how her parents 'had to stand outside the exhibition every day for ten days carrying a blackboard around their necks. At the time I was at my school. I couldn't leave because there were struggle sessions against me. There were close to eighty in total. They said that because of my family background I could never love socialism or the Communist Party.'

The aim was to eliminate all opposition and, as the logic of the revolutionary machine demanded, the means of elimination became ever more horrifying. The historian Michael Wood observed that 'the mass hysteria of the time snapped all bonds of humanity, as if violence took on a life of its own'.[9] In Guangxi, General Wei Guoqing gave instructions to 'put to death about one-third or a quarter of the class enemies by bludgeoning or stoning'. This injunction was carefully calculated. While it remained acceptable to commit a 'straightforward execution', Guoqing believed the best way to 'educate the masses' was 'to use fists, stones and clubs'. The result was the death of 3,681 people in Guangxi and, as the wave of cruelty grew bigger, 'denunciation rallies' were followed, in extreme cases, by cannibalism. Jung Chang and Jon Halliday describe how, after being slaughtered, 'choice parts' of the victims' bodies, 'hearts, livers and sometimes penises were excised ... and cooked on the spot to be eaten in what were called "human flesh banquets".'[10]

Millions died during the Cultural Revolution between 1966 and 1978. Such enormous losses were an inevitable consequence of a culture that prioritised ideological conformity over truth and competence. A few years earlier, during the Great Famine of 1958–62 when Mao sought to industrialise the countryside, about thirty-eight million people died from starvation and poor working conditions. Among the more absurd and damaging actions was the decision to eliminate sparrows, along with rats, mosquitoes and flies, as part of the Four Pests Campaign. Despite pleas from scientists to reconsider this ecologically devastating action, Mao persisted. He mobilised the masses to triumph over Nature by encouraging them to bang drums, gongs and pots to keep sparrows in the air until they dropped dead from exhaustion. Eggs were destroyed and sparrows shot and party officials in Shanghai celebrated the death of 1,367,440 of the birds. The main beneficiaries of this virtual elimination of sparrows were the insects that now multiplied freely and devastated crop yields. In Jingzhou, 15 per cent of the rice harvest was lost to an infestation of grasshoppers, while in Nanjing almost two-thirds of the fields suffered severe insect damage. In this collision between ideology and reality, there was only going to be one victor.

In the spring of 1960, when party leaders realised that sparrows ate insects, and so their elimination was not good for crop yields, they replaced them with bedbugs on the list of Four Pests. It was, of course, the correct decision, but predictably too late to stop millions of people from dying. From statues to people, the comedy and cruelty of Maoist China unleashed a tsunami of human suffering. By cleaving history in two, the time before Mao and the time after, the revolution set in motion an inevitable and deepening rift between communist ideology and the reality of its effects on the Chinese people. The attacks on the Four Olds and the Four Pests serve as symbols of this process, which happened before, during and after the Cultural Revolution.

The division between the old and the new found expression in many ways: old and young, past and future, class enemy and communist. As with all such tyrannies, the result was a deep excavation into the soul of the individual in order to eradicate any sense of self that was distinct from the collective. The risks to the revolution of a cultural environment where the individual took precedence over the group made it an absolute necessity to purge all forms of thought deemed to be 'counter-revolutionary', 'bourgeois' or siding with 'class enemies'.

The soil any tyrannical ideology needs to guarantee its fertility is that of group identity, where guilt is held in common, with equal culpability, across all members of a class. 'In class society,' Mao wrote in the *Little Red Book*, 'everyone lives as a member of a particular class, and every kind of thinking, without exception, is stamped with the brand of a class.'[11] This idea of class struggle, or any struggle between groups, is a zero-sum game. Only one group can triumph and victory comes at the other group's expense. Because of the stakes involved and the reduction of the nuanced individual into a caricature, the struggle can quickly descend into violence. Mao said, 'A revolution is not a dinner party, or writing an essay, or painting a picture, or doing embroidery; it cannot be so refined, so leisurely and gentle, so temperate, kind, courteous, restrained and magnanimous. A revolution is an insurrection, an act of violence by which one class overthrows another.'[12] It is these two strands, the collapse of the individual into the collective and the erasure of the past, that explain why it was so important for Mao to desecrate the grave of Confucius and publicly destroy his statue. Confucius was an archetype of the Four Olds and he had to be purged.

For Confucius, respect for the past was the only secure foundation on which to build a better future. To sever oneself from one's cultural past is to become rootless and incapable of shaping a coherent way forward. The past, in Confucian thought, is the source of our freedom, an idea that was heretical to the Chinese communists for whom the past had to be obliterated as the only way to liberate the future. At the beginning of *The Analects*, Yu Tzu, a disciple of Confucius, observes that 'an exemplary person devotes his efforts to the roots, for once the roots are established, the Way will grow therefrom'.[13] Without roots we have nothing on which to anchor our identity or construct our freedom.[14] For Confucius, it is the past that gives us the very possibility of freedom, which depends on the cultivation of 'character'. Yu Tzu ends his observation on the importance of roots by saying that, 'Being good as a son and obedient as a young man is, perhaps, the root of a man's character.' In the West, we tend to define 'obedience' in direct opposition to freedom. For Confucius this was not the case. Only by respecting the past and engaging in ritualised behaviours that honour that past, can we change our lives for the better.

The essence of Confucianism is practical. Confucius tells us to study hard and respect the knowledge passed down to us in order to apply what we learn to building a better world. These are the roots that allow us to develop our inner character and to embody it in our actions. Character, understood as the cultivation of virtues like trustworthiness, responsibility, filial piety and benevolence, means we take upon ourselves the arduous task of sorting ourselves out before we try to sort out the world: 'If a man manages to make himself correct, what difficulty will there be for him to take part in government? If he cannot make himself correct, what business has he with making others correct?'[15] This idea is beautifully summarised in one of the finest lines in *The Analects*, 'He did not sit, unless his mat was straight'.[16] In a Christian context this might read, 'Let anyone among you who is without sin be the first to cast a stone.'[17]

The manifold cruelties of Maoism are explicable, then, by the rejection of these injunctions. When we demonise groups, peddle the idea of collective guilt and imagine we are immune to exercising the dominance and cruelty we condemn in others, we open the floodgates to terror. The mass murders of landlords, teachers, intellectuals, rich peasants and entrepreneurs, were grounded in the communist belief that human beings are born as 'blank slates'. Given that premise, the differences between us, measured in status, capability or assets, can only be down to oppression or theft. It can have nothing to do with competence or genetic differences in traits such as conscientiousness and openness. The entire Maoist project can be summarised as an attempt to write new, more equitable scripts on that 'blank slate', with the aim of guaranteeing equity or equality of outcome between groups. 'A blank sheet of paper,' wrote Mao, 'has no blotches, and so the newest and most beautiful words can be written on it, the newest and most beautiful pictures can be painted on it.'[18]

These ideologies create a collective psychology grounded in what Nietzsche called *ressentiment*, where we become perpetual victims at the hands of those who must be held accountable for our failings. If we feel less than we believe ourselves to be, it cannot be our responsibility. It has to be somebody else's fault. The first step, then, in unlocking our power is to find out who is to blame and punish them. For the Maoists, it was old ideas, old customs, old habits and old culture that were at fault and this ideology gave ample scope for the settling of old scores. Recalling the teachers who humiliated her, Rae Yang wrote: 'When the Cultural Revolution broke out, I would have my revenge.'[19]

Confucius understood only too well how comforting the psychological position of victimhood, and the emotions on which it is built, can be: 'It is easy to hate and it is difficult to love. This is how the whole scheme of things works. All good things are difficult to achieve; and bad things are very easy to get.'[20] Perhaps the worst of the 'bad things' are status, power and influence, gained not through our own efforts, but through the shaming, denunciation and punishment of others. Nothing is more corrupting than this and, in the end, it consumes everyone. At one point, there were so many denunciations of class enemies written on posters that one Beijing resident complained the city had been 'submerged in a sea of paper'.

In their fervour, the revolutionaries did not see where this spiral of violence was taking them until it was too late. At the beginning of the Cultural Revolution, teachers denounced by their students turned on each other and it did not take long before Red Guards fought amongst themselves in an escalating struggle for status and survival. Seeing these conflicts erupt among her friends and allies led Rae Yang to grieve that, 'Hatred takes the place of the love we had for one another.'[21]

Eventually, Mao tired of the students who had delivered the civil war he craved and he exiled twenty million of them to the countryside to live among poor peasants. The conditions were harsh, as it always is for elites when stripped of their entitlement. A student in Hunan said he had 'lost interest in books and newspapers ... and mankind's dreams'. He complained he had been reduced to the status of 'a mere beast'.[22] At the beginning of the Cultural Revolution, Red Guards considered themselves to be 'professional revolutionary experts' whose purpose was to 'enlighten and organise the masses' and 'dig out hidden enemies',[23] but when they were sent to the countryside, the urban elite were shocked to discover that the rural poor cared little for ideology. The peasants 'never mentioned "class struggle", "guard against capitalist restoration"..."proletarian dictatorship"...[or]..."thought reform"'. Instead, as Rae Yang observed, 'they were just extraordinarily kind'.[24]

One of the great ironies of the tyranny of shaming and punishment is that the most radical elements believe they are acting out of love for the oppressed. Rae Yang believed she was building a 'society that is unprecedented in human history' where inequality between rich and poor, the urban elite and rural peasantry would be eliminated. She was, in fact, basking in the raw exercise of power as a means of displaying her piety, settling old scores and asserting dominance.

Similar patterns can be seen in the current clamour for social justice. Nellie Bowles, a journalist at *The New York Times* openly claimed the fastest route to cultural acceptance was to 'embrace … communal outrage'. Describing some stories as 'kills', she said she 'began to see myself … as a weapon'. One of her victims, as most victims of purges are, was 'a sweet and gentle man'. She regrets ruining him, as many Red Guards would come to regret their actions, claiming to 'feel sick when I think about him'.[25] Fearful of this weaponisation of ideas, the Chinese American Citizens Alliance Greater New York published an open letter in February 2021,[26] criticising the drift towards authoritarianism in American education. When Chinese parents found out third-graders in a school in California 'were told to check themselves off on a list of victimisation categories – race, gender, religion, family structure – to find out which made them *oppressors* and which made them *oppressed*', they said 'it reminded them of Mao's bloody Cultural Revolution'. In China, it led to teachers becoming afraid to correct their students' work and a dramatic rise in illiteracy, even among party officials. It will doubtless have the same effect in the United States.

If the past teaches us anything, it is that we should be wary of easy certainties and the psychological comfort they offer. The spiders in the title of Rae Yang's memoir, *Spider Eaters*, referred to the Cultural Revolution. Despite being 'poisonous', the spiders were 'a bitter medicine'. Those who ate them died but their suffering serves as a warning to future generations against repeating the mistakes of the past. Her own descent into intolerance taught Rae Yang to 'cherish freedom and value human dignity'. They opened her eyes to the true nature of the ideology she would once have sacrificed her life for. They taught her to doubt and be critical of her own thinking. As Confucius said, 'the asking of questions is in itself the correct rite'.[27] If we continue the noble labour of asking and doubting, then we may never have to bang a gong to kill a sparrow, denounce our teachers to assert our wisdom, dig up the dead to affirm an ideology or desecrate a statue to demonstrate our virtue.

LOUIS XV

BUILT: 23 February 1763

DESTROYED: 11 August 1792

On 10 August 1792, the day before the destruction of the statue of Louis XV, French revolutionaries massacred more than 600 Swiss mercenaries. The soldiers died defending the Tuileries Palace in Paris, where Louis XVI and his family were taken after their forced eviction from the Palace of Versailles in 1789. The battle was fierce and the victorious citizens of the revolution showed no mercy. They stuck the heads of the dead mercenaries on pikes, violated their bodies, cut off their genitals and stuffed them in their mouths or fed them to dogs. For the Jacobin leader Robespierre, the massacre was yet more evidence that the French Revolution was 'the most beautiful revolution that has ever honoured humanity'.[1] In the evening, when the victory of the revolutionaries was known, the Legislative Assembly stripped Louis XVI of the remnants of his constitutional powers.

On the following day, 11 August, the masses gathered in Place Louis XV to destroy the statue of his grandfather. A drawing from the late 1700s shows the equestrian statue of the king on the ground, with men hacking at the plinth on which it stood. Louis XV's headless horse lies upside down, pressing down on the broken body of the king. On the back of the drawing, the anonymous artist left an account of how the mob pulled the statue down:

'... the multiplicity of ropes were unable to pull out the statue of Louis XV. I heard a distinguished artist make this suggestion to a group: "Go to an ironmonger's ... Buy a saw ... Saw the left half of the left foot, saw the rear of the left foot in the same direction then pull in the opposite direction." The statue fell down in this way.'[2]

Commissioned in 1748 and made by the sculptor Edmé Bouchardon, the artistic execution of the statue was long and costly.

Bouchardon made hundreds of drawings, of which about 400 survive. His attention to detail was extraordinary. Determined to cast an equestrian sculpture worthy of a king, Bouchardon used a horse owned by Baron de Thiers as his model. He spent so long sketching the horse, they formed a close bond and the animal seemed untroubled by Bouchardon lying on the stable floor, sketch-pad in hand, taking in the smallest detail of its belly.

Bouchardon's friend, Pierre-Jean Mariette, described the stone used to line the casting pit, the time it took to cool the encased wax model (three weeks) and how long it took the labourers to pour molten metal into the mould (five minutes and four seconds). That such details were preserved for posterity shows the significance of the statue in the history of Enlightenment art. The monetary cost matched the artistic ambition and Bouchardon himself received more than 250,000 livres from the city of Paris, a little more than one-tenth of the cost of the statue. Even transporting the statue from the sculptor's studio and placing it on the plinth cost 20,000 livres.

Artistic merit and extravagant expenditure, though important, were not ends in themselves. The true significance of the statue lay in what it became after its inauguration in June 1763. More than a century earlier, François de Grenaille wrote that 'statues were invented in order to make one and the same person present in different places, to bring him to life in gold and bronze where he cannot be in person. In this way, the people may assuage their constant desire to see before them the prince that they adore'.[3]

If statues made 'the prince' present in two places, the ritual of inauguration brought the statue of Louis XV 'to life'. The inauguration began with Parisian notables, including the city's governor, meeting at the Hôtel de Ville, from where they made a ritual procession to Place Louis XV. When they arrived, they took off their hats, bowed and walked three times around the statue to the accompaniment of music, artillery and chants of *'vive le roi!'* Three days of festivities followed, which included banquets, firework displays and the distribution of food and money to the poor.

At the end of the inauguration, the statue of the king became what art historian David Freedberg called, 'the locus of the spirit'.[4] Elevated above profane works of art, it came alive at the intersection between the temporal and the sacred. At once a representation of a king and a symbol of dynastic power, Louis XV took on what the philosopher Louis Marin described as a 'transcendental permanence', which gave royal monuments a spiritual significance. He claimed that 'the representation of monarchy founds its model in the Eucharist. The phrase (doubtless apocryphal) *L'état c'est moi* functioned in a way similar to Christ's "This is my body"; it made the body of the king into a sacramental body.'[5]

Michel Foucault, commenting on the work of the historian Ernst Kantorowicz, agreed that the king had two bodies, 'the transitory element that is born and dies' and another body 'that remains unchanged by time and is maintained as the physical yet intangible support of the kingdom'.[6] Like Marin, he defined this 'double body' as 'close to the Christological'. To destroy the statue of Louis XV was, therefore, to violate the sacred.

Such a violation was inevitable given the logic of violent escalation that animates every revolution. As early as 1791, the defiance of royal power involved the statue. After Louis XVI attempted to escape from France in June, he was brought back to Paris. When his entourage passed the statue of his grandfather, the crowd blindfolded the statue and, according to one witness, 'pretended to mop his eyes as if he was crying at the sight of his grandson caught in the act of his third crime against the revolution'.[7]

When the statue of Louis XV fell in August 1792, the empty pedestal left what the art historian Andrew McLellan called, 'a symbol of a "sacred void"'. By destroying the statue of a dead king, the mob destroyed the transcendent power of royalty. It took less than six months before they took the life of a living king. On 21 January 1793, Louis XVI was beheaded by a guillotine placed symbolically next to where the statue of his grandfather had stood, an event described by the historian Lynn Hunt 'as close to a ritual sacrifice as anything in modern history'.[8]

Three months after the destruction of the statue of Louis XV, the Commission of Monuments, a body set up in 1790 to decide the fate of plundered works of art, hoped that 'spirits will calm down and one can then advise, after more reflection on the means of suppressing other sculptures, without starting trouble'.[9] The members of the commission would have done well to listen to the revolutionary leader Georges Danton, when he said that executions are necessary to 'appease the people of Paris ... an indispensable sacrifice',[10] or to Madame Roland who affirmed that 'there must be blood to cement revolution'.[11] Within a year, they would both learn the painful truth of their revolutionary ideals when they were themselves executed in Place Louis XV, by then renamed as the Place de la Révolution.

The naivety of the commission, Danton and Roland is understandable. It is mirrored by what the philosopher Slavoj Žižek called the wish of 'sensitive liberals' for 'a decaffeinated revolution'.[12] Elites, including those who started the French Revolution, believe that violence can be contained or, by permitting a moderate transgression, they can protect their interests and ideals from extremes of violence. They cannot. When Danton declared, 'Let us be terrible so the people will not have to be', he overestimated the power of the French revolutionary leaders to vicariously satisfy the vengeful instincts of the people. Revolutions do not have *rules*. They have *trajectories* that, as if moved by the force of an independent will, sink them in terror.

As the philosopher Georges Bataille wrote, 'once a limited licence has been allowed, unlimited urges towards violence may break forth ... for it is harder to limit a disturbance already begun'.[13] Bataille defined the period between the death of a king and the final

decomposition of the king's body, as a moment of maximum disturbance when the 'sense of rupture gets the upper hand and the sense
of disorder knows no bounds ... It ends when all the rotting flesh
has disappeared from the royal corpse ... when nothing is left of the
remains, but a hard, clean incorruptible skeleton'.[14] When the king,
however, has two bodies, a mortal body and a transcendent body, the
process of decomposition never ends. When the king, as the embodiment of an oppressive social order, is sacrificed to the people, the
remnants of that social order must be hunted down and sacrificed
in their turn. There is a remorseless logic to this process: as soon as
known enemies are purged, new ones must be found, turning the
decomposition of the social order into an endless task.

Speaking after the execution of Louis XVI, a tapestry weaver called
Laparra, now the head of a revolutionary club, warned that the 'terrible blow that you have struck has removed its principal head but it
is not yet dead, this monster that devours the entire universe'.[15] Such
a monster, of course, cannot be killed, only incessantly attacked. The
impossibility of ultimate victory creates a feedback loop that took the
people of France from the destruction of a statue to the beheading
of a king and, ultimately, to their own ruin. A revolutionary placard
written by Fabre d'Églantine captured the trajectory of escalating
terror: 'In the towns let the blood of traitors be the first holocaust
to Liberty, so that in advancing to meet the common enemy, we
leave nothing behind to disquiet us.'[16] More poetically, the Comte
de Ségur observed that 'we stepped out gaily on a carpet of flowers,
little imagining the abyss beneath'.[17]

The abyss opened because the ideals and expectations of the
people were incapable of being met. Idealists are always the most
dangerous members of any society because they seek to correct the
failure of the world to match their ideals. Frustrated by such failures,
they begin the process of purging society of those who corrupt the
social order, only to find, after each purge, that their ideals are no

closer to being realised. 'The people,' wrote the maverick revolutionary leader Mirabeau, 'have been promised more than can be promised; they have been given hope that it will be impossible to realise'[18] and the historian Simon Schama observed that 'asking for the impossible is one good definition of a revolution'.[19]

This collision of idealism with human frailty is the tragic contradiction at the heart of every revolution. As late as February 1794, five months before his own execution, Robespierre told the National Convention that the aim of the revolution remained 'eternal justice whose laws are engraved, not in marble and stone, but in the hearts of all men'.[20] But justice is imperfect and human hearts need scapegoats to explain its absence. Robespierre offered them the Terror, which he defined as 'prompt, severe, inflexible justice'. Like his fellow revolutionaries, in removing justice from the nuanced realities of human existence, he turned it into a transcendental ideal.

Detached from the world, the promise of eternal justice can never be delivered and there is no way back from this level of spiritual corruption. Three days before his own arrest and execution, Robespierre reminded the Convention of the noble ideals that ignited the revolution that was about to consume him, the 'deep horror of tyranny, that compassionate zeal for the oppressed, that sacred love for the homeland, that even more sublime and holy love for humanity'.[21] Even as he spoke of love and holiness, executions were increasing. When revolutions become *feverish*, they create an economics of terror where the supply of prisons, gulags and guillotines multiplies in a futile attempt to meet demand.

At the foundation of any revolution is the naive belief that people are essentially good and can build a just and equitable society, if only the oppressive social order in which they find themselves trapped can be dismantled. The French Revolution was no exception to this ideal, which found one of its purest expressions in the writings of the philosopher Jean-Jacques Rousseau, who died eleven years before the French Revolution began. Whilst his ideas were revered by revolutionaries, Rousseau's vision found a contemptuous enemy in a man who spent ten years imprisoned in the Bastille and went on to become a revolutionary judge before being thrown back into prison. His name was Donatien Alphonse François, better known as the Marquis de Sade.

Incarcerated in the fortress at Vincennes for sodomy and sexual violence, including crimes against children, Sade was moved to the Bastille in 1784. Held in a cell in the Tower of Liberty, he wrote every evening, hiding his manuscripts behind a brick in the wall. These years of imprisonment in the Bastille produced many of his most significant works including *The 120 Days of Sodom* and *The Misfortunes of Virtue*. Then, on 2 July 1789, as disorder spread through the streets of Paris, Sade saw his opportunity for freedom. He turned a funnel, designed to empty slops into a bucket, into a megaphone and shouted at the crowds gathered outside the Bastille: 'People of Paris, they are cutting the prisoner's throats!'

Two days later, Sade was moved to the asylum at Charenton. The suddenness of the move meant he did not have time to retrieve his manuscripts. For the rest of his life, he believed they were either lost or destroyed in the storming of the Bastille on 14 July 1789. Distraught at the loss of his work, Sade was kept in Charenton until 2 April 1790, when he was unexpectedly released.

A free man in the midst of a revolution, he and his mistress Marie-Constance Quesnet lived in the north of Paris. Because of his reputation and his aristocratic lineage, Sade was unable to earn a living from his plays. He knew he had to side with the revolutionaries or risk losing his life as well as his income. To serve that end, he became a member of the National Assembly and a prolific pro-revolutionary propagandist.

It must have struck Sade that the massacres following the revolt of August 1792 and the destruction of the statue of Louis XV, exceeded in their brutality anything he conceived in his books or enacted in his life. In one particularly gruesome episode, Princesse de Lamballe, a favourite of Queen Marie Antoinette, who had refused to take an oath of hatred against the king and queen, was hacked to death. Her clothes were taken to be sold at auction, while her head was cut off and paraded on a spike. When the mob arrived at a spot below the queen's window, they clamoured for her to show herself 'so you may know how the people avenge themselves on tyrants'.[22] Sade wrote to his attorney Gaufridy that 'nothing can equal the horrors which were committed'.[23]

In 1793, in a remarkable twist of fate, Sade found himself in the position of a revolutionary judge. Contrary to what might have been expected of him, Sade opposed capital punishment and sought to be lenient at every opportunity. He even pardoned the Montreuils, the family of his estranged wife who had been responsible for his incarceration, saying, 'Such is the revenge I take upon them.'[24]

On 8 December 1793, Sade's past, his reputation and his writings, caught up with him. He was arrested and charged with counter-revolutionary activities, which included his undue leniency as a judge. Confined in Picpus, a former convent turned into a prison, Sade began writing *Philosophy in the Bedroom*, which he dedicated 'To the Libertines'. Descriptions of violence and sexual excess are interrupted by a pamphlet titled, *Frenchmen, Some Effort If You Wish To Become Republicans*, in which he writes: 'Everything comes from nature's hands, and nature uses any and all possible methods to obtain, at an earlier moment, the unconditionally required raw materials of destruction.'[25]

For Sade, nature was synonymous with destruction. He believed our worst brutalities come not from indulging those natural inclinations, but in resisting them, judging them as immoral and taking vengeance on those who dissent. The revolution went against nature insofar as it condemned the crimes of priests and monarchists, even as it unleashed worse excesses in the name of its own 'virtue'. For this reason, Simon Schama was undoubtedly correct when he wrote, 'the violence which made the Revolution possible in the first place created exactly the brutal distinctions between Patriots and Enemies, Citizens and Aristocrats, within which there could be no human shades of grey'.[26]

Where nuance is removed, terror follows and for Sade, our highest moral duty was not to condemn violence in others but to see it in ourselves. Georges Bataille concluded a study on Sade with the observation that 'those things which repel us most violently are part of our own nature'.[27] By following Rousseau in eulogising a primal, uncorrupted state of nature, the revolution idealised its own motives and imagined impossible utopias. In doing so, it condemned itself to death. In the debate between contrasting concepts of nature found in Rousseau and Sade, the feminist writer Camille Paglia, saw only one victor: 'Simply follow nature, Rousseau declares. Sade, laughing grimly, agrees.'[28]

In the preface *to Justine or the Misfortunes of Virtue,* Sade asked for 'our readers indulgence for the erroneous ideas which we shall put into the mouths of our characters, and for the, at times, rather shocking events, which, out of love of truth, we have felt obliged to place before their eyes'.[29] If love was indeed Sade's motive, it was the toughest love of them all: to accept that we are no better than those we condemn, no more innocent than those we judge, no more virtuous than those we incarcerate and no different from those we hate. Such a vision of love is also a vision of tolerance. If the truth doesn't allow us to indulge our moral superiority then it demands that we look deeply at ourselves before we judge others. Perhaps the greatest crime we can commit is to be seduced by our own virtue and it is no coincidence that the intended final destination of revolutionary Terror was called the Republic of Virtue.

The ideals of the revolution proved as hollow as the statue of Louis XV. The writer Louis-Sébastien Mercier, who voted against putting the king to death, expressed surprise when he examined the fallen statue of the king's grandfather and discovered its hollow core. 'Yes,' he exclaimed, 'all was hollow, the power and the statue!'[30] He might have added, *and the revolution*, especially since he was himself to be imprisoned during the Terror.

Many stories exist about what happened to the surviving fragments of the statue of Louis XV. Some of the bronze was melted and made into cannon. The rest was put aside to be reused in a proposed statue of 'the people' to be sculpted by Jacques-Louis David. Yet it is the fate of the king's severed right hand that stands as one of the great ironies of the revolution. It was given to Jean Henri Latude, a former soldier who wrote a popular memoir about his years of imprisonment in the Bastille. In his memoir, Latude described the inhumane conditions in which he was held and how he took six months to build a rope ladder made of firewood, shirts and bed linen that helped him escape. After his rearrest three months later, the authorities put Latude in an underground cell infested with rats. His spirit unbroken, he trained the rats to eat bread off his plate and even gave them names. Describing the rodents as his 'little family', he made a flute from broken pieces of the iron grill that barred his cell and serenaded them. When Latude was released in 1777, he published his account. He was again rearrested before being finally released from the Bastille in 1784, the same year Sade arrived.

On Latude being given the severed hand of Louis XV, one newspaper commented that it was just reward because it was the same hand that signed the papers 'which put the unfortunate victim of despotism in irons for more than thirty years'.[31] It was, in fact, the king's mistress who signed the papers that condemned Latude, but she was acting on the authority of the king's dynastic or transcendent body. And when that body lay in ruins along with the statue that bore it, there was nothing left to protect the living king from the people or the people from themselves. The fight against tyranny became tyrannical, and the revolution became what Robespierre feared: 'just a noisy crime that destroys another crime'.[32]

The king's severed hand is now on display in the Musée de Louvre in Paris. Still clutching a broken baton of command, it stands as a relic of the past and a warning for the future.

FELIX
MENDELSSOHN

BUILT: 26 May 1892
DESTROYED: 9 November 1936

In 1936, the London Philharmonic Orchestra embarked on a controversial tour of Nazi Germany. On 9 November, the conductor Sir Thomas Beecham, accompanied by members of the orchestra, visited the Leipzig Gewandhaus concert hall. The following morning they returned to lay a wreath at the towering bronze statue of the Jewish composer Felix Mendelssohn. It was an act of respect, agreed in advance of the tour between Beecham and Dr Carl Friedrich Goerdeler, the mayor of Leipzig. Whilst historians are split on the extent of Goerdeler's anti-Semitism, there is no doubt that he fought to preserve the statue of Mendelssohn against a concerted hate campaign to have it removed or destroyed.

By 1936, Jews in Leipzig were facing harassment, discrimination and violence. In the months leading up to the visit by Beecham and the London Philharmonic, growing pressure to remove the statue had come from Goerdeler's deputy, Rudolf Haake, many other ideologically committed Nazis and the press. Bulletins of the Jewish Telegraphic Agency based in New York, included the 'Latest Cable Dispatches'. The bulletin of 8 October 1936 included this cable:

LEIPZIG NAZIS DEMAND REMOVAL
OF MENDELSSOHN STATUE

LEIPZIG, Germany, Oct 7. (JTA) – Local Nazi newspapers today joined in demanding removal of the Felix Mendelssohn-Bartholdi Statue from the Municipal Hall. It was suggested the statue of the famous composer be presented to the Jewish Culture League of Leipzig.

When Beecham and his colleagues returned to the statue to lay their wreath, Goerdeler was away in Finland. Before leaving, there are reports that he met with Hitler and Goebbels, the minister of propaganda, and agreed with them that the statue should remain standing. It was a futile request. In his absence, Haake took charge. By the next morning, it was clear there was to be no wreath laying, because the statue was gone. All that remained was an empty pedestal. Haake later remarked that he ordered the removal of the statue because a Jew could not 'be held up as an advocate of a German city of music'.[1] He ignored or considered of no consequence the fact that Mendelssohn had created Germany's first music conservatorium in Leipzig in 1843. For Haake, racial identity dwarfed all other considerations. Four months later, after failing to have the statue replaced, Goerdeler resigned.

Both Goerdeler and Haake met violent deaths. Goerdeler was executed in February 1945 for his alleged involvement in a plot to assassinate Hitler, and two months later American soldiers shot Haake in the town hall at Kelbra. The fate of the statue, however, remains unknown. One theory suggests it was taken to a nearby building and smashed to pieces. Another, that it was melted down and the bronze repurposed. The only certainty is that the statue of Felix Mendelssohn was a victim of Germany's escalating anti-Semitism.

The legacy of Mendelssohn's rivalry with the ferociously anti-Semitic composer Richard Wagner fuelled the zealous pursuit of his statue. When Mendelssohn died, he was hailed as one of the greatest German composers, yet his reputation soon declined. This was due in large part to Wagner's essay *Judaism in Music*, first published pseudonymously in 1850, three years after Mendelssohn's death. Wagner begins the essay by seeking to explain that 'unconscious feeling which proclaims itself among the people as a rooted dislike of the Jewish nature'.[2] A few lines later, his language is even stronger when he defines this 'dislike' as an 'involuntary repellence' that neither he nor anyone who truly knows the Jews for what they are, is able 'to rid ourselves thereof'. Familiar anti-Semitic tropes follow as Wagner berates the Jews for their love of money, their disagreeable looks, their voices that talk in a 'creaking, squeaking, buzzing snuffle'[3] and, above all, their lack of artistic merit.

In Felix Mendelssohn, Wagner found what he believed to be an exemplar of creative frivolity and lack of emotional depth, whose compositions fail 'to take the shape of deep and stalwart feelings of the human heart'. Rather, they emerge as 'washiness and whimsicality'. Mendelssohn's art 'is derivative and rotten' and he 'ends by deceiving himself as purposely as he deceives his bored admirers'.[4] For Wagner, the force that runs through the work of Mozart or Beethoven is entirely absent from the work of Mendelssohn as an individual composer and from Jews as a collective identity. Wagner knew that Mendelssohn had renounced his Jewish faith as a child and lived his life as a devout Lutheran. But to the anti-Semitic imagination, such conversions failed to touch the soul of a man tainted by generations of Jewish blood.

Wagner's vitriolic attack on Mendelssohn and Jewish music was also personal. In 1836, when Wagner was a struggling young composer, he sent a copy of his *Symphony in C Major* to Mendelssohn. Although the two composers were close in age, a vast gulf divided them in the esteem in which their music was held. Wagner was unknown. Mendelssohn, four years his senior, was one of the most celebrated German composers. Mendelssohn never replied or even acknowledged receipt of Wagner's work. As the composer, cantor and musicologist Abraham Zvi Idelsohn observed, Wagner's subsequent attacks on Mendelssohn 'sprang forth not out of analysis and conviction, but out of bitterness and envy'.[5]

Whatever the balance between his ideological and personal hatred for Mendelssohn, Wagner was unable to let it rest and, as anti-Semitism grew in Germany, in 1869 he republished his essay under his own name. It cemented his status as an ideologue, diminished Mendelssohn's reputation as a composer and, seventy years later, influenced the Nazis in banning Mendelssohn's music and destroying the statue that stood outside the Leipzig Gewandhaus.

In destroying statues, it is not the dead who are attacked, but the living. When Rudolf Haake destroyed the statue of Mendelssohn, there was no one alive in Germany who had known the composer. The attack on the statue was against a collective group the statue was deemed to represent: the Jews. Iconoclasm is never simply an attack on an individual historical figure. It is a symptom of an attitude, rooted in vengefulness, self-righteousness or both, that compels people to demand the collective punishment of a demonised group.

Wagner's *Judaism in Music* and the destruction of the statue of Mendelssohn were two of many markers on the path that led from prejudice to violence. It is a path well worn and welcoming to those who wish to take it. Our history of persecutions means we know the landscape through which the path winds its way. The first step on the journey is *segregation* between groups. In the case of Wagner and the Nazis, this meant creating first a psychological distance and then a physical separation between Aryan and Jew. The mechanism of this separation was to identify points of collective difference, such as money, speech, dress, taste, ritual, language, artistic capability. Once a distance was established, the basic human need to belong to a group, to co-operate with like-minded people and exert dominance over those defined as Other bred contempt. This is the primary emotion needed for segregation to become violence, and violence to become genocide. It is how the madness of crowds is engineered.

In *Ordinary Men*, a classic study of how a battalion of reserve police officers became mass murderers, Christopher Browning describes how the action against the Jews in the Polish city of Białystok began in June 1941 'as a pogrom: beating, humiliation, beard burning and

shooting at will'. In a desperate attempt to halt the escalating violence, Jewish leaders went to see General Pflugbeil, the head of 221st
Security Division. They 'knelt at his feet, begging for army protection'. As they pleaded, a member of the police battalion 'unzipped
his fly and urinated on them while the general turned his back'.[6]
At a time when collective identities dominate political and social
discourse, we should be mindful of how few psychological steps
it takes to display such contempt and how many fewer steps from
there to uncontrolled violence. The destruction of the statue of
Mendelssohn seems like an insignificant, almost irrelevant step on
this journey. It is not: minor violations are the necessary prerequisite
for major atrocities.

When the killing ends, usually as a result of exhaustion or military
defeat, we can heal the wounds or repeat the violence. This was the
choice faced by Jews in the aftermath of the Holocaust. In 1949, the
German philosopher Theodor W. Adorno wrote, 'to write a poem
after Auschwitz is barbaric'.[7] Yet if we allow cruelty to obliterate art,
writing and the creative imagination, to break the will of a people to
restore itself, what hope is there for renewal?

A response to Adorno's resignation comes from the Jewish philosopher Emil L. Fackenheim. In a remarkable book, *To Mend the World*,
he insisted we must 'face the fact ... that the unthinkable has been
real in our time'. Fackenheim considered it a 'moral and religious
necessity' to create a 'post-Holocaust *Tikkun*' or a *mending of the world*
after a great rupture. To this end, he created a new *mitzvah* or commandment, the 614th in Jewish law, 'forbidding the post-Holocaust
Jew to give Hitler posthumous victories'.[8]

But how, in the face of such enormous collective suffering, was
any Jew meant to act on it? How is *Tikkun* possible when, as the
Holocaust survivor Elie Wiesel wrote, the very 'Idea of Man' died at
Auschwitz? In Deuteronomy (6:5), God commands the Israelites to
'love the Lord your God with all your heart, and with all your soul,

and with all your might'. How, after Auschwitz, can such love be given and by what right can it be asked for?

The Jewish psychiatrist Viktor Frankl, himself a survivor of Auschwitz, believed he had found the answer. Taking his inspiration from Nietzsche that once 'a man has a "why" to live for, he can bear with almost any "how"',[9] Frankl developed a form of psychotherapy called logotherapy, whose aim was to help people find meaning in suffering. For the author of Deuteronomy, it is because we suffer that God insists we must continue to love: it is our means of survival, which we are commanded to give, with all our heart, despite the many reasons we have for withholding it.

Love is the ultimate leap of faith we take in the darkness of senseless suffering and another Jewish teacher, Rabbi Harold Kushner, sought to make sense of suffering when his son was born with progeria, a genetic illness that kills most of those afflicted in their teenage years. Distraught at the injustice of his son's illness, Kushner wrote a book that opened with the 'one question which really matters: why do bad things happen to good people?'[10] In search of an answer, Kushner turned to the biblical story of Job. When God claimed that Job was unique among men in his 'blameless and upright' character, Satan disagreed and taunted God that Job was obedient and lacking in sin only because God had blessed him with wealth and happiness. God then proceeded to inflict great suffering on Job. His property, livestock and children were killed. When Job accepted his losses stoically, without blame or recrimination, God restored Job's fortune and family.

For Kushner, we all share Job's suffering and he concludes his book with the reminder that 'everyone is our brother or sister in suffering. No one comes to us from a home that has never known sorrow.'[11] But many of us struggle to transcend that sorrow, let alone transform it into love. When millions of innocent people were displaced, tortured and killed during the Holocaust, Kushner asks the same question that we all ask when injustice rains down on us: why? Why didn't God send an earthquake to destroy the gas chambers or strike Hitler dead before the terror began?

Kushner concludes that, in giving us the freedom to choose whether to love or hate our neighbour, 'there was nothing God could do to prevent it'.[12] We, however, *can* prevent it and even in those moments when we are powerless before the malevolence of others, when we can no longer prevent the terror they inflict upon us and those we love, we can, even as our body suffers, refuse to allow the violation of our mind and our spirit. We can, indeed, become resilient public witnesses to our own suffering and the suffering of others. When we see individuals compressed into identity groups and the spectre of collective punishment passes before us as mobs destroy statues, we can bridge the distance between us and those we are asked to condemn. Out of the violence of collective guilt, we can preserve individual dignity, in all its nuance and complexity. This, perhaps, is the finest definition of heroism and Emil Fackenheim found it in the courage of the Catholic priest Bernhard Lichtenberg.

Lichtenberg walked through the streets of Berlin on the night of 9 November 1938 and saw the destruction of Jewish homes, businesses and synagogues that became known as *Kristallnacht* or the Night of Broken Glass. Horrified, he 'went back to his church and prayed publicly 'on behalf of the Jews and the poor concentration camp prisoners'. He prayed every day for the next three years until he was arrested. Given the opportunity to repent and save his life, he affirmed that 'I have not changed and would speak exactly as before.'[13]

Under questioning, he recalled the dilemma he faced during *Kristallnacht*. Knowing he was powerless to stop the violence, he asked himself what he could do that might help. His answer was to pray. Despite the apparent futility of such a gesture, especially to those who maintain the non-existence of God, Fackenheim insisted that 'it did help ... it went far towards closing the abyss' between Aryan and non-Aryan, Christian and Jew.

The power of Lichtenberg's prayers lay as an act of public and unconditional solidarity with those being persecuted. He understood his inability to bend the world to his will. In facing horror without acceding to it and publicly making a stand, regardless of the consequences for himself, Lichtenberg prayed only for that which was within his control: to make a public and personal connection to the persecuted Jews and to give himself the strength to continue his protest. In this, he stands alongside Harold Kushner who describes the prayers that God answers as being those that do not seek to avert a tragedy or change the course of events. They are prayers that help people discover 'the strength within you to help you survive the tragedy'.[14]

Lichtenberg resolved, after his release, to provide support for Jews in the Łodz Ghetto. He did not get the opportunity. He died on his way to Dachau concentration camp. Where Lichtenberg sacrificed his life by standing alongside the Jews, the Pope, safe in the Vatican, didn't once offer a public prayer in defiance of the Holocaust. Lichtenberg stood as a public witness to injustice, regardless of the cost to himself.

Kurt Huber, a psychology professor at the University of Munich, made the same stand. Arrested for distributing anti-Nazi pamphlets and for his association with the White Rose resistance movement, Huber, who was found guilty of insurrection and guillotined on 13 July 1943, concluded his final statement to the court with this passage from the philosopher Johann Gottlieb Fichte:

> *And act thou shalt as though*
> *The destiny of all things German*
> *Depended on you and your lonely acting,*
> *And the responsibility were yours.*[15]

This is a remarkable statement. Huber is taking responsibility, not just for his own actions, but for the destiny of Germany and all its people. The contrast between the 'lonely acting' and the magnitude of the responsibility marks out our best and only defence against tyranny, which is the capacity of the individual to accept unconditional responsibility for mending what has been ruptured. This responsibility is, of course, unjust and unreasonable, which is precisely why it is incumbent on us, as individuals, to shoulder the burden without any expectation that others do the same.

When the Czech playwright and dissident Václav Havel was imprisoned for subversion during the communist occupation of his country, he expressed this sentiment in a letter to Olga, his wife: 'I am responsible for the state of the world.' He reiterated the same view towards the end of his period in captivity. In August 1982, he wrote, that 'responsibility cannot be preached but only borne, and that the only possible place to begin is with oneself'.[16] His inspiration came from an essay by the Jewish phenomenologist Emmanuel Levinas, and without knowing anything about Levinas, Havel wrote it was 'perceptible in every line' that he had spent time in prison. Levinas had indeed been captured by the German army in Rouen in June 1940 and sent to a labour camp in Fallingbostel, near Hanover, where he remained until the end of the war. As a Jew, he was fortunate to avoid transfer to the nearby Belsen concentration camp. His family was not so lucky. After his release, he learned that his mother, father and two brothers had been executed in Kaunas, Lithuania, the place of his birth.

During his time in captivity, Levinas managed to write an extraordinary short work called *Existence and Existents* in which he describes a dark presence, an undifferentiated stratum of existence he calls the *il y a* (the 'there is'), defined by the 'total of exclusion of light'.[17] It is from this underworld that the self emerges without ever entirely freeing itself from it. The *il y a* threatens the self and the civilised social order of which it is a part, with collapse back into the impenetrable night from which they emerged. Doubtless drawing on the trauma of his own incarceration, Levinas goes on to compare this threat to the experience of insomnia, which he defines not as the absence of sleep, but as the terrifying presence of the night. He imagines the night as a malevolent presence invading the soul of the insomniac, bringing with it the threat of complete psychological collapse. This dark night is a metaphor for a world in which people are not valued as individual beings, but are submerged in a collective from which they are forbidden to escape. Having lost his family to a collectivist ideology, Levinas knew, from bitter personal experience, the price we pay for this erasure of a person's uniqueness.

Yet, like Kushner, Fackenheim and Havel, Levinas finds hope. In a short essay, he tells a story about a stray dog. During his captivity, Levinas was assigned to a forestry commando unit for Jewish prisoners of war. As the prisoners walked out to their place of work, the men, women and children they passed along the way treated them with contempt, they 'stripped us of our human skin. We were subhuman, a gang of apes'.[18] Then, for a few weeks, a stray dog came to greet the unit in the mornings as they assembled and he welcomed them back in the evenings, barking and jumping up and down with delight. The prisoners named him Bobby and in the eyes of this dog, Levinas writes 'there was no doubt that we were men'. A stray dog was able to mend what had been ruptured. He restored humanity to individual men who had been dehumanised by collective guilt. For Levinas, the restoration of the value of the individual being and the obligation that being has for the well-being of others, regardless of race, sex or creed, is the necessary foundation of civilisation. Like Václav Havel, he believed we are each of us responsible for the state of the world. This refusal to be a victim in the face of unspeakable cruelty is the true meaning of human dignity.

To take up our responsibilities as individuals in order to counter ideologies that feed off collective guilt is the essence of Emil Fackenheim's 614th commandment. Hitler, Mao, Stalin and Pol Pot can only be given posthumous victories if we refuse to learn the lessons history teaches us. Even those in today's open societies who would submerge the content of our character in group identities that define and divide us *collectively*, would do well to learn how easy it is to go from the destruction of statues to the killing of people. Felix Mendelssohn's grandfather, the philosopher Moses Mendelssohn, warned about this in 1784. He observed that the most prosperous societies can reach a pinnacle of prosperity before they turn in on themselves. For him, the key to progress was education and that required enlightenment, (the development of rational knowledge), and culture, (the application of that knowledge). He feared that in advanced societies, where enlightenment and culture diverged, corruption was inevitable. Of such societies, he wrote, 'The nobler they are in their blossoming, the more abominable they are when they deteriorate and decompose.'[19]

In 2003, Wolfgang Tiefensee, mayor of Leipzig and Professor Kurt Masur, honorary conductor of the Gewandhaus orchestra, agreed to rebuild the statue of Felix Mendelssohn. Inaugurated on 18 October 2008, the statue stands as a monument to our resilience, to those like Viktor Frankl and Emmanuel Levinas who survived internment by the Nazis, to the millions who did not and to the courage of people like Bernhard Lichtenberg and Kurt Huber.

It is one of the great ironies of musical history that two of the compositions most associated with love, *The Wedding March* and *Here Comes the Bride*, were composed by Mendelssohn and Wagner. Yet if you visit the statue of Mendelssohn in Leipzig, resist any temptation to assume the defeat of Wagner's legacy of hate. The drift, in the West, towards segregating people into racial groups and collectivising guilt, is pervading our cultural institutions, our universities, museums, opera houses and libraries. In 2020, Liz Jolly, chief librarian at the British Library in London, suggested that a bust of Mendelssohn might be removed from the Library or be subject to 'reinterpretation' on the grounds of his association with 'Western civilisational supremacy'.[20] A European Jew taken off a pedestal once, can be taken off again.

THE
CONFEDERATE
MONUMENT

BUILT: 1893

DESTROYED: 10 June 2020

On the night of 10 June 2020, less than three weeks after the death of George Floyd, protesters came to the Confederate Monument on the Town Square in Portsmouth, Virginia. Built on the site of a former slave whipping post, the monument stands 11 metres high. Almost half of Confederate statues feature a single soldier standing on top of a column, facing north towards enemy territory. Typically, he rests his hands on a gun, a knapsack on his back, waiting in silence for battle to begin. On the Portsmouth monument, whilst the iconography differs slightly, the symbolism is the same. It features three soldiers and a sailor, one on each side of a square, granite base. Each of the three soldiers holds a different symbol of Confederate defiance: a sword; a gun; and a sponge-rammer, one end used to prepare a cannon for firing, the other end used to put out the embers. The sailor stands with his arms folded, sword hanging on his left side.

To the accompaniment of a jazz band, protestors danced and cheered as they hacked at the four bronze figures until each one was beheaded. Someone lit a fire around the feet of one of the soldiers. Another was pulled down using a tow rope. The base and what was left of the figures were daubed in graffiti, flags and the branding of the Black Lives Matter movement that had erupted in the wake of the killing of George Floyd. Tragically, one of the granite heads fell on Chris Green, a protestor, causing a traumatic brain injury.

The base of the monument was laid in 1876, but it took a further seventeen years to be completed. It stands near a church and the Portsmouth Courthouse, unlike the earliest Confederate monuments, which were placed in cemeteries as symbols of grief and respect for the dead. This shift in location is significant. After the defeat of the Confederacy, middle- and upper-class women in the South formed societies such as Ladies Memorial Associations and the United Daughters of the Confederacy. Placing flowers and then monuments where their sons and husbands lay was their work of mourning, a private grief removed from the main public spaces of the town or city and a symbolic returning home of those who gave their lives to defend the Confederacy. By the 1890s, these monuments had moved into prominent locations, typically outside courthouses, which became the scene of racial violence and lynchings.

The number of monuments increased dramatically with 1911 being the peak year for the construction of Confederate monuments when forty-eight monuments were erected. The change in their physical location also marked a shift in psychology. Signs of grief tucked away out of public view now became symbols of Confederate ideals, a public statement of support for a collective identity that now had a new name: the Lost Cause.

The Lost Cause was a rewriting of history. No longer had the South broken away from the United States to preserve slavery. In this reinterpretation, the Civil War was fought to preserve states' rights and southern values, which were now embedded in an idealised and nostalgic vision of the Old South. Charles W. McLammy, a Civil War veteran, captured this vision when he looked back to the pre-war era as a time when 'no political convulsions had disturbed the peace! No gleaming bayonet had usurped the place of law! No remorseless tyrant had done violence to the plain and primitive principles of liberty.'[1] The transition from the private work of mourning to the public defence of freedom legitimised continued segregation in the name of preserving southern heritage. The Lost Cause actively forgot that the triumph of the Union freed more than 3.5 million slaves. Instead, it used the bitterness of military defeat to reignite a resurgent Confederate identity and building monuments asserted the resilience of southern culture in the aftermath of military defeat.

Despite their victory in the Civil War, the Union feared a resurgence of southern ideals and culture. This was the reason they were magnanimous in victory. They hoped for a lasting reconciliation and knew that humiliating a defeated enemy would be counterproductive. The terms offered to the Confederate leader General E. Lee were generous: every officer and soldier was allowed to return home and would not face prosecution for treason 'as long as they observe their paroles and the laws in force where they may reside'. They were also allowed to keep their horses, which Lee claimed 'will do much towards conciliating our people'.[2] Yet after the terms were agreed and the war was over, Ulysses S. Grant, the commander of the Union forces, wrote of his sadness at 'the downfall of a foe who ... had suffered so valiantly for a cause, though that cause was, I believe, one of the worst for which a people ever fought'.[3] It was also a cause whose wounds ran too deep for the South to forget. Caroline Janney writes in *Remembering the Civil War* that forgetting is what southerners 'feared most' because it meant the disintegration of their identity. They kept it alive by emphasising their difference from the northerners they opposed. A Confederate soldier remarked the North was 'a race which is and always has been antagonistic in every particular to us – of a different country & of different pursuits'.[4] For their part, northerners saw the South as a barbaric country, whose women took the ears and bones of dead northern soldiers to make them into necklaces and ornaments. These shared beliefs in irreconcilable differences bred a war whose depravities escalated with every passing month, leaving scars that refused to heal.

It was not only the labours of southern women that gave the South renewed purpose. Central to the Lost Cause was the ideal of the heroic veteran and in 1892, twenty-seven years after the end of the Civil War, Sam Watkins, a 'high private' in the Confederate army, published a memoir that was to become an enduring account of the horrors of the Civil War. With humility, he said his story was not the story of 'great achievements' by 'great men'. His aim was 'to tell of the fellows who did the shooting and the killing, the fortifying and ditching, the sweeping of the streets, the drilling, the standing guard, picket and videt, and who drew (or were to draw) eleven dollars per month and rations, and also drew the ramrod and tore the cartridge.'[5]

The rekindled memories of the war proved too much for Watkins. According to his daughter, he cried every morning as he wrote. Yet the raw honesty of his story and the emotions it stirred fed into the nostalgic revisionism of the Lost Cause. He restored pride and drew a revitalised manhood out of a narrative of defeat. His willingness to die for the southern cause and his sensitivity to the suffering of his fellow soldiers marked him out as the ideal of the Confederate hero. Walking into a field hospital, Watkins was overwhelmed by the 'pile of arms and legs, rotting and decomposing'. A wounded solider called out his name. At first, Watkins didn't recognise the weak voice and emaciated features of his friend James Galbreath. He walked over to his bedside and asked him if he was badly wounded. In reply, Galbreath 'only pulled down the blanket, that was all. I get sick when I think of it. The lower part of his body was hanging to the upper part by a shred, and all of his entrails were lying on the cot with him, the bile and other excrements exuding from them and they full of maggots. I replaced the blanket as tenderly as I could, and then said, "Galbreath, good-bye." I then kissed him on his lips and forehead, and left.'[6]

By the time Watkins' memoir was published, the South, driven by the zeal of affluent southern women, had reframed its monuments from memorials into celebratory symbols of southern heritage. The idea of 'heritage not hate' masked the pro-slavery roots of the Civil War and justified Jim Crow laws, which codified and legally enforced white supremacy. In 1903, Charles Bradley Aycock, Governor of North Carolina, claimed to have solved 'the negro problem' by affirming 'the unending separation of the races'. Whilst he claimed 'the negro ... has always been my personal friend,' Aycock insisted that this friendship must be based on a racial hierarchy that 'leads to the dominance of the Caucasian. When the negro recognises this fact we shall have peace and good will between the races.'[7] In reframing segregation and white supremacy as generosity, Aycock gave 'the negro a fair chance' on condition that he stand by southerners in their opposition to the 15th Amendment to the United States Constitution, which prevented any citizen from being denied the right to vote 'on account of race, color, or previous condition of servitude'.

As the Lost Cause re-engineered the identity of the South, statues proliferated and their meaning deepened. When Julia Jackson Christian unveiled a statue of her grandfather, General 'Stonewall' Jackson, in Raleigh on 20 May 1895, more than 20,000 people heard the Democrat politician Alfred Moore Waddell say, 'It is dumb granite, but it is not voiceless and will not be to our children, for it will be a perpetual appeal to their pride and patriotism.'[8] Hilary Herbert, who served as Secretary of the Navy, echoed these sentiments at the unveiling of the Confederate monument in Montgomery, Alabama, in 1898. 'We build monuments to heroes,' he said, 'prompted by the noblest impulses of the human heart, and that future generations may imitate their example'.[9] Children were to play a vital part in preserving these 'impulses'. The United Daughters of the Confederacy prioritised the instruction of children so they would become 'living monuments' to the Lost Cause and in the immediate aftermath of defeat in the Civil War, the southern politician George Wythe Munford described the preservation of southern culture, the building of monuments and, by implication, the right to keep slaves, as 'holy work'.[10]

As if to reinforce the 'heritage not hate' message of the Lost Cause, there were statues dedicated to 'faithful slaves' who sided with the Confederacy. The most notorious example of such a statue was *The Good Darky*, a statue of a black man tipping his hat, erected in 1927 in the centre of Natchitoches. Financed by Jackson Lee Bryan, a plantation owner who yearned for a return to the antebellum or pre-Civil War South, a dedication written on a plaque at the base of the statue read: 'Erected by the City of Natchitoches in Grateful Recognition of the Arduous and Faithful Service of the Good Darkies of Louisiana'. It was removed in 1968 after being attacked and vandalised.

Through the lens of men like Charles Aycock and Jackson Lee Bryan and the women who raised funds to build monuments to southern 'heritage', statues to 'faithful slaves' served as a reminder that the 'white man in the South can never attain to his fullest growth until he does absolute justice to the negro race'. It was, of course, also a reminder to the 'negro' to remember his place in the order of things and if he defied his southern masters 'there was death in the pot'.[11]

The brutality of that 'death' was documented in the 1890s by a black woman born into slavery in Mississippi during the Civil War. After the war ended, she moved to Memphis, became a journalist and began writing about the politics of the South after refusing to vacate a whites-only carriage on a train. Her name was Ida B. Wells and she wrote extensively, and at great personal risk, about the horrors of lynching, a practice defended by white southerners as justified retribution for the alleged rape of white women by black men. Rebecca Latimer Felton, a senator from Georgia, said in 1897, 'If it needs lynching to protect women's dearest possession from ravening beasts, then I say lynch, a thousand times a week if necessary'.[12] Wells documented the lack of evidence for these claims and the reality that lynching was an excuse 'to get rid of Negroes who were acquiring wealth and property'[13] and to mask male violence against women.

Black Americans were murdered by mobs for almost any reason, from quarrelling with white men to personal vendettas, at the rate of two to three lynchings per week, every week, for fifty years. With regards to rape – by far the biggest reason given for mob lynching – it was practically impossible for a black man to defend himself. 'The apologists for outlawry,' wrote Wells, 'insist that in no case has the accusing woman been a willing consort of her paramour.'[14]

In the conclusion to *A Red Record*, her longest essay on Lynch Law, Wells wrote that when members of an audience asked what they could do to help, her answer was always the same: 'Tell the world the facts.'[15] And the facts lose none of their force in the re-telling, 125 years later. Page after page documents the facts about Lynch Law cases, such as that of Henry Smith. Accused of murdering Myrtle Vance, the four-year old daughter of a white man in Paris, Texas, Smith fled the city. After being captured in Arkansas and brought back to Texas, he was handed over to what Wells describes as 'a surging mass of humanity 10,000 strong'.[16] They placed him 'on a carnival float in mockery of a king upon his throne, and, followed by an immense crowd, [he] was escorted through the city so that all might see the most inhuman monster known in current history'. Securely bound on a scaffold, Smith was tortured by 'the child's father, her brother and two uncles'. They burned his feet, stomach, back and arms with hot irons before thrusting the same irons down his throat. Every 'contortion of his body was cheered by the thickly packed crowd of 10,000 persons'. A pastor, Reverend King, on witnessing the horror, attempted to intervene to protect Henry Smith from the worst excesses of the mob. He was later forced out of Paris 'because I was the only man in Lamar county to raise my voice against the lynching ... and when I saw the poor wretch tumbling with fear, and got so near him that I could hear his teeth chatter, I determined to stand by him to the last'. As the torture progressed, King said of the mob that 'no one was himself now. Every man, woman and child in that awful crowd was worked up to a greater frenzy than that which activated Smith's horrible crime.' Smith's stepson, William Butler, was also lynched for no other reason than his connection to his stepfather.

Ida B. Wells exposed the violence at the heart of the Lost Cause and the racial hierarchy it protected. The proliferation of Confederate monuments between the late 1880s and the 1920s served to bolster the rewriting of Civil War history and redefine the South as the true protector of 'American values'. A Confederate veteran wrote in 1914 that when 'the historian comes to count the monuments builded [sic] to perpetuate the memories of heroes of the Confederate States, he will pause and question if his figures be really correct ... but in the end the sentiment, the loyalty, that marks those who constituted the Confederacy stands out as the most remarkable instance of love and gratitude and devotion of which human annals give an account'.[17]

To those who embraced the Lost Cause, monuments stood as symbols of love and devotion. For others, like the former Mayor of New Orleans Mitch Landrieu, they were symbols of hate and denial. After the removal of the last four Confederate statues from the city in 2017, Landrieu said, 'These statues are not just stone and metal. They're not just innocent remembrances of a benign history. These monuments celebrate a fictional, sanitized Confederacy – ignoring the death, ignoring the enslavement, ignoring the terror that it actually stood for.'[18]

These views were echoed by Warren and Jack Christian, the great-great-grandsons of the Confederate commander General 'Stonewall' Jackson. In August 2017, a few days after the killing of Heather Heyer during a Unite the Right rally in Charlottesville, they asked for the removal of the equestrian statue of Stonewall Jackson along with all other Confederate statues from Monument Avenue in Richmond. They argued that 'Confederate statues offer pre-existing iconography for racists ... [and] ... were never intended as benign symbols'.[19] They referenced John Mitchell, a black councilman from the 1970s, who said of the Lee Memorial 'that there will come a time when African Americans would "be there to take it down"'.

But how can the statues be taken down without fuelling the very tensions their removal seeks to eradicate? In beheading the Confederate figures at the summit or the base of monuments, as was done in Portsmouth, there is a danger that we fuel the ideology that drove southern women to erect the statues in the first place. The populism that animated the Lost Cause is the same populism behind contemporary southern heritage movements, such as The Heritage Preservation Association and the sociologist John Shelton Reed captured the southern sensibility when he wrote, 'They feel they don't get any respect, that their culture doesn't get any respect, and that their ancestors are being dissed.'[20]

Concern over the obvious psychological consequences of humiliating an enemy drove Abraham Lincoln's generosity to the defeated Confederacy. During his second inaugural address, Lincoln urged 'malice toward none'[21] and a hundred years later, Martin Luther King Jr, wrote that 'hate ... will bring us to destruction and damnation. Far from being the pious injunction of a Utopian dreamer, the command to love one's enemy is an absolute necessity for our survival.'[22] This love didn't mean 'ignoring what has been done or putting a false label on an evil act. It means, rather that the evil act no longer remains as a barrier to the relationship.'[23]

The alternative is to seek to crush our enemies, which only fuels the cycle of hate. The attribution of evil to those we oppose and goodness to ourselves and to those on 'our side', is naive and dangerous, which is why King urged us to remember 'there is some good in the worst of us and some evil in the best of us'.[24] He warned that 'devoid of intelligence, goodness and conscientiousness' people 'will become brutal forces leading to shameful crucifixions'.[25]

Ida B. Wells, too, understood we have to reason our way out of the temptation to hate. That doesn't mean we don't hate. It means we pause before we act on it. In *A Red Report*, Wells concluded that it is 'a well-established principle of law that every wrong has a remedy' and that 'no evidence (the accused) can offer will satisfy the mob; he is bound hand and foot and swung into eternity'.[26] Despite her fury, Wells was not a believer in retributive justice. But while she wanted a 'high moral ground,' she was also fearless in her determination to 'hit this issue head-on', which she did. She urged people to focus on 'the facts' and to refuse to invest capital where 'lawlessness and mob violence hold sway'. She demanded that the 'precepts and theories of Christianity are professed and practiced by American white people as Golden Rules of thought and action'. She insisted that America 'live up to its ideals, that "Equality before the law", must become a fact as well as a theory before America is truly the "land of the free and the home of the brave"'.[27]

In its unprecedented brutality, the Civil War gave us another definition of equality. It created what the historian Drew Gilpin Faust called a 'Republic of Suffering', in which soldiers and their families on both sides suffered equally. In 1862, a Confederate bishop observed, 'We all have our dead – we all have our Graves',[28] and the brutality of the war severed the distance between the living and the dead. It was said of General James Garfield, a future president, who witnessed first-hand the horrors of the war, that 'something went out of him ... that never came back again: the sense of the sacredness of life and the impossibility of destroying it'.[29] A Confederate widow spent 'every moment of quiet' trying 'to find truth at the bottom of this impenetrable darkness'[30] and the war did more than strip the Union soldier, Oliver Wendell Holmes Jr, of his moral beliefs. It 'made him lose his belief in beliefs'.[31]

When suffering collides with ideologies that divide us, when we have friends who are pure and enemies whom we consider polluted, we inevitably lose control of this descent into violence. The southern, pre-Civil War belief that 'a lady's thimble will hold all the blood that will be shed' was naive in its optimism. Alexander Stephens, vice president of the Confederacy, was more realistic: 'revolutions are much easier started than controlled and the men who begin them [often] ... themselves become victims'.[32] After over 23,000 men were killed in the Battle of Shiloh in April 1862, General Sherman described 'piles of dead soldiers' mangled bodies ... without heads and legs ... The scenes on this field would have cured anybody of war'.[33] Except there was no cure. The war went on, and three months later, at the Battle of Malvern Hill, a Union soldier described an 'appalling spectacle' where the smell of the dead was 'nauseating and so deadly that in a short time we all sickened and were lying with our mouths close to the ground, most of us vomiting profusely'.[34] In one of the most poignant passages in *Company Aytch*, Sam Watkins describes 'passing over the field of death and blood, with a dim lantern' where he 'came across a group of ladies looking among the killed and wounded for their relatives ... when one of the ladies screamed out, O, there he is! Poor fellow! Dead, dead, dead! ...My poor, poor darling! O, they have killed him, they have killed him! I could witness the scene no longer. I turned and walked away.'[35]

Shedding light on the horrors beneath our feet is one of the roles of a historian. When we see what the light reveals we can choose to act or look away. When the descendants of Stonewall Jackson call his, and other Confederate statues, 'symbols of racism and white supremacy', they are right. As such, the statues have no place to be on public display in diverse twenty-first century towns and cities. The civil rights activist W.E.B. Du Bois believed every Confederate monument should bear the inscription: 'Sacred to the memory of those who fought to Perpetuate Human Slavery'.[36] This uncompromising stance was echoed by a woman protesting the acquittal of a gas station attendant for the murder of civil rights activist Sammy Younge Jr in 1966. 'Let's get *all* the statues,' she shouted, 'not just one. Let's go all over the state and get all the statues'. But the greater the violence with which these statues are removed, the greater the resentment on the part of those who see such actions as an attack on their collective identity. Populism feeds off grievance and if we refuse dialogue with those we oppose, we must accept the consequences of that refusal. They, like us, have a voice that wants to be heard. If they believe they are being denied dignity and respect, resistance and intolerance will increase.

The black musician Daryl Davis became famous for engaging with members of the Ku Klux Klan and persuading them to abandon their white supremacist ideology through dialogue and friendship. He didn't succeed every time. There will always be those whose minds are closed. What matters is that we persist, regardless of the prospects of success, to question our own moral certainties, so that we can engage with those whose views may appal us. If, on the other hand, we cling to our moral purity and abandon even the hope of dialogue, we must accept our share of responsibility for the carnage that will ensue. 'History,' wrote F. Sheffield Hale, President and CEO of The Atlanta History Center, 'is never as simple or painless as you think.'[37] If the 'dim lanterns' are to shine on anything, it is on ourselves and in this murky half-light, full of shadows, it may be harder than we like to believe, to distinguish those we love from those we hate.

SIR JOHN A. MACDONALD

BUILT: 6 June 1895

DESTROYED: 29 August 2020

Two days after the death of John Alexander Macdonald in 1891, the leader of the Liberal Party, Wilfrid Laurier, stood up in the House of Commons and gave a speech in tribute to his great political rival, which began: 'I fully appreciate the intensity of the grief which fills the souls of all those who were friends and followers of Sir John Macdonald ... It is in every respect a great national loss, for he who is no more was, in many respects, Canada's most illustrious son, and in every sense Canada's foremost citizen and statesman.'[1] The next speaker, Nicholas Flood Davin, a conservative MP and political ally of Macdonald, concluded his speech by saying, 'should we never erect a statue to his memory, humanity would keep his memory green'.[2]

Davin need not have worried. Six days after Macdonald's death, the editor of the *Daily Citizen* in Ottawa wrote a short piece in which he asked the people of Canada 'to participate in his memory by erecting a People's Statue'. The editor suggested a contribution of 'say 25 cents'. A few days later, the *Daily British Whig* in Kingston ran an item on its front page headed 'A Fine Statue to Go Up' and the *Montreal Daily Star* confirmed the intention to build a monument in the city. However, the first statue to be erected was a bust of John Macdonald in St Paul's Cathedral, London, made by the British sculptor George Wade. During his last political campaign, which ended in victory three months before his death, Macdonald defended the British Empire, saying, 'A British subject I was born, A British subject I will die.' These words were inscribed around the base of the cathedral's bust.

When a budget of $20,000 was allocated to build a monument in Montreal, the scale of the monument proposed by George Wade enabled him to fend off competition from four Canadian sculptors. The result, unveiled on 6 June 1895, was a statue of Macdonald standing 21 metres high including its granite base, and protected against the elements by a canopy supported by twelve granite pillars. Four British lions sat on the roof of the canopy, along with youths representing the seven provinces of Canada. Despite criticism of the monument and Wade's complaints that he was £1,200 out of pocket, the Montreal Committee were satisfied that, by commissioning a British sculptor, they had served Canada's interests within the British Empire.

On a rainy Montreal afternoon in August 2020, to the accompaniment of chants to abolish the police, protestors tied a red rope around the chest of Macdonald's statue, pulled it off the plinth and cheered as it fell to the ground. The statue was decapitated when it struck the side of the granite base as it fell. A male protestor rushed forward and straddled the head, as if urinating on it. Other protestors kicked the head as it lay on the ground, and one man held it on his shoulder like a trophy. Within hours, the mayor of Montreal, Valérie Plante tweeted, 'I strongly condemn the acts of vandalism that took place this afternoon … Such gestures cannot be accepted nor tolerated.' Her views were echoed by many across the political spectrum, including Jason Kenney, premier of Alberta, who, while acknowledging that both 'Macdonald & the country were flawed but still great', tweeted, 'This vandalism of our history and heroes must stop.' The prime minister, Justin Trudeau, also condemned the protestors, declaring that 'acts of destruction are not the best way to advance the fight for equality'.

It was not, however, the first time this monument had been attacked. In 1992, unknown protestors beheaded the statue in protest at the hanging in 1885 of the indigenous leader Louis Riel. Shortly before the statue was toppled and beheaded for the second time, leaflets were handed out calling Macdonald 'a white supremacist who orchestrated the genocide of indigenous peoples with the creation of the brutal residential schools system'.[3]

Nicholas Flood Davin, who spoke so eloquently in tribute to Macdonald, was one of the architects of these Indian Residential Schools. His 1879 *Report on Industrial Schools for Indians and Half-Breeds* paved the way for legislation making attendance at them compulsory for First Nations, Inuit and Métis (of mixed indigenous and European descent) children. At the schools, administered by Christian churches, children were forcibly removed from their parents, given a number, a new name and forbidden to speak their language or practice any rituals associated with their own traditions. Parents who fought to keep their children faced up to six months in prison.

Expectations for the children were low. Davin's report concluded that, 'Little can be done with [the Indian child]. He can be taught to do a little farming, and stock-raising and to dress in a more civilised manner, but that is all.'[4] The children spent much of their school day learning practical skills such as carpentry for boys and sewing for girls to enable them to become 'functioning members of the emerging capitalist society'.

The fundamental aim of the schools was to hasten the disappearance of aboriginal cultures through cultural assimilation and conversion to what were seen as Christian beliefs and values such as thrift and industry. Duncan Campbell Scott, deputy superintendent of the Department of Indian Affairs, said the 'objective is to continue until there is not a single Indian in Canada that has not been absorbed into the body politic and there is no Indian problem'.[5] Macdonald agreed, saying that the schools allowed the indigenous children to 'be dissociated from the prejudicial influence by which he is surrounded on the reserve of his band'.[6]

The churches crafted a school environment that matched the government's aim of 'civilising' the Indians. They based their commitment to the residential schools on the conviction that spiritual salvation for the Indians was made possible by cultural assimilation. The churches called this process their 'civilising mission'. In a 1908 pamphlet titled *The Call of the Red Man for Truth, Honesty and Fair Play*, Archdeacon John Tims wrote 'that to deny even a few hundred Indians "the Bread of Life" … will be to be false to ourselves, our country and our church, and to be unworthy followers of the noble men who gave their lives as pioneers to the Indian work'.[7]

Tims' real concern was that the schools might be closed. He worried about the consequences of the *Report on the Indian Schools of Manitoba and the North-West Territories* published a year earlier by Peter Bryce, an official in the Ontario Health Department. The Bryce Report found that 24 per cent of the children died from tuberculosis, double the rate for the aboriginal population as a whole, and a report in the *Saturday Night* magazine claimed 'Indian boys and girls are dying like flies in … a situation disgraceful to the country'.

Whilst the churches managed to fend off calls for the schools to be reformed or closed, life for children trapped in the residential schools system was grim. Sexual and physical abuse were rife and the cultural theorist Lauren Berlant described the daily lives of the children as a 'slow death'.[8] The experience of Sue Caribou was typical of many. Taken from her parents in 1972 at the age of seven, Sue described how she was 'thrown into a cold shower every night, sometimes after being raped'. Despite the abuse, the children 'had to stand like soldiers while singing the national anthem, otherwise, we would be beaten up'. Catholic missionaries called Sue a 'dog' and forced her to eat rotten vegetables.[9]

Faced with the abuses of the residential schools and with little hope of change, some children tried to escape. On 1 January 1937, four boys, two aged eight and two aged nine, ran away from the Lejac Indian Residential School. Their clothes offered poor protection against the freezing temperatures and they froze to death before they could reach the safety of an Indian reserve. Three of the boys were found huddled together, while a fourth died alone less than 25 metres away from his friends.

Thirty years later, *Maclean's* magazine ran a story about the tragic death of twelve-year-old Chanie Wenjack who froze to death beside a railway track after he escaped from the Cecilia Jeffrey Indian Residential School in Ontario. He ran away in a futile attempt to walk over 600 kilometres in freezing weather to the reservation where his father worked. The police took five photographs of his body and they showed 'the thin, crumpled body of a twelve-year-old boy … lying on his back … When they found Charlie [sic] he didn't have any identification. All they got out of his pockets was a little glass jar with a screw top. Inside were half a dozen wooden matches. They were all dry. And that's all he had.'[10]

Estimates of the number of children who died in the schools before their closure in 1996 range from 1,000 to 6,000. The number is difficult to verify and may be much higher, since the government stopped recording aboriginal deaths in 1920 and some children were buried in unmarked graves.[11] Sue Caribou is certain the number of deaths at her school was much higher than official figures. She says, 'Remains were found all over the fields. But numbers do not reflect the reality. Many of my friends committed suicide after their release.'[12]

Among the traditional practices John Macdonald and successive governments sought to suppress was the ceremony of potlatch, practised by tribes of the Pacific Northwest coast, the Tlingit, Haida, Tsimshian and Kwakwaka'wakw. In April 1884, the Indian Act, which laid down regulations concerning the aboriginal peoples, was amended to read: 'Every Indian or other person who engages in or assists in celebrating the Indian festival known as the "Potlatch" or in the Indian dance known as "Tamanawas" is guilty of a misdemeanour, and liable to imprisonment for a term of not more than six nor less than two months.'[13]

Potlatch affronted church and state because it went against values of thrift, industry and utility. In capitalist societies, the aim is to accumulate wealth and to invest in order to increase it. Waste is scorned and financial losses are judged harshly. It is little wonder, then, that an ancient tribal system of gift exchange where rank and status are gained through the loss and destruction of property should have been met with misunderstanding and horror.

In his groundbreaking 1925 essay, *The Gift*, the sociologist Marcel Mauss defined the essence of potlatch as 'the obligation to give', because 'by giving one is giving *oneself*, and if one gives *oneself*, it is because one "owes" *oneself* – one's person and one's goods – to others'.[14] Potlatch was the means through which this 'giving of oneself' was ritualised. In the sacred winter months, tribes met for potlatch festivals where gifts were exchanged. These festivals were extremely competitive as each chief sought to outdo his rivals in generosity. The gifts exchanged had spiritual significance. They were considered to be alive with the souls of ancestors. The magnitude of the gift compelled rival chiefs to respond with even greater gifts of their own. According to Mauss, it wasn't just the receipt and exchange of gifts that imposed an obligation. What gave the ritual its power was the fact that every gift, even after it had been given away, still contained the residual presence of the giver. It was active with his spirit. This ancestral or spiritual power embodied in the gift demanded reciprocity. To refuse to return a gift with a greater gift of one's own was tantamount to a declaration of war. It was also to lose face and one Kwakwaka'wakw chief earned the derogatory title Qelsem or 'rotten face' for his refusal to hold a potlatch.

The spiritual power embodied in the gift and the fragility of the bonds that kept the peace between rival tribes meant that potlatch served as a protection against spiritual and social chaos. By giving all one had to another, one appeased the gods and stabilised relationships with other tribes. Rank or social status was measured by the capacity to wilfully suffer massive, often catastrophic losses, and the chief who squandered most goods gained the highest rank because he left his rivals in his debt. The more a chief gave, the more he obligated his rivals and the greater the risk to all of them. Given the high stakes, it is not surprising that festivity gave way to violence. This was common to all societies that practised potlatch, regardless of their geographical location. For example, the ethnographer Richard Thurnwald described a Melanesian potlatch where a chief invited a rival and his people to a banquet. After a long, sleepless night of ceremonial dancing, a casual remark made by the rival led to his murder, the massacre of his men and the rape and enslavement of the women of his tribe.

One of the ironies of the colonists' attempts to suppress potlatch was that the tribes used the additional wealth they were able to accumulate through labour to increase the size of potlatches and multiply the destruction of property. In 1849, one of the largest potlatches involved 240 animal fur blankets, twenty blankets, eight canoes and four slaves. By 1921, in one of the largest-ever documented potlatches, the exchange and destruction of gifts comprised more than 400 blankets, 300 oak trunks twenty-four canoes, five gas boats, two pool tables and vast numbers of basins, glasses, sewing machines, violins, gas lights, guitars, gramophones, sugar, clothes, cutlery, bedsteads, cash and 1,000 sacks of flour. Such extravagant waste demonstrated the irreconcilable difference between a culture where rank is based on utilitarian values and one based on extravagant expenditure. Mauss concluded that for 'a very long time man was something different, and he has not been a machine for very long, made complicated by a calculating machine'.[15]

For the tribes of the Pacific Northwest, the primary social and spiritual goods were rank and glory, acquired by the capacity to withstand enormous losses. In *The Notion of Expenditure*, an analysis of potlatch, Georges Bataille defined the 'states of excitation' characteristic of potlatch as 'the illogical and irresistible impulse to reject material or moral goods that it would have been possible to utilise rationally'.[16] In a brilliant observation, which explains the psychological basis behind our compulsion to break laws and transgress boundaries, Bataille wrote that 'human poverty has never had a strong enough hold on societies to cause the concern for conservation ... to dominate the concern for unproductive expenditure'.[17]

The reason for this behaviour is psychologically simple: there may be stability and virtue in thrift, but there is glory in waste. Glory gives people status or rank, and status is linked both to biological and psychological fertility. Bataille concludes that 'glory, appearing in a sometimes sinister and sometimes brilliant form, has never ceased to dominate social existence'.[18]

So, after the last Indian Residential School closed in 1996 and the Truth and Reconciliation Commission delivered its report in June 2015, a Reconciliation Pole – a totem pole standing at 17 metres – was unveiled at the University of British Columbia on 1 April 2017. The ceremony lasted five hours and gave indigenous and non-indigenous people the space to share stories, hope and understanding. Like all totem poles, the Reconciliation Pole tells a story. Reading from the bottom up, it begins with a tribal myth of a shaman enacting a ritual to ensure the return of the salmon that symbolise the cycle of life and death. This leads to a Bear Mother holding her two cubs, and then to an Indian Residential School house and children wearing school uniforms, their feet unseen to symbolise the lack of grounding during that time. One of the children's faces is smooth and uncarved to represent the unknown victims of the schools. Copper was the gold of First Nations people and at the top of the pole, Four Coppers (traditional copper shields) stand for cultural diversity and an eagle represents a collective will for a sustainable, harmonious future. The pole is studded with copper nails in remembrance of the children who died at the residential schools, each nail representing one child.

The nails were hammered into the pole by survivors of the schools, their descendants and contemporary school children.

In looking towards the future, the master carver and hereditary chief of the Saanggalth Stastas Eagle Clan, James Hart, said, 'We still need to move forward ... Canada needs to stand up ... not just apologising, but really acknowledging what happened in the past, so it doesn't ever happen again'.[19] It was for this redemptive hope that activists claim they destroyed the statue of John A. Macdonald. When we look at the scenes of the statue falling on that rainy afternoon in Montreal and the mob assaulting its severed head, the destruction shares with potlatch both its extravagant expenditure and its dominance displays. It has little in common with the impulse to conserve and reconcile. Despite its fragility and violence, potlatch formed part of a spiritual belief in the mechanics of cosmic order. Rank, hierarchy and dominance, acquired through the exchange of gifts, was a means, despite appearances to the contrary, to prevent that order from sliding into chaos. The people, mostly young, white and angry, who beheaded the statue of John Macdonald had no spiritual anchor to make sense of the destruction. There were no gods to appease. The cheers, chanting and festivity as the statue fell, the race to be the first to violate the severed head, remained, however, a race for glory that, as Bataille predicted, continues to dominate our social existence. That glory may be a pale potlatch, a shallow imitation of displaced indigenous rituals, but it still carries meaning. It stands as a symbolic statement of power and dominance, a utopian vision of a changing social order where the oppressed rise to cast the oppressors off their pedestals. But this drive to acquire glory is impossible to contain. As the struggle for rank grows in intensity, the boundary between the festivity and violence of protest breaks down.

Chaos overwhelms revolutionary movements because they overestimate their ability to control the consequences of their actions. When those consequences become clear, they are unable or unwilling to pull back from the brink. Collapse breeds further collapse until everything is in ruins. As this cycle of instability deepens, polarisation increases, compelling people to make a choice: *are you with us or against us?* When we reach this dark place, demands for social justice lose all nuance. Comforting ideals of Good and Evil take possession of us, where the ancient and marginalised are identified with Good, and the recent and normative associated with Evil. The outcome is the erasure of dialogue and doubt. In such a psychological and social landscape, the temptation to acquire rank by demonstrating commitment to an apocalyptic moment of reckoning becomes irresistible. But even as we tear apart the ties that bind us, we can pause long enough to acquire the glory of advancing social justice without descending into tyranny. It means we have to embrace the risk, embodied in potlatch, of an unstable exchange in which we are all part of a unifying cosmos, each of us having an obligation to the other. Potlatch teaches us the cosmos is riven with conflict, sometimes violent, as we struggle for status and glory. First Nations people celebrated the inevitable disparities in rank and power that result from this struggle. They are common to every social order. If, on the other hand, we are so mired in hypocrisy and narcissism that we become wilfully blind to our individual need for status, we will fight (and *be seen* to fight) for the elimination of all disparities. The hypothetical end of this struggle is the *Utopia of Equity*, where we not only betray the wisdom of our indigenous ancestors, we also reject their ideal of reciprocal obligation. In doing so, we place demonised identity groups outside the circle of exchange, where they exist only to justify the terror we unleash upon them.

Human biology and psychology mean there is no place where the individual is free from the need to acquire status. Our best defence against the excesses of this impulse is a deep understanding that our judgement is partial and flawed, that our lives, if lived well, will deepen our ignorance as we advance our knowledge. On this journey, we need the ideas of those we oppose, since our well-being is as dependent on them as theirs is on us. The fragile dialogue that ensues is the true meaning of reciprocity, a gift in return for a gift.

The *Utopia of Equity*, on the other hand, means the silencing of those we oppose and the levelling of difference. John A. Macdonald, because of his flaws, understood the dangerous impracticality of this view of the world. 'I am satisfied,' he said, 'not to have a reputation for indulging in imaginary schemes and harbouring visionary ideas that may end sometimes in an annexation movement, sometimes in Federalism, and sometimes in a legislative union, but always utopian and never practical'.[20] When Utopianism gains the upper hand, the relative peace of gradual change is sacrificed in a revolutionary clamour to overthrow the entire social order. In such situations, there is no Reconciliation Pole that can withstand the hunger for glory and the chaos it brings in its wake.

EDWARD COLSTON

BUILT: 13 November 1895

DESTROYED: 7 June 2020

On 7 June 2020, a rope tied around its neck, protestors pulled the bronze statue of Edward Colston off its plinth and cheered as it crashed to the ground. After it fell, the protestors pounced on it, with one man laying his knee on Colston's neck, before the crowd threw the statue into Bristol harbour.

The statue had stood for 125 years on Colston Avenue, just around the corner from the Colston Hall concert venue. The original plaque on the Portland stone plinth celebrated Bristol-born Colston as 'one of the most virtuous and wise sons of the city'. His name dominated Bristol. A residential tower block, a school, a street and even a bun, traditionally eaten on Colston Day (13 November), were all named after him.

The 'virtue' that immortalised Edward Colston came from his philanthropy. A wealthy businessman and Tory MP, he donated money to charities and institutions throughout England. His main contributions were, however, to the city of Bristol where he founded schools, almshouses and made financial donations to local churches and to the cathedral. In his will he left £71,000, the equivalent today of more than £8,000,000, to charity. Described by the historian David Hughson as 'the great benefactor of the city of Bristol',[1] Colston's philanthropy changed many lives for the better and the Colston Society, established shortly after Edward Colston's death in 1721, continued his charitable work. It held commemorative services to remember him and organised fund-raising events, involving local schools and churches, raising and donating an average of £20,000 a year between 2015 and 2020.

The reason for the destruction of Colston's statue had nothing to do with his philanthropy. It centred on the source of his wealth:

Edward Colston was a slave trader. A member of the board and eventual deputy governor of the Royal African Company in 1689, he made his money from the Atlantic slave trade. It is estimated the company transported more than 80,000 Africans from West Africa to the Caribbean and the Americas, with almost a quarter of them dying in the atrocious conditions on board the slave ships.

Colston's links to the slave trade were well documented and his statue had been the focus of repeated attempts at removal. In the weeks before its destruction, more than 10,000 people signed a petition demanding the statue's removal, with Olivette Otele, Professor of the History of Slavery at Bristol University, describing it as 'a provocation for many people, not just those from the Black community'.[2] The historian David Olusoga agreed, protesting that 'the statue should have been taken down and it should have been a great collective day for Britain and Bristol when the statue was peacefully taken down and put in a museum, which is where after all, we remember history properly'.[3]

Attacks on the statue began in 1998 when the words 'slave trader' were written on the base. In 2018, attempts were made to reinterpret the statue by adding a second plaque to explain Colston's involvement in the slave trade. However, Marvin Rees, the first mayor of African descent of a major UK city, withdrew from the project. He complained that the Society of Merchant Adventurers, an organisation with its own history of involvement in the slave trade and active in preserving Colston's memory, had attempted to 'have the final say on the words for a new plaque ... without reference to the communities of descendants of those Africans who were enslaved and treated as commodities by merchants like Colston'.[4] The struggle was typical of that between many who believe they are preserving 'heritage' against those who fight for change, almost regardless of what the 'heritage' signified or who were its beneficiaries. While the negotiations over the wording were going on, Colston's face was spray-painted white, and a ball and chain were attached to his leg. In October 2018, a stone replica of the layout of a slave ship, with stone figures lying flat on the ground to represent the position of the slaves, was laid out at the foot of the statue. Around the side of the slave ship, labels identified work such as kitchen work or sex work that is still being done today by people sold or trafficked into slavery.

When the end came and the statue was toppled, it was sudden and decisive. Those who had defended its right to exist found themselves retreating. The Society of Merchant Adventurers vowed 'to continue to educate itself about systemic racism' and the writer and performance artist Vanessa Kisuule, marked the fall of Colston in a poem, 'Hollow', which ends:

> *Colston, I can't get the sound of you from my head.*
> *Countless times I passed that plinth,*
> *Its heavy threat of metal and marble.*
> *But as you landed, a piece of you fell off, broke away,*
> *And inside, nothing but air.*
> *This whole time, you were hollow.*[5]

Hollow men is T.S. Eliot's preoccupation in a poem[6] of the same name, penned seven years after the end of the First World War. In a letter written in 1936, Eliot described it as his 'one blasphemous poem … because it is despair'.[7] The hollow men are neither alive nor dead. They exist in a 'twilight kingdom', where they cannot even complete their prayers. Spiritually dead, their spectral lives, drifting into nothingness, serve as a mirror of the fate of the world, which Eliot claims will end, 'Not with a bang but a whimper'. Two epigraphs frame the poem. The second, *A penny for the Old Guy*, is a reference to Guy Fawkes, fit for nothing but the flames. But the first epigraph, *Mistah Kurtz – he dead*, takes us to the world where Edward Colston made his money and helps us makes sense of his hollowness.

Kurtz, a fictional ivory trader in the Congo Free State at the end of the nineteenth century, was the central figure in Joseph Conrad's masterpiece, *Heart of Darkness*. He based the novella on his own experiences in the Congo during its colonisation between 1885 and 1908 by Leopold II, King of the Belgians. The book has faced its share of criticism. In a 1975 address at the University of Massachusetts, the Nigerian novelist Chinua Achebe called it an 'offensive and deplorable book'. Dismayed by what he saw as the appropriation of the continent of Africa 'as props for the break-up of one petty European mind', he described Conrad as 'a thoroughgoing racist'.[8] Yet as the historian Adam Hochschild wrote in *King Leopold's Ghost*, 'the moral landscape of *Heart of Darkness* and the shadowy figure at its center are the creations not just of a novelist but of an open-eyed observer who caught the spirit of a time and place with piercing accuracy'.[9]

Conrad uses the device of a narrator, Charles Marlow, to tell the story of the search for the mysterious Mr Kurtz, the company's most successful ivory trader. As would be expected, the only eyes Marlow has are his own and he sees the Congo through those of a European colonist, which is why Hochschild resists the temptation to follow a tradition of psychological or spiritual interpretation. For him it is 'a book about one time and one place ... a precise and detailed description of ... King Leopold's Congo in 1890, just as the exploration of the territory was getting underway in earnest'.

Conrad himself described Leopold's colonisation of the Congo as the 'vilest scramble for loot that ever disfigured the history of human conscience'.[10] But King Leopold considered it his right to have 'a slice of this *magnifique gâteau africain*'.[11] The natural resources of the Congo included copper, rubber, gold and diamonds. They were of such magnitude that a Congolese boxer, Papa Marcel, imagined God travelling the world 'placing precious minerals in the earth, a little gold here, some diamonds there. When he came to Congo he was tired and left everything that he had beneath the soil.'[12]

Leopold was determined to dig up what God left in the soil of the Congo and take it back to Europe. In the process of doing so, he killed as many as ten million Africans, or half the population of the Congo Free State. The brutality he unleashed seemed boundless in its cruelty. Whilst rubber production increased from 100 tonnes in 1890 to 6,000 tonnes in 1901, villagers who failed to hit their quotas were beaten, imprisoned or had their hands severed. A Congolese man called Tswambe described Léon Fiévez, a state official, as 'the Devil of the Equator'. With the bureaucratic banality that Hannah Arendt defined as evil a century and a half later, Fiévez 'wanted to see the number of hands cut off by each soldier, who had to bring them in baskets'.[13] A report in a German newspaper in 1896 claimed that 1,308 hands were brought to Fiévez in a single day. Another state official, Simon Roi, boasted that his soldiers were required to bring back a severed hand for every unused cartridge. The British consul Roger Casement, a staunch abolitionist later executed in 1916 for his support for Irish Republicans, reported that some soldiers cut off the penises from the Africans they killed. This was to prove to their white superiors that they were able to kill men: a severed hand, after all, could be, and often was, the hand of a woman or a child.

Torture, rape, forcing young villagers to kill or rape their mothers and sisters, looting, the burning of villages, killing on an industrial scale, were the daily horrors of Leopold's colonial regime. On Saturday 17 December 1898, the *Saturday Review* printed a story about Captain Léon Rom, a river station chief who decorated the flower beds in his garden with twenty-one African heads. Joseph Conrad may well have read it. The following day, he began writing *Heart of Darkness* and, as with Captain Rom, severed heads on poles mark Marlow's arrival at Kurtz's Inner Station.

It is entirely reasonable to make Conrad's *Heart of Darkness* into a straightforward morality tale, an attack on the violence and moral bankruptcy of European colonialism. If this is how we read the novella, we can sit in judgement on Kurtz without finding our moral compass duly disturbed. Like Eliot's 'hollow men' and Kisuule's 'hollow' statue, Kurtz is 'hollow at the core', a 'hollow sham', who ends his methodical report for the International Society for the Suppression of Savage Customs, with a 'luminous and terrifying' phrase, that struck 'like a flash of lightning in a serene sky: Exterminate all the brutes!'[14]

This phrase formed the title of Sven Lindqvist's tale of his own journey into the Congo, where he recalled the white, European supremacy that defined the cultural environment Edward Colston shared with Captain Rom. In the nineteenth century, even abolitionists like Robert Knox and Social Darwinists like the philosopher and biologist Herbert Spencer, agreed on the superiority, and inevitable triumph, of European civilisation. In a speech delivered at the Albert Hall in London on 4 May 1898, Lord Salisbury, the prime minister, expressed this view succinctly: 'One can roughly divide the nations of the world into the living and the dying.'[15] The path from a belief that inferior cultures die out to exterminating 'brutes' already destined for extinction, is a short one. It was exemplified by Commander Bedford Pim in a speech to the Anthropological Society in 1866, where he said there is 'mercy in a massacre'.[16]

We should, however, beware of apparently self-evident moral certainties and the asymmetrical moral worlds, one good, the other evil, that define them. At the beginning of *Heart of Darkness*, Marlow observes that the 'conquest of the earth, which mostly means taking it away from those who have a different complexion or slightly flatter noses than ourselves, is not a pretty thing when you look into it too much. What redeems is the idea only. An idea at the back of it; not a sentimental pretence but an idea; and an unselfish belief in the idea – something you can set up, and bow down before, and offer a sacrifice to.'[17]

The darkness at the heart of Conrad's novella is the impossibility of such an 'idea'. There are no values in play here, simply human desire stripped of all restraint. Profit may have been the motive that brought the ivory traders to the Congo. Once there, that motive of accumulation collapsed because of its own inner logic: the hunger for more, ultimately consumes itself. So, when Marlow reaches the Inner Station and sees the heads on spikes, the manager informs him that 'there was nothing exactly profitable in these heads being there. They only showed that Mr. Kurtz lacked restraint in the gratification of his various lusts, that there was something wanting in him.'[18]

But isn't there 'something wanting' in us all? Random historical events may divide victims from aggressors but each one of us is capable of performing either role. Just over fifty years after the death of Leopold II, the country then known as Congo-Léopoldville gained independence from Belgium. Patrice Lumumba, an independence leader, became the first prime minister of the newly freed state. On the sixth day of independence, the Congolese army mutinied after a recalcitrant Belgian General, Émile Janssens, refused to acknowledge that independence meant any change in the military chain of command. To make his point he wrote on a blackboard, 'Before Independence = After Independence'. The reaction was immediate and violent. White Europeans were humiliated, beaten and raped.

Lumumba, young, inexperienced and erratic in his decision making, was incapable of exerting control. On 15 August 1960, as his country disintegrated, Lumumba decided to crush revolt against his rule in the diamond-rich province of South Kasai. His troops massacred hundreds of Baluba tribesmen and created more than 250,000 refugees. Already racked by civil war, the country descended further into chaos when army chief-of-staff, Colonel Joseph Mobutu, ousted his former friend and ally and took power on 14 September.

Two months later, as Lumumba tried to flee the country, he was captured and brought before Mobutu who spat in his face, saying, 'you swore to have my skin, now it is I who have yours'. On 17 January, after being beaten and tortured, Lumumba was shot by a firing squad under the command of a Belgian officer. His body was dissolved in sulphuric acid but not before a Belgian police officer, Gerard Soete, removed two of Lumumba's teeth with pliers. He took them back to Belgium and kept them in a matchbox in his house in Bruges.

Mobutu, growing increasingly confident and ruthless in the exercise of power, ruled the country he renamed Zaire for thirty-two years. During his time in power, Mobutu presided over a violent and corrupt regime. As his country descended into bankruptcy, he amassed a vast personal fortune and often chartered Concorde as a private jet. His many properties included the magnificent Chateau Fond'Roy in Brussels, built, ironically, by King Leopold II.

The crisis that led to his fall from power began in 1994. In neighbouring Rwanda, a civil war broke out that resulted in the killing of 800,000 Tutsis and moderate Hutus by Hutu militias and the army. When the Hutu regime crumbled, the Tutsi Rwandan Patriotic Front came to power and more than a million Hutu refugees sought sanctuary in an ethnically complex region of Zaire. As tensions and violence soared, an alliance of Angola, Uganda and Rwanda overthrew Mobutu in 1997.

A year after he ousted Mobutu, President Laurent Kabila, fearing a coup against him by the Tutsi government in Rwanda, sanctioned the massacre of Tutsi refugees in Zaire. He used the same tactics to mobilise mass violence as the Hutus had used to instigate the Rwandan genocide. Congo state radio urged listeners to use 'a machete, a spear, an arrow, a hoe, spades, rakes, nails, truncheons, electric irons, barbed wire ... to kill the Rwandan Tutsi'.[19] They did what was asked of them and thousands of Tutsis were butchered. In an echo of colonial brutality, Papy Kamanzi, a Tutsi military commander, claimed he could kill more than 100 'dissidents', including women and children, in a day. When asked why he killed so many people, he replied that for soldiers 'killing comes easy. It has become part of our lives ... You have to understand the history of my family – how we were persecuted ... how we were denied citizenship and laughed at at school. How they spat in my face. Then you can judge me.'[20]

The massacre of Tutsis was not enough to save Kabila from assassination in 2001, while Congo's gold, diamond, petroleum and timber resources became the subject of predatory wars fought by its neighbours, Angola, Zimbabwe, Uganda and Rwanda. In 2000, Rwanda and Uganda fought three wars to gain control of the diamond trade in the northern city of Kisangani. By 2002, a year after the assassination of Kabila, five years of civil war had killed more than five million people.

There is no doubt that colonial powers and Cold War rivalry destabilised newly liberated African countries. Does this legacy remove responsibility from African civilians and soldiers for the atrocities that followed? Adam Hochschild believes it does not. He says the reasons for the violence and social disintegration 'go far beyond the colonial heritage'. They include the 'abysmal position of women' in African society, the 'hero-worship of strongmen like Mobutu' and 'the long history of indigenous slavery' that is still 'woven into the social fabric'.[21]

It is comforting, for those seeking a simple narrative of Good and Evil, to take away from those who suffered under colonialism all responsibility for their own actions. In this narrative, Africans are dehumanised a second time: first, they were deemed uncivilised and now they are stripped of agency and a mature humanity – even when they make an individual decision to kill, it is the colonial ghost-in-the-machine that is responsible for their behaviour, not the killers themselves. This is an illiberal and dehumanising perspective. Africans and Europeans, black and white, Papy Kamanzi and Edward Colston must all be held to the same standards. Holding white people to higher standards of moral agency than black people is classic white supremacy that yields, as it has always done, a soothing supply of self-righteousness to those who peddle it.

The easy moral certainties of *Heart of Darkness* are, then, a misreading of the text. Kurtz's last words, 'The horror! The horror!',[22] are not an expression of moral disgust. The horror Kurtz carries with him to the grave is not that people may sink 'deeper and deeper into the heart of darkness' but that we never truly emerge from it. The ease with which liberators become tyrants and noble ideals collapse into barbarism, is the struggle each of us faces, in myriad small and large ways, throughout our lives.

T.S. Eliot's 'hollow men' are trapped in a half-world between life and death, neither damned nor saved. Similarly, Conrad offers us little hope of escaping this struggle. When Marlow says of Kurtz, 'There was nothing either above or below him', he has moved beyond Good and Evil. What remains is the amoral rhythm of life in all its random brutality, which, through Kurtz, Marlow had glimpsed. Kurtz is 'hollow at the core' because he has seen beyond the 'hollow sham' of 'all the appearances of success and power' and discovered the 'diabolic love' and 'unearthly hate'[23] that make us what we are. This is Nietzsche's *amor fati*, or love of fate, whose random, often unjust, consequences we have to bear.

When a station manager tells Marlow that Kurtz spoke 'of love', Marlow is surprised: 'Ah, he talked to you of love!' I said much amused. "It isn't what you think" he cried, almost passionately. "It was in general. He made me see things – things."'[24] This dark vision of love contrasts with the closing scene of the book when Marlow visits Kurtz's 'Intended' to tell her what happened to him. 'I knew him best,' she says. 'I loved him – I loved him – I loved him.' When she asks Marlow what Kurtz's last words were, he lies to her: 'The last word he pronounced was – your name.' He lies because the truth would have been 'too dark – too dark altogether'.[25] The lies of colonialism are mirrored in the lies of romantic love. Nothing is pure.

Did the protestors who toppled the statue of Edward Colston have the courage to dismantle the lies they tell themselves? Do any of us possess such courage? Or do we cling to comforting illusions about our own purity and the moral ascendancy it gives us? If we choose comfort, we choose ignorance. 'Everywhere in the world,' Sven Lindqvist wrote on the last page of *Exterminate All the Brutes*, 'where knowledge is being suppressed, knowledge that, if it were made known, would shatter our image of the world and force us to question ourselves – everywhere there, *Heart of Darkness* is being enacted.'[26]

The consequences of such dishonesty are catastrophic. As H.G. Wells warned in *War of the Worlds*, published the same year Conrad began writing *Heart of Darkness*, choosing moral elevation over truth eventually leads to social collapse: 'In the case of every other predominant animal the world has ever seen, I repeat, the hour of its complete ascendancy has been the eve of its complete overthrow.'[27]

A month after the statue of Edward Colston had been toppled and pushed into the harbour, a black resin sculpture of Jen Reid, a protestor, arm raised in a Black Power salute, appeared in its place. This, too, was removed, quietly, by the council, without any of the violence of the previous month. The sociologist Frank Furedi wrote about the destruction of the Colston statue that 'what was really disturbing was not the actual tearing down of the statue but what happened afterwards ... it was almost as if what was being dragged was a person not a statue'.[28] And that, as if we didn't already know, is the true heart of darkness that beats wherever people breathe.

CHRISTOPHER COLUMBUS

BUILT: 1904

DESTROYED: 12 October 2004

On 12 October 2004, protestors in Caracas, Venezuela, climbed onto a stone plinth, tied a yellow rope around the neck of a 10-metre bronze statue of Christopher Columbus and pulled it to the ground. After it fell, they dragged the statue, its arm severed, through the streets, the rope still wrapped around its neck. When it arrived at the Teresa Carreño Theatre, indigenous people sang and danced before putting the statue on trial. When a guilty verdict was passed, protestors hung the statue upside down from a tree and chanted, 'Justice for the people! Justice for the people!'

The date of the destruction, also known as Columbus Day, was the anniversary of his arrival in 1492 on the island of Guanahaní[1] in the Bahamas. Built by the nineteenth-century Venezuelan sculptor Rafael de la Cova, the statue of Columbus stood for 100 years before it was pulled down. The destruction was the work of supporters of the Venezuelan leader Hugo Chavez, who sought to 'undo the symbols of our oppressors'. Angel Montiel, leader of an indigenous movement, called it an 'act of symbolic justice' against a man who represented 'invasion and genocide in our land'. After the trial and 'execution' of Columbus, the protestors who claimed responsibility for the act released a statement rejecting the idea that they were vandals, before going on to say they were 'absolutely proud of what we have done, since [our actions] finally destroyed … one of the strongest symbols of what has been the genocidal, exploitative, dehumanising, deconstructive, and truly vandalic exercise of all the imperialisms that have plagued this planet of misery … And in particular the conquest and extermination of more than 70 million human beings … and the death of more than 30 million original inhabitants of Africa, brought as slaves, from the day the Spanish "national hero" put his boots on these lands.'²

Perhaps because of the coup against him two years earlier and the fear of fuelling more conservative opposition support, Hugo Chavez and his government at first condemned the removal of the statue. Freddy Bernal, mayor of Caracas, said the 'anarchic actions do not accomplish one possible objective. We agree that history has to be rewritten and we are doing it. We reject honouring Columbus, but that is one thing, anarchy is another.'³

Despite his otherwise radical policies, it was only when he felt the political environment was safer for his government that Chavez came out in support of the destruction of the statue. In 2007, during a televised address, he protested against any reverence for Columbus, complaining that 'they taught us to admire Christopher Columbus' and in 'Europe they still speak of the "discovery" of America and want us to celebrate the day'.⁴ He renamed 12 October as the Day of Indigenous Resistance.

When Columbus, a Genoese man of humble origins, set out from the Spanish port of Palos on 3 August 1492 and headed West, he believed he was sailing towards Asia. Convinced by the writings of the Venetian explorer Marco Polo, he went in search of an island 2,400 kilometres off the coast of China called Cipangu where there are 'tremendous quantities of gold. The king's palace is roofed with pure gold, and his floors are paved in gold two fingers thick.'⁵

Columbus also drew inspiration from Marco Polo to support his argument against the ideas of the second-century Roman mathematician and astronomer, Claudius Ptolemy who believed the world was a sphere of such magnitude as to make any crossing of the Atlantic an impossibility. Even at the time of his fourth and last crossing, Columbus was still adamant that the land he had colonised was in Asia and, therefore, Ptolemy must have been incorrect in his calculations. 'The world,' he wrote, 'is not as big as the common crowd say.'⁶

As for the gold, he had, by that time, discovered plenty of it. Gold mining, undertaken by indigenous labour, yielded fifty million mara-vedis[7] between 1505 and 1507. 'With gold, said Columbus, 'one may do what one wishes with the world'. But what did Columbus wish for?

For many, the phrase 'God, gold and glory' covers the three main dimensions of the conquest of the Americas. However, Columbus's quest for wealth was not driven by an appetite for earthly gain. Of course, like any human being, he valued recognition for his efforts and the status this brought with it. To that end, he signed an agreement in April 1492 with the Spanish monarchs, Ferdinand and Isabella, giving him the title of grand admiral and a ten per cent share of any produce and merchandise from the new-found lands. He also asked to become viceroy of any colonised territories, a request that was granted him, but he was denied the right to pass the title on to his descendants in perpetuity.

Yet earthly riches and recognition were secondary to Columbus's sense of his divinely ordained mission. During his voyages from Spain to the New World, he prayed daily, kept canonical hours and bestowed a religious significance on the islands he colonised, giving them names such as San Salvador (the Saviour) and La Isla de la Trinidad (Island of the Trinity). 'I do not endure the hardships,' he wrote during his third voyage in 1498, 'to gather treasure nor find riches for myself, for, to be sure, I know that all is vanity that is accomplished in this world, save what is to the honour and service of God, which is not to build up riches or causes of pride or many of the other things we use in this world to which we are better affected than to the things that can save our souls.'[8]

It was Columbus's fervent wish that the riches of the Indies should go to the Crown to hasten the Second Coming of Jesus Christ. He wrote in the log of his first voyage that he sought to compel the Spanish monarchs 'to conquer the Holy Sepulchre ... to spend all the profits of this my enterprise on the conquest of Jerusalem'.

'Gold' observed Columbus in 1503, was simply a means to 'send souls into Paradise.'[9]

This vision had its roots in the work of Joachim de Fioré, a twelfth-century Calabrian abbot, who found patterns in the Bible that enabled him to prophecy the future. He saw history as a gradual ascent through three successive ages, each overseen by one element of the Holy Trinity. History passed through the first age of the Father, associated with Law, the second age of the Gospel, where the Son became the central figure and the third age of the Spirit, where people would, for the first time, be free.

According to Joachim, the first age 'was lived in fear, the second in faith, the third will be in love ... the first was lived in starlight, the second in the dawn, the third will be the perfect day'.[10] He even dated each age, the first extending from Adam to Abraham, the second from the prophet Elijah to Christ and the third, not yet upon us, which would bring God's decisive intervention in history.

Taking the biblical narrative as his guide, Joachim calculated that, from the time of his writing in about 1185, there were 155 years left before the third and final age. The fact that, according to Joachim's calculations, the third age ought to have begun by the time Columbus set sail on his first voyage to the Indies in 1492, gave him an increased sense of urgency and of the significance of his personal mission. He quoted Psalm 137, 'If ever I forget the thought of thee, Oh Jerusalem, let my tongue cleave to the roof of my mouth.'[11] This obsession with conquering Jerusalem explains why Columbus clung, against all the evidence, to the idea that he was in Asia, since that was surely the route to Jerusalem.

His belief that the Second Coming was at hand made it a matter of utmost urgency to save as many souls as possible before the Final Judgement. A Papal Bull issued by Pope Innocent VIII in 1496 gave Ferdinand and Isabella title over the new territories on condition they evangelise and bring the natives to God. On a voyage from Hispaniola to Cuba in 1494, one of Columbus's crew claimed to have seen a man dressed in white. Columbus told the crew the man must have been Prester John, a mythical Christian king and descendant of one of the three Magi, who ruled a lost kingdom variously thought to have been located in India, Asia or Ethiopia. There were also the prophecies of Maria de Santo Domingo, an illiterate peasant who found herself summoned before the king. In his presence she confirmed her vision that he would not die before he had conquered Jerusalem.

Such was Columbus's certainty of his mission that he ignored any arguments to the contrary, relying only on 'holy, sacred Scripture and certain prophetic texts by certain saintly persons, who by divine revelation have had something to say on this matter'. As if to reinforce his sense of purpose, Columbus convinced himself he was close to the Garden of Eden. A combination of his belief that he was in Asia, sudden changes in climate and the position of the Pole Star, convinced him the world was 'in the shape of a pear' and he was sailing to Eden. In 1502, at the risk of being deemed to have betrayed the confidence of the Spanish Crown, Columbus wrote to Pope Alexander VI claiming he had discovered Eden and that the conquest of Jerusalem would soon take place.

To the late medieval European imagination, the idea that worldly actions or political ambitions had a divine or prophetic meaning was taken for granted. In the mind of a woman like Queen Isabella it led to her opposing the enslavement of indigenous people and, in one instance, sending slaves back from Spain to the Indies. This was done not out of an abhorrence of slavery as a practice, but out of what she saw as a legal obligation to people living under a Spanish jurisdiction and out of a firm conviction that only a person free in mind and body could convert to Christianity.

If the conflation of the political and the spiritual, the temporal and the eternal, could lead to acts of mercy, it could also lead to barbarism. Bartolomé de Las Casas, a Spanish landowner who would later became a priest and Dominican friar, arrived on the island of Hispaniola in 1502. In *A Short Account of the Destruction of the Indies*, written forty years later, he recounted in graphic detail the mistreatment of indigenous people by the Spanish colonists. Las Casas describes indigenous tribes as being 'without malice or guile' and displaying 'exceptional patience and forbearance'. It was 'upon these gentle lambs ... that from the very first day they clapped eyes on them, the Spanish fell like ravening wolves upon the fold, or like tigers and savage lions who have not eaten meat for days'.[12] The result was genocidal with the population of Hispaniola declining from 'some three million' to 'only two hundred'. He gives the total death toll at 'more than fifteen million'.[13]

The colonists inflicted upon them 'a diet of robbery, murder, violence and all other manner of trials and tribulations'. In Hispaniola, 'they forced their way into native settlements, slaughtering everyone they found there ... They hacked them to pieces, slicing open their bellies with their swords as though they were so many sheep herded into a pen ... They spared no one, erecting especially wide gibbets on which they could string their victims up with their feet just off the ground and then burn them alive thirteen at a time, in honour of our Saviour and the twelve Apostles.'[14]

In Xaragua, one of the indigenous kingdoms of Hispaniola, Las Casas tells the story of Queen Anacaona. During her brother's reign, the people of Xaragua had done great service to the Spanish Crown, and after her accession to the throne she assembled hundreds of her people to welcome the governor of the island, Nicolas de Ovanda who brought with him 'sixty horse and a further three hundred men on foot'. Ovanda asked the leaders of the Xaragua to gather together in a straw building, which they dutifully did. He then 'ordered his men to set fire to it and burn them alive. All the others were massacred, either run through by lances or put to the sword. As a mark of respect, and out of deference to her rank, Queen Anacaona was hanged.'[15]

Las Casas was not alone in his condemnation of the colonists' violence. In an extraordinary sermon delivered on 21 December 1511 to the 'best people' of Hispaniola, Friar Antonio de Montesinos thundered his disapproval at the settlers. Calling himself 'a voice crying in the wilderness' he warned the congregation 'this is going to be the strangest voice you have ever heard, the harshest and hardest and most awful and most dangerous that ever you expected to hear'. After telling them they were all in 'mortal sin' because of 'the cruelty and tyranny you use in dealing with these innocent people', he demanded to know on 'what authority have you waged a detestable war against these people, who dwelt quietly and peacefully on their own land? ... Are these not men? Have they not rational souls? Are you not bound to love them as you love yourself?'[16]

Predictably, Montesinos faced fierce retaliation for his sermon. The head of the Dominican Order in Peru, Friar Jeronimo de Loayza said 'because of your words ... all of this might have been lost'. Yet Montesinos, inspired by the writings of the fourteenth-century mystic Catherine of Siena stuck to his doctrine of love, mindful of Catherine's belief that 'love carries the soul'.[17]

This strand of Dominican thought that emphasised common humanity and a divinely ordained obligation to the Other, made it impossible for Las Casas and Montesinos to remain silent whilst the indigenous population was being enslaved and butchered. However, as we have seen throughout this book, people who commit atrocities are ordinary men and women with the same capacity for generosity and cruelty as the rest of our species. It is often puzzling to witness good people do bad things, and that was how Las Casas felt about Columbus. He was perplexed how 'a man whom I have to say had a good nature and meant well, should be so blind in such a clear matter' as the cruel treatment of indigenous people.

Such blindness had its roots in the belief, which Columbus held, that the New World was not on earth but in heaven. Seen through this lens, evangelising was an act of compassion. He wrote in October 1492 that the natives, because of their gentle nature, 'were a people who would be better freed [from error] and converted to our Holy Faith by love than by force'. This was a view he shared with Las Casas and Montesinos. In his sermon, Montesinos asked the settlers 'what care do you take they should be instructed in religion?' and this evangelising impulse was also central to Las Casas' works on Spanish cruelty. He wrote *A Short Account of the Destruction of the Indies* 'in order to help ensure that the teeming millions in the New World, for whose sins Christ gave his life, do not continue to die in ignorance, but rather are brought to knowledge of God and thereby saved'.[18] Neither man saw any value in the existing beliefs and rituals of the indigenous inhabitants of Hispaniola. Even the finest of the Europeans were, despite their good intentions, misguided at best. The love and kindness of Las Casas and Montesinos and the eschatology of Columbus were aimed at eradicating what they believed to be the spiritual poverty of the natives.

The Chavistas who tore down the statue of Columbus in Caracas shared a similar wish to eliminate poverty. Their leader, Hugo Chavez, a devout Christian, anchored his political identity in a mission to protect and enhance the lives of the poor. In this, Chavez had much in common with Liberation Theology, a movement that began in the late 1960s in the Catholic Church in Latin America.

Gustavo Gutiérrez, a Dominican priest who gave the movement its name, believed those who followed the teaching of Christ had to make a commitment in solidarity with the poor and in protest against poverty. He wrote that the 'poor are anonymous ... They are born and die without being noticed. They are disposable pieces in a history that eludes their grasp, and excludes them.'[19]

For Gutiérrez, the essence of the Christian message is the obligation we have to elevate the poor out of their anonymity. The Gospel of Luke contrasts a rich man 'dressed in purple and fine linen' with 'a poor man, named Lazarus, covered with sores' who lay at the rich man's gate. Yet, despite his poverty, it is Lazarus who has a name. The rich man is anonymous. This reversal bears witness to what Gutiérrez calls God's 'preferential option for the poor',[20] who may be anonymous to the world at large, but are known to God by their names.

Despite this sanctification of the poor, Gutiérrez warned against turning 'the poor themselves into a kind of idol', of forgetting that 'the poor are human beings pierced by both grace and sin'.[21] He saw the danger of dehumanising the poor in the name of an ideology, where the poor, once again, lose their identity, and risk being told by ideologues what is best for them.

Chavez ignored Gutiérrez's warnings. He embraced a revolutionary eschatology and when he came to power in 1999, he proclaimed 'a new national existence'. In his inaugural speech, he said the people are breathing 'the winds of resurrection, we are coming out of the tomb'.[22] He identified himself with Christ, claiming he would be prepared to die, like Jesus, in the name of truth. He also extended his identification with Christ to include the people. He dedicated himself to 'fighting for the Venezuelan people, whom I love more than my life'. Christ, he said, 'is in the people' and the poor would come 'rising from hell'.

Chavez stripped liberation theology of its nuances, of what one commentator called its 'eschatological reserve'.[23] He defined the world as a battleground between two forces, one despotic, the other liberating. Inevitably, such an emaciated analysis of the lives of individual people led to the division of the world into friends and enemies: 'To be with the oppressed is to be against the oppressor'.[24] He identified the oppressors as the rich and the powerful. Comparing them to the merchants Jesus expelled from the Temple in Jerusalem, he claimed 'our homeland's temple was taken by looters, by merchants who turned it in to a brothel; and into a den of thieves, bandits and mafia'.[25]

By dividing Venezuela into the deserving poor and malevolent elites, Hugo Chavez urged his supporters to 'build together and without fear the crucial cornerstones of Latin American freedom'. He looked back at past 'humiliations' in order to construct a populist message anchored in identity politics, which framed a final political struggle between rich and poor, patriots and antipatriots. 'Every day,' he said to the people, 'I love you more.'[26] In return for that love, he demanded loyalty. He saw 'hegemonic forces' of oppression everywhere and he urged his brothers to unleash the 'sword of truth', which would take the people to the Promised Land of justice and dignity. His solution was to mark a radical break between a capitalist past and a socialist future. The means to get there was to 'demolish the old values of individualism, capitalism and selfishness' and he compared Judas Iscariot, the 'first capitalist', with Jesus Christ, 'the first socialist'.[27]

Ideologies grounded in such binary distinctions between Good and Evil are, by definition, utopian and unrealisable. They force individuals and societies into imagining the Kingdom of Heaven on Earth. After his re-election in 2007, Chavez addressed the National Assembly, giving them an ultimatum: 'Fatherland, socialism – or death. I swear it. I swear by Christ, the greatest socialist in history.' When socialism failed to arrive, the circle of blame and persecution expanded. Every 'all or nothing' ideology will ultimately consume its own children: 'either,' claimed Chavez, 'we will all leave the misery, poverty, colonialism, and underdevelopment, or else nobody will leave it'.[28]

Columbus and Chavez shared a vision of defending and elevating the poor. They both claimed they acted out of love and saw the true significance of their actions as lying in a vision of a final eschatological event, the promise of an End Time of justice and liberation. But, as Gutiérrez warned, the 'idealisation of the poor ... does not lead to liberation'.[29] On the contrary, it leads to its opposite.

The activists who tore down the statue of Columbus on 12 October 2004 may have felt hope when the imperialist fell. Chavez's successor, Nicolas Maduro, even replaced the statue of Columbus with a statue of the indigenous *cacique* Guaicaipuro. The date of inauguration was 12 October 2015, the Day of Indigenous Resistance. Yet, the indigenous population of Venezuela continued to suffer. Nicolas Maduro sanctioned 'armed groups' to subdue the population by 'threatening them with weapons'. According to Javier Tarazona, head of Funda Redes, state-sanctioned drug trafficking, corruption and money-laundering forced indigenous communities to migrate to ensure their safety. 'Even now,' said the indigenous leader Wilber Flores, 'they conceive of us as animals, as dogs. That has got to change, which is what we are fighting for – to be recognised as equal citizens, with equal rights.'[30]

Whether we seek to alleviate material or spiritual poverty, we must approach the task with humility and a recognition of the fallibility of our own judgement. For Gutiérrez, 'a humble and open identity, is an essential component of spirituality'[31] and if we are to change anything for the better we must be mindful of idolatry in all its forms, especially the worship of our ability to dismantle societies and rebuild them in our own image. Without humility, we will suffer the fate of Columbus, Chavez and many others, and end by magnifying the poverty we seek to eradicate.

CECIL RHODES

BUILT: 1912

DESTROYED: 12 July 2020

They smashed his head in the night. When dawn broke over Table Mountain, all that was left was a hollow shell and the remnants of what was once his chin. His right hand, still intact, rested against his cheek that no longer belonged to a face. Paint spattered his jacket. No one claimed responsibility, and whoever destroyed the bust of Cecil Rhodes was never caught.

It was not the first time that the Rhodes Memorial had been attacked. In 2015, his nose was sliced off with an angle grinder. On one side of the bust the words, 'Racist, thief, murderer' ..., were sprayed along the wall; on the other, 'Your dreams of empire will die.' Graffiti covered the last verse of a poem, 'The Burial' by Rudyard Kipling, which was carved onto the plinth on which the bust stood. Except for the word 'nose', the text of the graffiti was indecipherable. The stanza of the poem read:

> The immense and brooding sprit still
> Shall quicken and control.
> Living he was the land, and dead,
> His soul shall be her soul!

Of all the many statues and memorials dedicated to Cecil Rhodes, the memorial in the foothills of Table Mountain in Cape Town, South Africa, stands as the 'most grandiose of all'.[1] Designed by the English architect Sir Herbert Baker and completed in 1912, ten years after Rhodes' death, the memorial is laced with meaning. Forty-nine steps, one for each year of Rhodes' life, lead to a temple in which his bust looks north towards the distant city of Cairo. In life, Rhodes imagined the British Empire stretching all the way from Cape Town to Cairo and, in death, his vision became immortalised. A bronze horseman, displaying the muscular masculinity that Rhodes admired, adorns the entrance to the memorial and behind him eight sphinx-lions, four on either side, mark the path of the pilgrim to the temple and the bust of Rhodes. The memorial binds the future of the British Empire to the might of Greece and Rome, with Rhodes serving as the mediating link. He had always admired the busts of Roman emperors. Baker once observed him looking at a photograph of the Emperor Titus and remarking, 'He has a fine forehead.' As he said this, Baker noticed that Rhodes 'hand [was] passing unconsciously over his own'.[2]

A short distance away from the Rhodes Memorial, at the University of Cape Town, stands another statue of Rhodes. In 2015, the political activist Chumani Maxwele threw excrement at the statue before joining other activists in a *toyi-toyi*, a traditional protest dance. This was the inception of the Rhodes Must Fall movement. It began as a protest against statues of Cecil Rhodes and quickly morphed into a demand to 'decolonise' South African education. A month later, as university officials discussed whether to remove the statue, protestors chanted the anti-apartheid mantra, 'One Settler, One Bullet'.

Even Rhodes' grave has been threatened and attacked. After his death in 1902, more than 30,000 people paid their respects by filing past his coffin as it lay in the hall at Groote Schuur, his home near Cape Town. The coffin was then moved to the parliament building in Cape Town before being transported 2,250 kilometres by train to Bulawayo. From there it made its long ascent to its final resting place in the Matopos Hills in Zimbabwe, then known as Rhodesia. A team of oxen carried his body to the summit of Malindudzimu where, amid a circle of boulders, he was laid to rest, a short distance away from the burial site of Mzilikazi, a king of the Ndbele (Matabele), a people whom Rhodes had crushed in battle. Despite this, a chief of the Ndebele paid tribute to Rhodes, saying, 'I was content to die knowing that my people would be safe in the hands of Mr. Rhodes, who was at once my father and my mother. That hope has been taken from me, and I feel that the sun has indeed set.'[3] Ndebele warriors gave him the royal salute and the bishop of Mashonaland recited Kipling's 'The Burial', the final verse of which would be carved a decade later into the memorial at Table Mountain.

Three weeks after the burial, Rhodes' brother entrusted the grave to the Ndebele 'as a proof that I know that the white man and the Matabele will be brothers and friends for ever ... I charge you to hand down this sacred trust from generation to generation and I know that if you do this my brother will be well pleased.'[4] The inscription on the tomb reads: 'Here Lie the Remains of Cecil John Rhodes'. No epitaph. No dates. Rhodes rests, as he intended, beyond time.

In 1928, the South African writer Dorothea Fairbridge called the burial site, 'Rhodesia's "Valhalla"'. Decades later, the British High Commissioner Lord Alport, called the site 'a haunted, sinister, pagan place'.[5] It was also the site of protests against Rhodes and his legacy. During the struggle for independence in the 1960s, a petrol bomb was thrown at the grave and the future dictator of Zimbabwe, Robert Mugabe, threatened to dig up the grave and send the bones of Cecil Rhodes to England.

The venom directed at Rhodes after his death matched the grandiosity of his imperial ambitions. Enormous financial success amassed through ruthless business practices was not enough for Rhodes. Niall Ferguson writes in *Empire* that Rhodes 'aspired to be more than a money maker. He dreamt of becoming an empire builder.'[6] Rhodes himself said, 'I would annex the planets if I could.'[7] In *The Origins of Totalitarianism*, Hannah Arendt claims that Rhodes 'believed less in profits than in expansion for expansion's sake'[8] and cites Rhode's contemporary Leander Starr Jameson as saying 'he expected to be remembered for at least four thousand years'.[9]

Rhodes was just seventeen in 1870 when he joined his brother in South Africa where, with the backing of the Rothschild Bank, he made a fortune in diamonds and gold. Money bought him power. 'Without money, you can do nothing,'[10] he told the editor of the *Pall Mall Gazette*. With money, Rhodes believed he could restore the might of the British Empire, bring the United States of America under British rule, and extend the empire across the entire continent of Africa. In an early version of his will, Rhodes called for the establishment of a 'Secret Society, the true aim and object whereof shall be the extension of British rule throughout the world'. His justification for this ambition was his conviction in the racial and cultural superiority of white Anglo Saxons: 'We are the first race in the world, and the more of the world we inhabit, the better it is for the human race.'[11] Influenced by men like the biologist Thomas Henry Huxley, Rhodes saw black Africans as 'children', incapable of raising themselves to the intellectual and cultural level of white men.

Determined that death should not impede his ambitions of creating a revitalised British Empire, he wrote seven wills. The final one, completed in 1899, set up an institution that would become his most enduring and controversial legacy: the Rhodes Scholarships. He outlined his plans for 'the education of the colonists at one of the Universities in the United Kingdom' with the aim of 'instilling into their minds the advantage to the Colonies, as well as to the United Kingdom of the retention of the unity of the Empire'.[12]

The 'Colonial Scholarships' were to be the means for Rhodes to establish his 'Secret Society', a highly educated network of 'two or three thousand men in the prime of life scattered all over the world, each one of whom would have had impressed upon his mind in the most susceptible period of his life the dream of the Founder'.[13] This army of Rhodes scholars was his route to immortality. 'I find I am human,' Rhodes complained, 'and I should like to go on living after my death'.[14] The scholarships were a means for Rhodes to bridge the gulf between his finitude and his attachment to earthly glory, which is why the historian Philip Ziegler called them his 'true legacy'.

Rhodes stipulated the type of men who deserved to receive a scholarship. Although 'literary and scholastic attainments' were important, the men were not to 'be merely bookworms'. He emphasised success 'in manly outdoor sports such as cricket football and the like' and 'qualities of manhood truth courage devotion to duty sympathy for and protection of the weak kindliness unselfishness and fellowship'. (Sadly, punctuation was not among the virtues he valued). Finally, Rhodes insisted on 'moral force of character and instincts to lead' because the ideal man to whom he entrusted his immortality had to 'esteem the performance of public duties as his highest aim'.[15]

Having described the qualities he sought in a Rhodes scholar, he weighted each of them.' He allocated the highest proportion to 'literary and scholastic attainments', before changing his mind, and making 'qualities of manhood' their equal. He also added an instruction on the award of the scholarships, which appears strange considering his misogyny and position on white supremacy: 'No student shall be qualified or disqualified for election to a scholarship on account of his race or religious opinions.'[16] Whilst the question of religious belief was a genuine opening for diversity, the instruction on race was not. Even if a black man applied for a scholarship, he posed no threat to the white man who, in Rhodes' opinion, would always demonstrate his superiority in educational achievement, cultural sophistication, sporting ability and character. In 1906, the president of the University of North Carolina made the point more bluntly: 'A man of the coloured race would be of little to no value … a wasted opportunity'.[17]

A year after Rhodes' death, the president of the University of Iowa compared his achievements to those of Shakespeare and praised Rhodes' dream of creating a 'spiritual federation of the world through the common republic of letters'. In deciding which university the scholars would attend, Rhodes settled on his alma mater, Oxford. A 1906 article by H. Rushton Fairclough in the *Journal of Education* celebrated that Rhodes scholars would study 'at the cradle of Anglo-Saxon intellectual life'. He believed that Oxford developed 'character ... a life of "plain living and high thinking"'. For those reasons, Fairclough concluded that 'a Rhodes scholarship is one of the greatest prizes that could fall to the lot of any young man'.[18] A recipient of the award echoed this view when he told *The New York Times* in 1983, 'Winning a Rhodes Scholarship is one of the few things that you can do at 22 that they will chisel on your tombstone.'[19]

Ironically, Rhodes wasted much of his own time at Oxford. He did the minimum required of him and made few friends. Yet he expected his scholars to use the advantages of Oxford to create a global, interconnected elite. Rhodes is alleged to have told Lady Warwick that 'dreamers and visionaries have made civilisations'.[20] For others, however, the practicalities of realising this vision were challenging. In 1962, Edgar Williams, the Warden of Rhodes House at Oxford, admitted it was a 'tall order' to 'discover an elite with a conscience – with compassion and without arrogance'.[21]

Yet, many of today's educational elite believe they have achieved the ideal of a transitional, compassionate elite, while standing in opposition to everything Rhodes sought to achieve. The Rhodes Must Fall movement spread quickly from the University of Cape Town to the University of Oxford, with demands being made for the removal of the statue of Rhodes situated above the entrance to Oriel College. The protests began three months after the 2015 attack on the statue in Cape Town. The rage of the protestors was about more than Rhodes as a person: it was about the ideal of white dominance embodied in his will. Students at Oxford demanded the 'decolonisation' of the campus and the curriculum. They wanted less Eurocentricity and more women and people of colour represented on university reading lists, as well as the immediate removal of the statue.

The university authorities replied by acknowledging the grievances of the students whilst resisting their demands to remove the statue. They claimed they might lose £100 million in gifts if the statue was removed and pointed out that more than 8,000 students, of all races, have benefited from Rhodes Scholarships. The university also received 'an enormous amount of input' from students, academics, alumni and heritage bodies, as well as 500 written responses, with the majority in support of keeping the statue in place. The Conservative MP Jacob Rees-Mogg, an Oxford alumnus, said 'apologising for the past is one thing, but destroying symbols of the past is quite another'.[22]

The statue remained in place for four more years, but in 2020, after the death of George Floyd, student protests intensified and eleven Oxford professors and three associate professors demanded 'a full and frank accounting for Britain's history' rather than the 'selective commemoration of "great men" whose wealth was made through white supremacy'.[23] Faced with a new wave of demonstrations, the university agreed to begin consultations to remove the statue.

The Rhodes Scholarships have been awarded to men and women of all creeds and colours, who have gone on to become presidents, prime ministers, Supreme Court judges, NASA scientists, Booker and Pulitzer prize winners, corporate executives, politicians, academics, sports people, humanitarians and leaders in their chosen fields. The scholarships have contributed to an international elite that has taken a very different form from the one foreseen by Rhodes. As the historian Christopher Lasch pointed out, the new, highly educated, affluent elites have all the benefits to which Rhodes aspired for his own scholars, but without any sense of duty. They 'retain many of the vices of the aristocracy without its virtues. Their snobbery lacks any acknowledgement of reciprocal obligations between the favoured few and the multitude.'[24] They have contempt for socially conservative working-class communities whose traditions and values they identify as racist and oppressive.

Unlike the elite that Rhodes envisaged, the new, international, educated elites feel no obligation to contribute to the communities or societies that raised them. On the contrary, their impulse is moralistic, not civic, and their esteem and cohesion as a group is derived from pointing out pervasive violence against marginalised or racial groups. In a vicious irony of which they seem unaware, the largely white elites predicate their virtue, not on freeing those groups from oppression, but on keeping them in a state of permanent grievance. They have, according to Lasch, abandoned the historic mission of education, which is 'the democratisation of liberal culture'.[25]

By condemning Western culture, into which they entered in a position of privilege, they stand up for minorities while 'denying those minorities the fruits of the victory they struggled so long to achieve: access to the world's culture'.[26] Above all, they speak of love and compassion, of the elimination of a multitude of evils from 'hate speech' to 'patriarchy', yet that love vanishes when their movements are challenged. Lasch concludes that 'When confronted with resistance to their initiatives, they betray the venomous hatred that lies not far beneath the smiling face of upper-middle-class benevolence … They become petulant, self-righteous, intolerant. In the heat of political controversy, they find it impossible to conceal their contempt for those who stubbornly refuse to see the light – those who "just don't get it," in the self-satisfied jargon of political rectitude.'[27]

This hate, masquerading as love, finds expression in extraordinary ways. An example is when the privileged, white elite attack the minorities they claim to defend, if individual members of minority groups haven't learned to know their place in the social order. In New York in July 2020, a white, college-educated protestor mocked African American police officers, shouting at them, 'You know a hairdresser has to go to school for longer than you do' and 'half of you don't even have a college education'. The protestor then walked closer to them, yelling in their faces, 'You can't even read a fucking history book' before telling one of the officers that he is a 'Black Judas' and a 'traitor to your people'.[28]

If the incident was an isolated one, not representative of the moralising of the new elite, it might be put aside as an aberration. Except that it is not. It is one of many such instances. A week earlier, a white, college-educated protestor in Washington DC was caught yelling at black police officers. When she was asked if she felt if it was problematic for a white woman to be standing in judgement on black police officers, she replied, 'No I don't. Just because I'm white and haven't experienced racism myself doesn't mean I can't fight for justice.' Pointing at the officers, and raising her voice, she continued, 'They're a part of the system, they're a part of the problem ... Racism is a white person's problem, racism is my problem and I need to fix it.' She also confronted a female African American police officer, holding a placard in her face and filming her on her iPhone. As she did so, she said, with contempt, 'Smile for Breonna Taylor'.[29] The black officer, who may not have had any of the protestor's inherited privileges, appeared shocked and humiliated.

In 2020, a team of four psychologists from the University of British Columbia published a study in the *Journal of Personality and Social Psychology*[30] demonstrating that emitting 'signals of victimhood and virtue' allows the people who do it, to 'pursue an environmental resource extraction strategy that helps them survive, flourish and achieve their goals in situations that are responsive to their claims'. Put simply, this means that people who can convince others they are both victims and morally good people, are likely to be rewarded with preferential treatment at work or with educational opportunity without having the same expectations of competence placed upon them as their peers. They may also obtain symbolic rewards such as status, respect, compassion and love.

Crucially, these 'virtuous victims' may also be able to extract the right to take revenge on those who inflict verbal, moral or physical harm on them. The authors of the study suggest that the reason these behaviours are so prevalent in Western democracies is because these societies hold egalitarianism and the alleviation of suffering as paramount values. This allows people to equate comparative disadvantage, frustrated ambitions, or any form of conflict, with harm.

Given the enormous rewards the virtuous victim can extract, it is not surprising that the study finds they are more likely than the rest of the population to exhibit what psychologists call Dark Triad behavioural traits. These are Machiavellianism, narcissism and psychopathy, which means virtuous victims are more likely to be manipulative, grandiose in their opinion of themselves, and to exhibit a general disregard for social norms. Dark Triad traits give the social justice warrior the ability to emit false or exaggerated signals of victimhood and virtue, whilst leaving them 'unencumbered by the bite of conscience'. It explains why largely white educated elites are able to stand up for racial equality while mocking African American police officers and black Trump voters. They see themselves as victims of victims: not only do they have to fight for racial justice, they have to suffer the injustice of having to enlighten those who suffer racial injustice, but who have the temerity to refuse to see themselves as victims.

Rhodes' dream of finding an 'elite with a conscience' is more distant than ever. Modern elites, including many who seek the destruction of his statues, display qualities that bear remarkable similarity to those they condemned in colonialists, white supremacists and patriarchs.

Real victims of discrimination, prejudice and intolerance need to be distinguished from those who seek status and reward from playing the part of virtuous victims. Those who struggle against immense oppression know it takes courage, strength and humility to effect meaningful change. That is why Nelson Mandela supported the Rhodes Scholarships and put his name to ten Mandela-Rhodes Scholarships. Mandela saw combining his name with that of the arch colonialist as 'the closing of the circle and the coming together of two strands of our history'.[31] Virtuous victims have an investment in keeping the oppressed in their state of degradation, so they may extract rewards from their activism. Those, like Mandela, who live in a more nuanced world, know that progress is the art of compromise and the result of a long, often disheartening, struggle.

Elites, be they Cecil Rhodes or social justice activists, who harbour grand visions of ideal societies, will do worse than fail: their narcissism will deepen mistrust between people and increase polarisation. Poles act like magnets that collapse the centre ground. As we are pulled to extremes, we become strangers to each other, with nothing in common but belief in our own righteousness and a sense of having been wronged.

Whether we accept it or not, our survival and prosperity depend on our ability to talk to those we do not understand and with whom we have substantive disagreements. In *Talking to Strangers*, Malcolm Gladwell analyses the strategies we use to translate the words and intentions of strangers. The misunderstandings that ensure often result in tragedy. These are the last lines of the book: 'Because we do not know how to talk to strangers, what do we do when things go awry with strangers? We blame the stranger.'[32]

We cannot stop the blaming, because the rewards of virtuous victimhood are so great. Such a cynical psychological ruse, where the aggressor self-identifies as the victim, keeps those who adopt this strategy in a state of intellectual adolescence. They are neither willing nor able to cope with opinions that differ from their own. As the classicist Mary Beard observed of Rhodes Must Fall: 'The battle isn't won by taking the statue away and pretending these people didn't exist. It's won by empowering those students to look up at Rhodes and friends with a cheery self-confident sense of unbatterability.'[33] Judging by a large segment of our educated elites, such a victory is both distant and seen as undesirable.

GEORGE
WASHINGTON

BUILT: 4 July 1927

DESTROYED: 18 June 2020

The protestors wrapped an American flag around the head of George Washington, set it on fire and celebrated as it burned. After the flames consumed the flag, they wrapped strong cord around his neck and pulled the bronze statue off its plinth. Daylight showed it lying face down, daubed in graffiti. The red paint covering the back of his head looked like blood, and tiny, broken fragments of his body littered the ground. 'You are on Native land', read a sticker attached to the top of Washington's head. 'GENOCIDAL COLONIST', written over three lines, covered one of the four sides of the plinth. '1619', sprayed on Washington's right hip, marked him with a reminder of the date a ship docked in Point Comfort in the British colony of Virginia carrying the first African slaves to arrive in North America. Messages written in festivity and rage adorned the plinth with a list of grievances. 'BIG FLOYD' referenced the killing of George Floyd and it wasn't clear if 'MURDERER', scrawled along one side, referred to George Washington, police officer Derek Chauvin, convicted of the murder of George Floyd, or whether it stood as a general indictment to be directed at whomever the viewer saw fit to accuse. 'FUCK COPS' in bright blue letters took one entire side of the plinth. 'DON'T SHOOT' and 'NO GOOD COPS' were positioned below. 'Damn White Men', teetered on the edge of the base, around the corner from 'BLM', both dwarfed by the biggest two words, the first sprayed in gold, the second in orange: 'WHITE FRAGILITY'.

An hour, perhaps two, before the destruction of the statue, three groups of protestors had gathered in different locations in Portland, Oregon. It was the twenty-first day of protests demanding racial justice and police reform. A peaceful group held a rally at Jefferson High School before dispersing. A second group of demonstrators blocked

Southwest 3rd Avenue and attacked the Justice Center, while a third group ran down Northeast Sandy Boulevard at about 11.30 pm and destroyed the statue. There were no arrests.

In the febrile atmosphere after the death of George Floyd, the descent into identity groups, each with its own grievances, deepened. The following day, as the battered body of the first president of the United States was loaded onto the back of a truck, the city of Portland, along with the rest of the country, celebrated Juneteenth, the anniversary of the day in 1865, eight weeks after the defeat of the Confederacy, when slavery ended in America. One hundred and fifty-five years later and 221 years since the death of George Washington, the latter's ownership of slaves was sufficient to bring his statue to the ground.

Washington's slave ownership began after his father fell ill after going out riding and died soon after at the age of forty-eight. Included in George's inheritance were ten slaves. Despite having to wait seven years, until he turned eighteen, before he could exercise control over them, more slaves soon followed. He inherited six slaves after the death of his brother Lawrence and a further five when his sister-in-law died. His marriage in 1759 to a wealthy widow, Martha Custis, along with his own slave trading, meant that by the time the Revolutionary War began in 1775, Washington owned more than 150 slaves. During and after the war, his attitude towards slave ownership changed and in 1786 he claimed 'there is not a man living who wishes more sincerely than I do, to see a plan adopted for this abolition of [slavery] – but there is only one proper and effectual mode by which it can be accomplished & that is by Legislative authority'.[1] Despite this intention, Washington owned slaves throughout his life. He freed them only after his death, but even this was a complicated and uneven affair.

Washington was never a utopian. He was a practical man, concerned with profit, propriety and posterity. The historian Edmund Morgan described him as having a 'constant, wary and often cold eye on making a profit'[2] and he had become increasingly concerned at the cost of owning slaves. By the time of his death, he either owned or had responsibility for 317 slaves. His estate manager, James Anderson, told him that less than one third of his slaves worked and Washington himself believed the ownership of so many slaves had become an economic burden. A relative, Dr David Stuart, warned Washington that keeping slaves 'costs a great deal. Their work is worth little if they are not whipped'. However, freeing his slaves also presented a problem. Stuart concluded that they could 'all agree to free these people, but how to do it with such a great number?'[3]

Three months before his death, Washington wrote that he was unwilling to sell his slaves 'because I am principled against this kind of traffic in the human species', nor could he 'hire them out' because that would mean splitting up families as the slaves would be relocated without consideration of their own ties of family and friendship. 'What then must be done?' he asked. He had no answer to his own question, ending the letter, 'Something must or I shall be ruined.'[4]

If Washington was left grinding his teeth over this dilemma, even those teeth belonged to his slaves. Known for having troublesome teeth, a scar below Washington's left cheek on Charles Wilson Peale's 1779 portrait marks the place of an abscessed tooth and, five years later, Washington paid for nine replacement teeth at a cost of six pounds and two shillings. The teeth belonged to one of his slaves and the dentures onto which they were transferred are now on display at Mount Vernon. The method of extraction or the willingness of the donor are not recorded, but such practices were common in the eighteenth century. At the time Washington was having his slave's teeth removed, the English artist Thomas Rowlandson painted a sketch showing a malevolent and incompetent dentist pulling teeth from an impoverished young chimney sweep in order to transplant them into the mouth of a fashionably dressed, if rather grotesque, young lady. Two young children can be seen clutching their mouths as they leave the surgery, their teeth already having been extracted and transplanted into the mouths of the two other wealthy adults in the room.

If the teeth of the poor and enslaved were easily removed, their yearning to be free was more difficult to get rid of. In 1798, Washington complained that his slaves were 'growing more and more insolent and difficult to govern'. When Caesar, a quiet, middle-aged slave, escaped, Washington appeared baffled since he had fled 'without having received any correction, or threats of punishment, or, in short, without having any cause whatever'.[5] Determined to find a resolution to the problem of what to do with his slaves after his death, Washington drafted his final will in July 1799. He catalogued his slaves, and was shocked to learn that almost 100 were under the age of twelve, while a further ninety were married and likely to produce children of their own. But he was also concerned for his wife's financial well-being and the impact on her should his slaves be freed. He concluded that the best course of action was to free his slaves only after her death, making it known that the young slaves should, before being freed, 'be taught to read and write and be brought up to some useful occupation'.[6] He made one exception. His personal assistant, Billy Lee, was to be freed immediately and given an annuity of $30 with an option to stay at Mount Vernon. This is what Billy chose to do, living there for the rest of his life.

Washington's primary concern, as he neared the end of his life, was his legacy. He wanted to ensure that 'no reproach may attach itself to me when I have taken my departure for the land of spirits'. Perhaps freeing his slaves was one step towards achieving this end. Another was a bequest to found a university where students could shed 'their local attachments and state prejudices'. Washington feared tribalism and understood the difficulty of holding together a fledgling Union composed of disparate beliefs and values, which might fragment at any moment.

During the course of his life, Washington's humility and commitment to building a peaceful and enduring Union had been put to the test by the plaudits he received. From the moment he took over as commander-in-chief of the Continental Army in 1775, towns and ships were named after him, handkerchiefs bore his initials and poems were composed in his honour. One of these, written by the enslaved poet Phillis Wheatley, held out the promise of kingship:

Proceed, great chief, with virtue on thy side,
Thy every action let the goddess guide.
A crown, a mansion, and a throne that shine,
With gold unfading, WASHINGTON! be thine.[7]

Whilst his public image and the regard in which he was held were important to him, Washington neither sought nor wished to be the head of a monarchy. His commitment to the republic was deep and immovable. Despite this, the eulogies grew in number. Another poet, Francis Hopkinson, wrote that had Washington 'lived in the days of idolatry he had been worshipped as a god'. The historian Gordon Wood called him 'an extraordinary heroic man'. Many considered him an 'American Moses' leading his people to the Promised Land, and the congressional delegate Benjamin Rush claimed 'there is not a king in Europe that would but look like a *valet de chambre* by his side'.[8]

It is one of the ironies of revolutionary movements that they erect new icons as soon as they topple the old ones. While clamour grew for Washington to adopt the mantle of a king, love for the British King George III quickly turned to hate. On 9 July 1776, about forty American soldiers, having listened to the newly issued Declaration of Independence, made their way to Bowling Green park in Lower Manhattan and pulled an equestrian statue of George III to the ground. The lead statue was made into 42,088 musket balls and the

New York Postmaster, Ebenezer Hazard, wrote that the statue of the king 'has been pulled down to make musket ball of, so that his troops will probably have melted majesty fired at them'.[9]

Wherever Washington went, he was greeted with adulation. Women threw flowers at his feet and in 1780, as the British forces advanced from the South, a member of Congress wrote of the 'necessity of appointing General Washington sole dictator of America ... as the only means under God, by which we can be saved from destruction'. Again, Washington refused to bend principle to populism and in 1797, two years before his death, he retired to Mount Vernon, still preferring principle to power.

Washington was by no means a democrat in the way we understand the term today. He was a Federalist who feared the mob. He saw no role for the people to criticise their elected officials and his paternalism came under attack, notably from a French minister, Edmond-Charles Genet, whose arrival in South Carolina in April 1793 served as the impetus for the formation of Democratic-Republican Societies. Within a year, more than thirty were established and Washington feared they were, as the Federalist Fisher Ames claimed, 'born in sin, the impure offspring of Genet'.[10] Washington's tolerance was not helped when a newspaper ran a cartoon of him with his head in a guillotine.

When the Founding Fathers sought to build an enduring republic they turned to classical Greece and Rome for inspiration. They were particularly concerned about learning lessons from history about how to prevent the emergence of tyrants from within the republic itself. Washington's favourite play, *Cato*, told the story of the Roman statesman, Cato the Younger, who committed suicide rather than submit to tyranny. Washington's fear of the tyranny spawned by democratic rule had another famous classical precedent. In *The Republic*, the Greek philosopher Plato argued that democracies inevitably become tyrannies. This happens because the 'insatiable desire for what democracy defines as good overthrows it … [The] insatiable desire for freedom … prepares the ground for tyranny'.[11]

In democracies, the permanent extension of freedom is at the same time the engine of tolerance, the measure of progress and the mechanism of collapse. 'In the end,' wrote Plato, 'the very beasts are imbued with anarchy'. He describes how democracies destroy hierarchies and disrupt all forms of order. The parent fears the child and the old imitate the young for fear of being 'disagreeable or despotic'.[12]

The crisis in democracy comes when the fruits of this freedom are distributed unevenly and a mass of people feel they have been cheated out of what is rightfully theirs. Determined to bring down the elites, they turn to the tyrant to protect them. To consolidate his power, the tyrant, even though he is one of the elite, pretends he is on the side of the people. His survival is dependent on having an enemy to consolidate his power. In this way, he energises the love the people have for him. If he triumphs over his enemies, he must find new ones, so he is fated to 'constantly stir up wars, in order that the people may need a leader'.[13]

In analysing the emergence of a tyrant, the mistake is to make the tyrant responsible for tyranny. Of course, it appears that way because the tyrant stokes fear and division. But the desire for that fear and division comes first from the people: tyranny is an emergent property of mobs, not the other way around. They take to the streets to demand the freedom they believe they have been denied, only to find they spawn a cult leader who will take away the freedom they already possess. David A. Bell wrote that the 'cult of the commander in chief' that grew up around George Washington, 'derived less from his own achievements than from the longings of his fellow citizens'.[14]

Washington was able to resist sanctification by the people and the temptation of tyranny, but other leaders have no desire to do so. Indeed, like Donald Trump, they feed off it. As Trump prepared to host religious leaders for the National Day of Prayer, his campaign

manager Brad Pascale tweeted, 'Only God could deliver such a saviour to our nation.'[15] The evangelical preacher Jerry Falwell justified
his endorsement of Trump by comparing him to King David, 'a
man after God's own heart, even though he was an adulterer and
murderer'. Trump's press secretary, Sarah Huckabee Sanders, told
Christian Broadcasting Network News that 'God calls all of us to fill
different roles at different times, and I think that he wanted Donald
Trump to become president'. Almost half of all Trump supporters
believed God had chosen him to be president and his secretary of
state, Mike Pompeo, agreed with an interviewer who suggested that
Trump had been 'raised for such a time as this, just like Queen Esther,
to help save the Jewish people from the Iranian menace'. QAnon
conspiracy theorists believe that elites throughout the world are
abusing and killing children and that Donald Trump has been sent to
defeat them. Part of their strategy to defeat Trump, QAnon followers
believe, was to win the 2020 election by fraud. When Democrats
made it easier for people to vote by mail, Q, the mysterious founder
of the cult, posted, 'These people are sick! Nothing can stop what
is coming. Nothing.'[16] Except, of course, Donald Trump, who will
lead the 'Great Awakening', free children from abuse and redeem
the dispossessed. The storming of the Capitol building that followed
was apocalyptic to its core.

The Canadian historian, Timothy Naftali described the sanctification of Trump as depriving his followers of their freedom. In fact,
the reverse is true: Trump had no freedom other than to magnify
what he is in order to retain the love and support of the people. This
creates a vicious paradox: to sustain his power, an authoritarian leader
has to deprive the people of the freedom he promises them. As he
consolidates this power at their expense, he feigns to be on their side,
always mindful that the people must never be sufficiently free to free
themselves from him. The invasion of the Capitol by Trump supporters, who even turned on Vice President Mike Pence, threatening to

hang him for his certification of Joe Biden as president, was a warning that, ultimately, the people can consume the tyrant himself.

There are those who see reason as a protection against the sanctification of ideologies and political figures. The philosopher Immanuel Kant, who lived at the same time as George Washington, defined the 'motto of enlightenment' as: 'Have courage to use your own understanding!'[17] He warned against the 'laziness and cowardice' of submerging the individual will into the collective. He called it a 'lifelong immaturity' for which we pay a high price. If an autocratic dictator is overthrown, unless the people reach a state of intellectual maturity, a new director will emerge as 'new prejudices just like the old ones they replace, will serve as a leash for the great unthinking mass'.[18] The answer for Kant was for each individual to use the freedom to think as a secure defence against tyranny. If the individual 'is only allowed to use freedom, enlightenment is almost inevitable'.[19]

Kant's vision may be our only hope that democracies may survive the current turbulence, but increasingly it looks like a forlorn one. In *Democracy in America*, first published in 1835, Alexis de Tocqueville wrote that people are driven 'by the most demanding of all necessities, that of not sinking'.[20] When economic growth stalls and people lose faith in the future, they will invest the present with intolerance and violence. As Edward Luce wrote, 'the West's souring mood is about the psychology of dashed expectations rather than the decline in material comforts'.[21] As the gulf between the educated elite and the mass of ordinary Americans widens, the hope for civility declines. The top 1 per cent send more of their children to elite American universities than the bottom 60 per cent. They emerge from these universities with contempt for the social conservatism of large swathes of working-class America whose fury found a voice in a president who told them, 'I love the poorly educated!' This dynamic of love and hate, fuelled by identity groups that no longer understand each other, creates digital echo chambers where we speak only to those who speak like us. The first casualty of these chambers is any possibility of shared truth, and without this truth the centre cannot hold. The escalating hate and contempt will not even be eased by economic prosperity since growth is no longer equated with more jobs.[22]

The educated elites are also subject to the logic of decline. More than a third of STEM graduates are doing jobs that don't require that standard of education and there are three times as many law graduates as there are jobs in the legal profession. We see the future stretching out ahead of us and it belongs to the vanishing few who profit from the algorithms and technologies they develop. Activism, on the right and left, the violence of Trump supporters and the illiberalism of elite identity politics, are products of the same despair.

Kant's hope for tolerance and 'understanding', of building effective coalitions with those with whom we disagree, is ruined before it begins. 'I know your pain. I know your hurt. We love you. You're very special', said Donald Trump as he basked in the chaos his followers unleashed on the Capitol Building. The attack on the Capitol was the mob returning their leader's love through an act of transgression. When people feel deprived of love, dignity and an acknowledgement of their identity, they are ripe for submission to an authoritarian leader who promises them a world where he will lift them out of their misery – and punish their enemies.

Secularism can formalise the separation of powers, but it can't remove the human desire for transcendence and revenge. Bitter with resentment and hate, the mob looks to the tyrant to punish the elites and open the gates to a new world where wrongs are put right. This explains why the transition from democracy to tyranny is accompanied by apocalyptic dreams and conspiracy theories. Both of these elements are embedded in QAnon, which is both a cult and a millenarian movement. Trump didn't start QAnon, nor did he believe it, but he recognised its utility and harnessed its message to serve his political ends.

The historian Norman Cohn described the typical millenarian narrative as an evil power of 'boundless destructiveness … [that] … will become more and more outrageous, the sufferings of its victims more and more intolerable – until suddenly the hour will strike when the Saints of God are able to rise up and overthrow it'.[23] In modern America, the Saints of God are replaced by Donald Trump, as QAnon believers await The Storm, when cannibalistic, child-killing Democrats, Hollywood stars and officials of the 'Deep State' are rounded up and executed. After the executions, a Great Awakening will take place, where children will finally be safe and the voiceless will have their voice. 'Q gives us hope. And it's a good thing to be hopeful,' said Shelly, a middle-aged QAnon follower. Observing that Q occasionally quotes scripture, Shelly believes the movement is 'very biblical and that this is Armageddon'.[24]

As Plato predicted, these dreams and theories keep the people vigilant and protective of the tyrant whom they see as their salvation. They follow him slavishly to the Promised Land, even if the cost of that journey is the descent of everything into chaos. In 1953, the year of Joseph Stalin's death, the Polish writer Czesław Miłosz warned the West to be mindful of believing it was immune to tyranny. He warned that if 'something exists in one place, it will exist everywhere'.[25] He believed that we are creatures of habit who lack the imagination to believe that the tyranny we condemn at a distance will one day come to our own cities. We behave 'like Charlie Chaplin in *The Gold Rush*, bustling about in a shack poised precariously on the edge of a cliff'.[26] What stops us from falling is, in large part, the goodwill and restraint of those who have the ability to convert their power into tyranny, but refuse to do so.

Trump may have left office and moved to Florida but he did so reluctantly, having exhausted all avenues to maintain his power. The next president elected in his image may not be so easy to dislodge. Washington, on the other hand, retired to Mount Vernon and died having sacrificed his own vanity for the good of the republic he was instrumental in creating. His story is often compared to that of the Roman consul Lucius Quinctius Cincinnatus who left his farm in 458 BCE to lead the Roman army to victory against the invading Aequi. Appointed dictator of Rome, he retained his position only as long as it took to restore order, before willingly surrendering it and returning to his farm.

When, therefore, we tear down the statue of George Washington, we may choose to condemn him for owning slaves, but we should also remember his humility. Our best defence against tyranny is, like Washington, to tame the tyrant in ourselves before we scorch the earth on which we stand.

JOSEPH STALIN

BUILT: 18 December 1951
DESTROYED: 23 October 1956

S tatues bear witness to truth. Before they can stand, two spaces must be cleared: a space in a park, a street, a square or a building, and a space in the minds of the people. The first is easy to find. The second is hard to sustain.

Preparing the ground for truth is a brutal affair. In Hungary, it began with the occupation of the country by the Soviet Union after the defeat of Germany in the Second World War. Despite getting less than a fifth of the vote in Hungary's first free elections on 4 November 1945, the communists, led by the stalinist Mátyás Rákosi, sought to take control of the country. To this end, they adopted what Rákosi called 'salami tactics'. He explained that their 'demands were always modest at first – and were then increased',[1] stealth paving the way to terror. As their influence increased, the communists set up the AVO[2], the Hungarian equivalent of the KGB, under the sadistic libertine Gábor Péter. Their aim was to silence and eliminate opposition. Their methods were as effective as they were crude. Lieutenant-Colonel Gyula Prinz, a bald, pot-bellied former fascist who was reputed to have tortured more than 25,000 people, served as the party's main interrogator. His ingenuity and the pleasure he took in his work can be seen by his treatment of the writer Paul Ignotus. Forced to stand facing the wall and to hold a pencil between his nose and upper lip, Prink asked him why he didn't 'use a writer's imagination and write a writer's confession'. When the pencil dropped, Ignotus was beaten until his 'whole body was swollen with purple bruises and a couple of teeth were kicked out'.[3]

By 1948, most of the opposition had been crushed, but the Catholic Church remained defiant. In a bid to silence ecclesiastical opposition, Rákosi arrested Archbishop Mindszenty, the head of the church in

Hungary. Before his arrest, recognising the possibility that torture might break him, Mindszenty told his followers that if they should 'read or hear it said that I have made admissions, or that I have resigned, or even that my signature is used to try to authenticate such confessions, this must be put down to my human weaknesses'.[4] It was with scepticism, therefore, that Catholics read his confession about using American aid to overthrow the Hungarian republic. He had been tortured for days before confessing his treason.

Other Christian denominations were attacked. A leading Lutheran Bishop was jailed and when the Greek Orthodox Bishop János Ödön Péterfalvy refused to sign a confession, his interrogators ripped his toenails out. When this didn't break him, they threatened to arrest and torture his elderly father. Péterfalvy confessed and spent ten years in a Siberian labour camp.

After the torture and execution of his rival László Rajk on 15 October 1949, Rákosi's grip on power tightened, and he unleashed the Great Terror. Between 1950 and 1953, over a million Hungarians were prosecuted on bogus charges and almost 2,500 were executed. With such meticulous and ferocious preparation, the political space had been cleared for the erection of a statue in honour of Joseph Stalin. A final act of preparation was the blowing up of the votive church of Regnum Marianum on 23 September 1951. On 18 December 1951, a bronze statue of Stalin emerged out of the ruins of the church. The statue and the stone plinth on which it stood, reached a height of 25 metres. His left foot forward and his right hand outstretched, the statue portrayed Stalin as an approachable, paternal figure.

Stalin stood, dominating Heroes Square, for less than five years. On the afternoon of 23 October 1956, 100,000 people marched on the statue. A young communist lieutenant frantically called his boss, asking what he should do. When he said he had only twenty-five men at his disposal, his boss told him to let the crowd destroy the statue, which was easier said than done. Ropes were of little use and shortly before 10 pm, after much deliberation, three cranes pulled the statue to the ground. Stephen Vizinzcey, a student, recalled 'several thousand people sighing with joy' when the statue fell and the sense they were 'making history. We thought the whole world is looking at us and the whole world is happy.'⁵ A sign over Stalin's mouth told the Russians to go home and someone scrawled W.C. on his left cheek. All night, demonstrators attacked the ruins of the statue. Factory workers brought blow torches and flame-cutting machines to cut its remains at the boots before it was dragged to Blaha Lujza Square. The severed head ended up on Grand Boulevard where the crowds attacked it, thrusting an implement through its forehead. Over the following days, the people hacked at what was left of the fallen statue, breaking pieces off in a slow and deliberate decomposition.

In that brief fragment of time, it seemed that the Hungarian people would free themselves from Russian occupation, something that would have seemed unthinkable just a few years earlier during the Great Terror. The first event that made the Hungarian Revolution possible was the death of Stalin in March 1953. Then, in February 1956, his successor Nikita Khrushchev gave a speech to a closed session of the Twentieth Congress of the Communist Party of the Soviet Union. Known as the Secret Speech, it was the first time any senior communist official, let alone the president, had dared to denounce Stalin in public. It was an event of such magnitude that people had heart attacks while they listened and there were reports of suicides for days afterwards among those faithful to Stalin.

In the speech,⁶ Khrushchev criticised Stalin for demanding 'absolute submission' and for condemning those who resisted him to 'physical annihilation'. Stalin's idea of the 'enemy of the people' gave him the freedom to unleash the 'most cruel repression' against the people of the Soviet Union. Khrushchev observed that, despite the triumph of the revolution, Stalin persisted in using 'extreme methods and mass repressions' to consolidate his power. In what would become

Khrushchev's most famous phrase, he accused Stalin of ignoring the 'Leninist principle of collective party leadership' and creating a 'cult of personality'. He mocked Stalin's 1948 biography for its 'dissolute flattery' and its 'loathsome adulation'. Finally, warning against releasing any details of his speech to the outside world, Khrushchev concluded that 'we must abolish the cult of the individual decisively'.

As details of the Secret Speech found its way to Hungary, the arch-Stalinist Rákosi took comfort in the belief that Khrushchev would soon be ousted. It was unthinkable that the Soviet Union would tolerate such historical revisionism. The majority of Soviet citizens still regarded Stalin as a father figure and they were being asked to believe that not only were they wrong, but that Stalin was a tyrant.

Rákosi, too, was wrong. Khrushchev survived and elements within the Hungarian Communist Party that wanted an end to Stalinist terror began openly mocking Rákosi. In what became known as the Khrushchev Thaw, reformist communists, emboldened by the denunciation of Stalin, demanded freedom of political and artistic expression. A spontaneous movement without a centralised leadership structure began to undermine the foundations of Stalinist Hungary.

The movement found its voice in a group of young intellectuals based in Budapest known as the Petöfi Circle. Named after a Hungarian poet who disappeared after the Battle Segesvár during the Hungarian Revolution of 1848, the Petöfi Circle began as a series of small meetings held at the Kossuth Club in 1954. After the Secret Speech, attendance increased. Notable attendees included the composer Zoltán Kodály, who spoke at one of the meetings, and, on 14 June 1956, four months before the toppling of the statue of Stalin, the Marxist György Lukács recommended reading non-Marxist philosophers like Plato and Schopenhauer.

Two weeks later, an event took place that would finish Rákosi: Júlia Rajk, the widow of the former leader executed by Rákosi, spoke at the Petöfi Circle. 'I stand before you, she said, barely able to stop herself from crying, 'deeply moved after five years of prison and humiliation ... Not only was my husband killed but my little baby was torn from me ... Murderers should not be criticised – they should be punished. I shall never rest until those who have ruined the country, corrupted the Party, destroyed thousands, and driven millions into despair receive their just punishment. Comrades, help me in the struggle!'[7] When she sat down, the room burst into thunderous applause.

The thirst for freedom was unstoppable. The Petőfi Circle spoke openly about 'structural mistakes' and the need to remove the communist leadership. A blacksmith captured the mood of the people when he wrote, 'I'm not a child, I'm an adult ... I want to be able to speak my thoughts without having anything to fear'.[8] In July, Rákosi resigned, and on 6 October more than 100,000 people witnessed the reburial of László Rajk and four of the men who had been hanged alongside him in 1949. The atmosphere grew increasingly frenetic. On 23 October, protestors tore down the statue of Stalin. The revolution was chaotic, spontaneous and uncoordinated. Some members of the AVO were lynched, but there was relatively little violence given the number of people involved. A list of sixteen demands were made, pinned on trees and walls and broadcast on radio. The army, ordered to crush the rebellion, instead sided with the rebels. The Soviet army tried and failed to quell the dissent. A week after it started, the revolution appeared to have succeeded.

It was, according to the political theorist Hannah Arendt, a battle fought for 'Freedom and Truth'. She quoted a young Hungarian girl describing how she was 'brought up amidst lies. We continually had to lie. We could not have a healthy idea because everything was choked in us.'[9] This was the essence of Stalinism: the subordination of truth to ideology and the preservation of the lie through terror. A Hungarian joke told the story of a party official who visited a farmer and asked him who created the world. The farmer took a moment to think carefully before speaking. 'God made the world,' he replied, adding, 'with the help of Soviet experts.'

The Party determined truth and enforced it on the people. Paul Ignotus, the writer tortured by General Prinz, described how the communists manufactured 'outright lies, elevated to the status of truth through forced or forged confessions'.[10] The Hungarian nobleman George Paloczi-Horvath suffered a similar fate to Paul Ignotus, and he described this collapse of truth into ideology in his biography, *The Undefeated*. Despite being a committed communist, he was jailed in 1949 and shared a cell with Ignotus and other imprisoned intellectuals. In the first week of his captivity, he described the 'hideous feeling to be jailed by my own state, to realise that I, a good Communist, was confined in a Communist jail'.[11] A colonel attempted to explain away Horvath's confusion at his incarceration on, as yet, unspecified charges: 'Anyone we pull in is guilty. We never make mistakes.'[12]

Horvath illustrates this ideological collapse of truth into absurdity through the story of his friend, the poet George Faludy, who confessed to spying and sending back information to his superior officers, Edgar Allan Poe and Walt Whitman. During questioning, he said to General Peter, 'You know that I am innocent.' The General replied, 'Yes, of course … [but] … now that you are here, you'll die here'.[13]

When lies are repeated enough times, people will actively accept what is false as true. They will even condemn their own families. Magda, a Jewish Holocaust survivor, described how her husband was arrested for actions against the Communist Party. She explained her acceptance of his fate because 'as a zealous communist I should know that he must have done something awful! That's why the party had to imprison him! Eradicate him! Because he betrayed it! The Party!'[14] When the Party is Truth, dissent is a lie, punishable by imprisonment or death. The ability for such cognitive distortions to grow, like parasites in the human brain, is well evidenced and Horvath described how, to appease his accusers and unburden his soul, he was forced to repeatedly write his autobiography in the form of an extended self-criticism. If he was to be executed, it was having found inner peace as a good communist. Just as for those accused by the Church in the Middle Ages, truth didn't matter when salvation was at stake. This loss of psychological reality explains why people sentenced to death by Stalin chanted 'Long Live Stalin!' at the moment of their execution. 'If', wrote Horvath, 'it was true, as the wall telegraph informed me, that László Rajk's last shout was "Long live the party!" then he too preferred to die at peace with the party.'[15][16]

When lies become truth, terror is inevitable. In a brilliant essay called 'The Death of Gods', written in the same year as the Hungarian Revolution, the Polish philosopher Leszek Kołakowski describes how 'at the ripe age of eighteen', he became a communist. Writing with the benefit of weariness and hindsight, he mocks the utopianism of his younger self who believed that 'socialism would automatically eradicate all social inequalities ... [and] lead to the swift and total disappearance of national hostility, nationalist prejudice and tribal conflict.'[17]

What sustained the idealistic Kołakowski in these beliefs was the ingenuity of the communist system in explaining away inconvenient facts with 'ideological myths'. Kołakowski compares a communist society to 'a heap of stones flung into a sack and bound together with the string of military discipline'.[18] He notes the power of this sack, especially its ability when necessary to 'smash skulls'. The aim of the discipline is to convince the stones they are in the sack of their own free will. From the outside, this seems impossible. but when you're in the sack, you can't see out. This explains why men like Horvath, even while he languished in prison, would still defend Marxism-Leninism in discussions with his fellow prisoners and was 'proud that no amount of suffering could shake our belief'.[19] Eventually, Horvath lost his faith. He called himself an 'erudite idiot',[20] unable to understand his previous fervour and tormented by the 'monstrosity' he had allowed to infect his mind and which he passed on into the world.

In 1956, having been freed during the thaw, Horvath participated in the Hungarian uprising. With rebellions against communist rule taking place at the same time in Poland and Hungary, Kołakowski wrote 'we are now witnessing the funeral of this mythology'.[21] However, this was a funeral unlike any other because the deceased refused to believe in its own death. When an ideology is defeated, when the gods that lie and call it truth are killed, we can never be so sure they will not return 'in a new incarnation'. These are dangerous gods, whose death is perpetually deferred, even as the corpse is buried and soil raked over the grave.

This is the meaning of the famous story told by Nietzsche about a madman who lit a lantern and ran into a market square, shouting, 'God is dead. God remains dead. And we have killed him.'[22] God, the symbol of metaphysical truth had been killed because his creatures refused to stop asking difficult, impertinent questions. They refused to accept that the quest for truth should stop at the word of God, so they pushed beyond it. Realising the implications of this crime, the madman wanted to know how 'shall we comfort ourselves, the murderers of all murderers? ... Must we not become gods simply to appear worthy of it?' Despairing that people were not able to live without the need for certainty and the comfort of new gods, the madman smashed his lantern on the ground. He extinguished the light that shone after the death of God. Nietzsche feared, as did Kołakowski, that in killing gods we descend into nihilism and brutality, only to resurrect new gods as the means of our salvation.

Despite this pessimism, Nietzsche saw the possibility that the death of God, the hunger to push beyond lies masquerading as truth, offered hope: 'at long last our ships may venture out again, venture out to face any danger; all the daring of the lover of knowledge is permitted again; the sea, *our* sea lies open again; perhaps there has never yet been such an open sea'.[23] Kołakowski agreed, writing that 'the death of the gods is the liberation of man'.[24]

This hope for liberation was what drove the Petőfi Circle and the Hungarian revolutionaries. They fought for a society in which facts and truth mattered. The reformist Tibor Meray described the 'telling of truth' as 'our most imperative inner necessity'.[25] The Party could treat people like stones in a sack, but it couldn't stifle dissent. It couldn't erase facts. All it could do was suppress them. Despite this, getting stones in a sack to think for themselves isn't easy, as exemplified by those who praised Stalin as he executed them. When external, ideological compulsion is transformed into self-denunciation, when we accept the lies we are told as truth and then turn that truth against ourselves, we are completely and utterly lost. We are lost, too, when we free ourselves from oppression only to use the lies that oppressed us in order to oppress others. They will, of course, be different lies: it may be that we expose the lies of the 'old Party' only to create some new ones in the name of the 'new Party' and use the new lies to repeat old patterns of oppression. Modern Hungary, under the leadership of the former anti-communist revolutionary Viktor Orbán, is an example of a liberator taking on the methods of the tyranny he helped to depose.

On 4 November 1956, Soviet tanks swept into Hungary and crushed the revolution. As the tanks entered Budapest, the moderate Hungarian leader, Imre Nagy put out a message over the radio to inform the people that 'Soviet troops attacked our capital with the obvious intention of overthrowing the legal Hungarian democratic government. Our troops are in combat. The government is at its post.' He ended the broadcast with this carefully worded phrase: 'I notify the people of our country and the entire world of this *fact* [emphasis mine]'.[26] In similar vein, the last message broadcast by Hungary on Radio Station Kossuth was spoken by the playwright Gyula Háy: 'We appeal for help to all intellectuals in all countries.

You all know the facts. There is no need to review them. Help Hungary. Help!'[27]

A month after the invasion, amid the rubble and terror of Budapest, 30,000 women dressed in black marched in silence through the city mourning the death of the revolution. Within a few months, almost 200,000 people, mostly young, had fled the country. The new Stalinist leader, János Kádár, set up People's Courts, which imprisoned 22,000 people and ordered the executions of more than 300. Imre Nagy himself was put on trial, charged with plotting to overthrow the state, and hanged at dawn on 16 June.

The Hungarian Michael Polanyi wrote that the communists 'detested everything', yet convinced themselves that the 'total destruction of existing society and the establishment of their own absolute power on its ruins would bring total happiness to humanity'.[28] Like gruesome alchemists, the communists turned hate into love, vengeance into compassion, ruin into progress. After the triumph of the Soviet invasion of Hungary, the Party was, once again, the bearer of truth.

Of all possible worlds that we can imagine, however, the worst is not the one where lies are turned into truth in the name of the Party or in the name of God. That is, at least, a world in which there will still be facts able to expose our subjugation if only we choose to search for them. In describing what he calls the 'communist neurosis'[29] as the 'contradiction between ideals and reality', Horvath believes there is still a reality to which those who fight for freedom can anchor their actions. When the statue of Stalin fell, it was like a sudden burst of that reality through the veil of ideology. Ultimately, the statue, for all its tyrannical presence, was hiding truth.

Far worse, perhaps the worst of all possible worlds, is the one defined by what Hannah Arendt calls the 'terrifying impossibility of agreeing about facts'.[30] This is a world where we can't persuade each other 'to recognise facts as they are and to come to terms with the factuality of the world as it is'. It is a world without truth of any sort, just an endless supply of competing ideologies fuelled by self-serving biases. In such a world, there will be tyrants at every turn, each one passing off lies as truth and even if a few still have the courage to scramble in the dust for facts, they will fail to find any or, if they do, they will no longer be able to recognise them for what they are. In George Orwell's *Nineteen Eighty-Four*, Syme, who works at the Ministry of Truth, explains the ultimate purpose of *Newspeak*, the ideologically correct language of the party: 'Don't you see that the whole, purpose of Newspeak is to narrow the range of thought? In the end we shall make thoughtcrime literally impossible, because there will be no words in which to express it.'[31]

Today, we live in a multiverse of competing linguistic dystopias, each one believing its own 'truth'. All that remains of the statue of Stalin in Budapest are his boots, a symbol of the defeat of tyranny. However, it is far more likely they are waiting, patiently, for many, more deadly, feet to fill them.

YAGAN

BUILT: 11 September 1984
DESTROYED: September 1997

On 31 August 1997, an Aboriginal delegation accompanied the boxed-up head of a Noongar warrior onto a flight from London to Australia. As the plane approached its destination, chanting, singing and dancing flooded through Perth International Airport. Voices rang out, 'I tell you, our people, our brother he come home, we lay his head down ...'[1]

Fourteen thousand kilometres away in Paris, a black Mercedes-Benz W140 moving at more than twice the legal speed limit to escape pursuing photographers entered a tunnel. The driver lost control. The car hit a stone wall. The driver and a male passenger were declared dead at the scene. The woman, still conscious but fatally wounded, murmured, 'Leave me alone.' Three hours later, she was dead.

The head belonged to Yagan, a leader of the Noongar tribe, killed in 1833. The woman was Diana, Princess of Wales. The link between them is more than the coincidence of these two events. It is also more than their iconic status for their respective communities. What binds them are the words of Ken Colbung, one of the Noongar leaders who brought back the head of Yagan to his people. He described the death of Diana as 'Nature's revenge'[2] for the killing and beheading of Yagan by the British colonists.

To make sense of Colbung's claim, we have to go back to events leading up to the murder of Yagan. Born a few years after the first British ships arrived in Botany Bay in 1788, Yagan was the son of Midgegooroo, a prominent elder of the Noongar tribe. By the 1830s, he had become a fearsome figure in the imagination of the colonists, some of whom called him the 'Black Napoleon'.[3] In April 1833, Robert Menli Lyon, one of the earliest defenders of Aboriginal rights, described Yagan as 'among the princes of the country. He has greatly distinguished himself as a patriot and a warrior. He is in fact the Wallace of the age.'⁴ The Perth *Daily News* also compared Yagan to the thirteenth-century Scottish independence leader in an article titled, 'Yagan, "Wallace" of the Aborigines'.⁵ Written on the 100th anniversary of Yagan's death, it described the gradual escalation of conflict between the colonists and natives, as the former appropriated Aboriginal land. This was more than a struggle over resources. It was a conflict of cultures that failed to understand each other.

In his groundbreaking book on Aboriginal farming, Bruce Pascoe claimed if 'we are to attempt to understand Indigenous philosophy, it has to begin with the profound obligation to land'.⁶ For men like Yagan, land was not something you owned. It was a space marked by myth. For a people who looked back to the deep past to make sense of the present, rocks, trees, rivers and mountains, the sun, the sea and the stars, all had a sacred significance. A Noongar creation myth tells the story of *Waugal*, a Noongar word meaning 'soul' or 'spirit'. In the Dreamtime, *Waugal* took the form of a Rainbow Serpent that wound its way over the land, forming the landscape as it went. Such myths reminded the Noongar they are custodians of the land, a land that is inseparable from the unity of the cosmos and from the connection of Aboriginal people to their ancestors, who first breathed life into it.

The British idea of the individual ownership of land was incomprehensible to the Aborigines. When the British punished theft or damage to property, Yagan replied that the 'wild black fellows do not understand your laws, every living animal that roams the country, and every edible root that grows in the ground are common property. A black man claims nothing as his own but his cloak, his weapons and his name … He does not understand that animals or plants can belong to one person more than another.'⁷

Land was not the only marker of misunderstanding between colonists and natives. In 1836, after their vessel struck a coral reef, Eliza Fraser, her husband and members of the ship's crew rowed until they landed on an island, now known as Fraser Island. Heavily pregnant, Eliza gave birth and lost her baby on the voyage. Years later, Eliza described the 'cruel abuse' she suffered at the hands of the Ka'bi Aborigines. She claimed she was stripped of her clothes, forced to undertake menial tasks and beaten severely for the 'least resistance'. She complained at having to carry 'wood, water and bark' and 'all we had to subsist upon was a kind of Fern root which we were obliged to procure ourselves in the swamps'.[8] She accused the natives of throwing a spear at her husband 'which entered his shoulder a little below the blade-bone'. When he died, 'they dragged him away by the legs and buried him'. Eight days after 'this brutal affair, the same cannibals also killed Mr Brown, the chief officer, by holding firebrands to his legs'.[9]

While many suspect Eliza exaggerated her account, Aboriginal interpretations of the story have pointed out the indigenous dislike and mistrust of fully clothed bodies. As for the labour, Eliza was only being asked to do what was expected of Aboriginal women. Also, the Ka'bi people believed white people to be 'ghosts from the world of Spirits'[10] and were unsure how to behave around them. As for the alleged murder of Mr Brown, it is likely that the Ka'bi applied heat to soothe the ulcers on his legs and back: they were trying to heal him, not kill him.

It is unsurprising, given these misunderstandings and the colonial belief in the right to take ownership of land and resources, that violence escalated between indigenous people and the colonists. During the colonial period, which began in 1788 and continued into the early 20th century, the Aboriginal population declined from 750,000 to fewer than 50,000. By 1835, the indigenous Tasmanian population had fallen from as many as 15,000 to fewer than 400.[11] These patterns were a result of the violence and disease brought to Aboriginal society by the colonists. To many of them, the Aborigines were 'indiscriminating Savages' and 'the connecting link between man and the monkey tribe'.[12] Their 'war whoop' signalled 'a war of extermination, even of defenceless women and children'. By temperament, they resembled 'the cold malignity of a wicked spirit', a view reinforced by newspapers that described them as 'cunning ... black devils' and 'bloodthirsty savages'.[13] A Wellington clergyman despaired at the possibility of civilising indigenous people, saying that 'our giving instruction to them is like writing on the sand, the impression of such may be effaced by the first breeze or wave that passes over it'.

Stories of Aboriginal brutality, real and imagined, amplified these perceptions. Aboriginal warriors broke the legs of sheep, raided farms and attacked colonists as a means to protest the theft of their land and to get the colonists to leave their farms. In 1841, a man was found staked to the ground with his limbs ritually defleshed and *The Queenslander* reported a 'spectacle never before witnessed' of a 'well-built township, surrounded by magnificent gardens ... with a stately courthouse, a recently completed Commissioner residence, with luxurious bathrooms ... one of the finest assembly rooms in the North ... and much more being abandoned in favour of the blacks, whose murderous hostility and great numbers render the place no longer hospitable'.[14]

The Aboriginal as Other to the civilised and outnumbered colonists was a myth reflected in contemporary descriptions of Yagan. He was seen both as an incarnation of Rousseau's 'noble savage' and a savage possessed by malevolence. When a fire broke out at the bungalow of a Mrs Birkett in March 1833, the *Perth Gazette* described how Yagan, 'the daring chief of the tribe' helped extinguish the flames.[15] A magazine called *Clare's Weekly* called him 'a man of Herculean proportions' who stood, improbably, at '6ft 10in, his shoulders square and massive'. The article contrasted his physical power with his moral degeneracy, the appearance of civility with the soul of a barbarian. When 'calm and peaceful, his countenance betokened honesty', but his temper was 'easily ruffled' and showed 'signs in deep muscular contraction, pressing of lips, in looks of scowl and defiance which often melted into airs of ineffable contempt'.[16] In 1915, an edition of the *Western Mail* looked back at the life and death of Yagan. It praised him for having the 'character of a gentleman ... Tall, slender and well-fashioned, he is of pleasing countenance'. It concluded he was a 'person of great charm' who 'recognised the importance of good clothes in a civilised community'. His manners were more than matched by his athleticism and physical power. When a rabid dog was on the loose, Yagan 'entered on a vigorous pursuit and eventually transfixed it with his spear on the verandah of Mayo's hotel'.[17] An article in the *Daily News* called him 'a splendid specimen' but warned about his character 'in whom two personalities seemed to alternate',[18] one courteous, the other impudent and aggressive. These two personalities embodied the awe, disgust and terror the indigenous warrior evoked in the colonial imagination.

Yagan fought the British because they violated ancestral lands and abused and murdered his people: 'You came to our country – you have driven us from our haunts, and disturbed us in our occupations. As we walk in our own country, we are fired upon by the white men, why should the white men treat us so?'[19] In Aboriginal culture, people were inseparable from their relationship to the land they foraged. Bound into a complex tradition, which they understood through practice not theory, small groups were connected to clans, which, in turn, formed tribes, which could become larger confederations made up of multiple language groups. Because kin and land defined a person's place in the cosmos, the world was divided into friends and enemies, those inside and outside the kinship group. While conflict between friends was, on the whole, contained by kinship, death was believed to be the result of sorcery cast by outsiders. When vigilance and bush medicine failed to stop an attack, Aboriginal people believed in retributive justice against enemies who caused suffering and death to their kin.

As the early, reasonably cordial, relationships between settlers and indigenous people descended into mistrust and confrontation, Yagan's fury erupted into violence. In June 1832, he fatally wounded William Gaze at Kelmscott, near Perth, and on 4 May 1833, the *Perth Gazette* accused him of the murder four days earlier of Thomas and John Velvick, servants to a local farmer. The report claimed a witness saw Yagan 'pulling the spear out and repeatedly thrusting it into the body of Thomas Velvick'.[20] A reward of £30 was put on Yagan's head. It was soon to be collected.

Three weeks after the Velvick murders, Yagan's father, the tribal elder Midgegooroo was captured and convicted of murder. Colonel Frederick Irwin, serving as acting governor in the absence of Governor James Stirling, attended his execution on 22 May, at which Midgegooroo was 'blindfolded and bound to the outer door of the jail'.[21] When Irwin lowered his sword, a firing squad opened fire. On 11 July, William Keats, an eighteen-year-old boy from the local workhouse, shot and killed Yagan before being killed himself by an Aboriginal warrior called Heegan. William's younger brother James survived the attack and collected the reward. Two days after the killing of Yagan, the *Perth Gazette* reported that 'one sentiment prevails as regards the death of Yagan, which is that of satisfaction, and with some even of exultation, but it is generally lamented that the youth should have fallen a sacrifice to his boyish daring'.[22]

Yagan's head was hacked from his body and the skin, bearing his tribal tattoos, flayed from his back and kept as a trophy. His head, wedged into a tree stump, was preserved in the smoke of gum leaves. In a final humiliation, string was wrapped around his head and cockatoo feathers added in a mocking reference to his status as an Aboriginal leader. In September, Yagan's head was acquired by Ensign Robert Dale, who transported it to England, where he hawked it about as an 'anthropological curiosity'. The gruesome relic was exhibited in fairs and shows as *The Head of a Barbarian*. In 1834, Dale loaned Yagan's head to Thomas Pettigrew, a surgeon who displayed it at a society gathering held at his London home. A review of the event in the *Perth Gazette and Western Australian Journal* described 'crowded rooms' where 'many objects of exceeding interest were exhibited to the scientific visitors'. One of the objects was 'a head peculiarly preserved, which is said to be that of Yagan. The reporter observed that his 'features are well-preserved, his skin is a deep jet black and the hair upon his chin very crisp – that of his head is soft and lank'. As if to add an artistic flourish, to reflect the sophistication of the event, the reporter concluded that a 'very interesting panoramic drawing of the settlement accompanied this curious specimen'.[23]

The head found its way to the Liverpool City Museum in 1894 via the Insect Room at the Royal Institution of Liverpool. Over the years, Yagan's head deteriorated, and a decision was made to bury it in a cemetery in Everton. In the spring of 1964, an undertaker lowered the head into its resting place along with the remains of a Peruvian mummy and an unknown Maori warrior.

In the decades that followed, the Noongar people persevered in their efforts to locate Yagan's head. If they failed to find it, his spirit would not be free to enter the Dreaming. They also fought to honour his memory. In 1984, a life-size bronze statue of Yagan was erected on Heirisson Island in Perth. He is naked, a spear held across his shoulders, his left leg forward. He looks out towards the horizon, ready to face whatever comes his way. For thirteen years, the statue remained undisturbed. That changed when his head returned to Australia in 1997.

The journey to repatriation was difficult. When the Noongar community finally located Yagan's head, the British government denied them the right to exhume it. More than twenty stillborn babies lay buried in the same plot and parents of one of them refused to agree to the disturbance of their baby's resting place. In time, the parents relented but another objection came from an unexpected source. Corrie Bodney, a member of the Noongar people, claimed to be the sole descendant of Yagan and objected to the exhumation of his ancestor's remains, claiming it went against Aboriginal custom. When Bodney lost the court case that followed on 29 August 1997, he threatened to flog Ken Colbung, a leading member of the delegation sent to London to collect Yagan's head, with a traditional fighting stick. Readers sent letters to newspapers mocking this display of Aboriginal disunity. A cartoon titled *Alas Poor Yagan* told the story of the in-fighting and ended with Yagan's head shouting out of a box on the floor, 'Crikey – give me a warm beer in a quiet Pommy pub any day …'[24]

In the days before the head was handed over by the British to the Aboriginal delegation, Colbung described Australia as 'a racist country … They don't really recognise us as having our own traditions, our own religion and our own rituals.'[25] It was then, as Yagan's head landed at Perth International Airport, that Colbung described the death of Princess Diana as 'Nature's revenge'. As the world united in an extraordinary outpouring of grief for Diana, an unknown assailant, describing himself only as a 'British Loyalist', beheaded the statue of Yagan. It was not the first time the statue had been attacked. On three separate occasions, vandals had thrown paint over it, its spear had been stolen and its genitals mutilated. In a gruesome irony, there were now two heads of Yagan, one bronze, one bone, both detached from his body.

If Ken Colbung saw retributive justice in the death of Diana, he missed the true unity of the 'Black Napoleon' and the 'People's Princess'. Colonists suffered the wrath of Yagan with a mix of admiration and terror, branding him a noble warrior and a savage killer. A similar ambivalence surrounded Diana, a beautiful woman born into an aristocratic family. Yet, despite her status, when news broke of her engagement to Prince Charles, she blushed when photographers captured her on her way to work in a nursery. The blend of power and vulnerability captivated a nation. It was, of course, all projection. We didn't know Diana. We only believed we did. The colonists didn't know Yagan. They drew a picture of him in their imagination and stamped that picture on his body. We did the same with Diana. What these immense figures meant to us was more important than who they were. The delegation who brought Yagan's head back to Australia didn't know him either. The long-decayed head was a symbol of who they believed themselves to be, the restoration of an ancient connection, rooted in myth.

In 2017, the novelist Hilary Mantel wrote that 'myth ... works subtly to shape its subject'.[26] Be it a statue or the head of a dead warrior, we shape our icons into who we want them to be and inscribe our dreams on their remains, regardless of whether those remains are made of flesh, stone or steel. Of Diana, Mantel writes, that the 'princess we invented had little to do with any actual person'. In the end, she became a 'hollow vessel, able to carry not just heirs but the projections of others'. After her divorce, Diana claimed an 'affinity ... with the rejected' and isn't it acceptance, respect, dignity, that we spend our lives seeking? And when we are denied this acknowledgement, how many of us can resist the desire for retribution?

Of course, the targets of our anger may be no more deserving of our hate than a 'hollow vessel' was deserving of being filled to overflowing with our love. But despite, or perhaps because of, what we are, we can't stop grief and its consequences. Our projections make angels and demons out of people, who stand as proxies for the emotions we might otherwise be incapable of expressing. And when an angel dies, we are overwhelmed with grief, not just, or even primarily, for the one who has died, but for ourselves. Mantel concludes that, after Diana died, 'a crack appeared in a vial of grief, and released a salt ocean'. As we are buffeted by the waves, we can find the sorrow of others comforting. Collective grief breaks our emotional isolation. It helps us draw 'the shape of loss. It is natural and necessary and there is no healing without it'.

All too often, however, our pain confirms the absence of the love we believe we are owed. It leads to the transformation of that absence into hate and despair. We want to know 'Why?' We want someone to pay the price of our grief. Above all, we are terrified of the injustice and ugliness of the world. Writing[27] after the death of his wife, C.S. Lewis found himself haunted, not by the fear of losing his faith in God, but that God might have deceived him, that God, now that grief had lifted the veil of illusion, might turn out to be malevolent.

One of the signs of that malevolence is a terrible feeling of isolation, that there is no longer anyone to soothe our pain. In a moving eulogy for his friend and teacher Emmanuel Levinas, the French philosopher Jacques Derrida reminds us that death is 'not, first of all, annihilation, non-being or nothingness but a certain experience for the survivor of the "without-response"'.[28] It's not the absence of those we love that we grieve for, but the awful silence that greets us when we call out their name. In this abyss of silence that opens under our feet, we grasp at the first hand that reaches down to us. Love is a matter of survival, not reason, and we are poor judges of those who stop us from falling. The temptation to blame and to hate is at least as great as our grief and if the hand that helps us belongs to a tyrant, then we will grasp it nonetheless and give him our love.

The real danger, then, of Ken Colbung's balance sheet, where the debt owed for a beheaded Aboriginal warrior is repaid by the battered body of a 'fairy-tale princess', is that it perpetuates the cycle of hate. 'Nature's revenge' simply means that someone has to pay a price for our grief. It is what we mean by 'healing'. Whether the price is paid or not, those upon whom the demand is made, unless they can find other ways to soothe their pain, will want revenge of their own. Perhaps that explains why, after the head on the statue of Yagan was reinstated, it was hacked off again before being put back on his shoulders for a second time. There is no equivalence between grief and retribution. They do not cancel each other out. They create a deepening asymmetry of grief and terror. And that is Nature's true revenge.

SADDAM HUSSEIN

BUILT: April 2002

DESTROYED: 9 April 2003

In the spring of 2003, statues of Saddam Hussein began falling. Hands, hammers, saws, chains, ropes, mattocks, crowbars, fists, feet, all played their part in an orgy of destruction. When bronze, stone, marble and metal icons of the dictator crashed to the ground, the desecration began. Sandals, shoes and stones struck the face and body of the fallen dictator. Many urinated on his remains. Decapitated heads served as seats for photo opportunities.

Amidst the chaos, the fall of one statue stood out as a symbol of the end of Saddam Hussein's regime in Iraq. In the late afternoon of 9 April 2003, American tanks arrived at Firdos Square in the centre of Baghdad. Sergeant Leon Lambert, driving an M88 Hercules, noticed the 12-metre-tall statue of Saddam Hussein, erected the previous year to celebrate the Iraqi leader's sixty-fifth birthday. He asked Captain Lewis if he could use the M88, which was equipped with a crane for towing tanks, to bring the statue down. Lewis refused. He needed to be sure the square was secure. As the Americans consolidated their control of the area, a few Iraqis made their way into Firdos Square. Lambert tried again. He told Lewis the Iraqis wanted to destroy the statue. This time, Lewis agreed. Lambert gave the Iraqis a sledgehammer and rope from the M88, stood back and watched. On live television, a power weightlifter and motorcycle enthusiast began swinging at the base of the statue with a sledgehammer. Kadhim Sharif al-Jabouri had good reason to hate Saddam Hussein. He used to look after the motorcycles of Saddam and his sons, but ended up spending eleven years in prison. Saddam had killed more than a dozen of his family because of their support for the Communist and Shia Dawa parties. Al-Jabouri laboured in vain in the burning sun. Only a few blocks of plaster fell away from base of the statue. Someone threw a rope over Saddam's neck. It had no effect.

The Americans understood the psychological impact of destroying Saddam Hussein's statue. At the beginning of the war, British troops tore down a statue of the dictator in Basra. They hoped it would incite an insurrection, but the absence of a televised record of the event limited the impact. This time, the world's media were gathered in the Palestine Hotel facing the square. The commanding officer, Lieutenant-Colonel Bryan McCoy, grasped the potential of the moment. He ordered Captain Lewis to help the Iraqis topple the statue, on condition they were careful that no one got killed by falling debris. As the M88 moved into position with its crane, Corporal Edward Chin climbed up the statue and covered Saddam's face with an American flag. Al-Jabouri recoiled when he saw the flag there. McCoy shared his horror. They were the optics of an occupying power, not a liberating army. The action was being streamed live and Major-General James Matthis, perhaps under orders from the Pentagon, beat McCoy in telling them to take the flag down immediately. Al-Jabouri claimed he got an Iraqi flag to replace the Stars and Stripes. The Americans wrapped a chain around Saddam's neck and the statue fell. As it crashed to the ground, Iraqis swarmed over it, beating it, breaking it into pieces.

The toppling of the statue was, however, a smaller, orchestrated outburst of rage rather than the symbol of mass support for the American army that the media portrayed. The CNN anchor Bill Hemmer gave a rousing commentary, 'You think about seminal moments in a nation's history ... indelible moments like the fall of the Berlin Wall, and that's what we're seeing right now'.[1] With a foretaste of the unrest to come, Ann Garrels from NPR painted a very different picture: 'There are so few people trying to pull down the statue that they can't do it themselves ... Many people were just sort of standing, hoping for the best, but they weren't joyous.'[2] A reporter from the *San Francisco Chronicle* filed a similarly downbeat report only to find his editor retold the story featuring 'a jubilant crowd' shouting 'We are free! Thank you, President Bush!' In fact, some of the crowd were chanting the name of Mohammed Sadiq al-Sadr, a Shia cleric assassinated in 1999 as his car left a mosque.

The conflicting narratives of the destruction of the statue at Firdos Square illustrate the symbolic value of iconoclasm. The image of a statue being toppled suggested victory, the erasure of a dictator, closure. The CNN report, mirrored across other networks like Fox News, elevated an uncertain, nuanced event into a seminal, historical revolt, analogous to the collapse of the Berlin Wall. The journalist Shahira Fahmy assessed the media response to the top-pling of the statue. She analysed[3] the visual framing of the event in photographs published by forty-three newspapers across thirty countries on the five days following the destruction. She found that some newspapers favoured close-up shots of Iraqi civilians cheering and embracing US soldiers, while photographs published online showed a sparse crowd of no more than 200 people, many of them indifferent to the fate of the statue. However, Fahmy's overall con-clusion was that the findings of the study were interesting because of 'the patterns they did not produce'. In other words, coverage in the US and elsewhere failed to produce a coherent interpretative pattern within or between countries. For instance, in the UK, *The Times* portrayed the event more negatively than the Iranian daily newspaper *Etella'at*.

The difference between a small hesitant crowd and a jubilant mob shows how easy it is for us to see what we want to see. Where one person sees a celebration of an American ideal of freedom, another sees the opening of sectarian wounds, covered over for decades by the rule of a fallen dictator. What is beyond doubt is that the inter-pretation of an event is inseparable from the event itself and that these interpretations have real effects on behaviour. In his account of the interrogation of Saddam, the former CIA leadership analyst John Nixon described how one of the soldiers who captured Saddam punched him, saying, 'That's for 9/11!'[4] The soldier may have felt it was all he could do, one small act of vengeance set against the massacre of thousands. Except it wasn't true. Saddam Hussein had nothing to do with 9/11. Iraq's foreign minister Naji Sabri claimed that Saddam's first reaction after 9/11 was to believe the attack on the Twin Towers would be good for him. The Americans would seek revenge against al-Qaeda, and he ran a secular regime hostile to all forms of Islamic extremism. He also saw himself as a counterweight to the Islamist regime in Iran, which threatened military conflict and the smooth passage of oil to the United States.

Saddam's hostility to al-Qaeda was reciprocated. Even as coalition forces amassed on the borders of Iraq, bin Laden attacked both the US and Saddam, whom he described as a socialist: 'It is not harmful in such conditions for the Muslims' interests and the socialists' interests to come along with each other during the war against the crusade, without changing our faith and our declaration that socialists are infidels wherever they are, either in Baghdad or Aden.'[5]

The misperception of Saddam's relationship with bin Laden was one of many, on both sides, that paved the way for the invasion of Iraq. John Nixon describes how easily the Bush administration accepted 'the crude caricature of Saddam as an evil butcher who must be stopped at all costs'[6] and there was, of course, plenty of evidence of Saddam's butchery against his own people. In his history of Baghdad, Justin Marozzi described accounts of unimaginable depravity committed in the name of the regime and concluded that 'in all the terrible history of death and violence in Baghdad, there had been nothing as perverted as this'.[7] The White House put many of these accounts on its website to justify the removal of the Iraqi leader. The crimes are variously attributed to Saddam's torturers, executioners and sons. Sticks of dynamite were placed in the pockets of prisoners and detonated. Athletes were smeared with faeces, beaten and jailed. A man was placed in a sarcophagus with the nails pointed inwards, so they punctured him to death. Dogs tore men to pieces. Uday Hussein, Saddam's eldest son, kept monkeys in a floor-to-ceiling cage so they could watch him as he raped young virgins. Men were thrown knee-deep in sewer water and told to swim. They were pushed down with a stick when they came up for air. Men were dragged over gravel and broken glass. Two students were thrown into a cage of lions, where they were eaten alive. A man was asked to catch ten flies and ten mosquitoes during the night. If he failed, he was beaten and tortured. If he succeeded, he was asked to say how many of the insects are male and how many female. When, inevitably, he answered incorrectly, he was beaten and tortured. The depravity was endless.

This focus on the figure of Saddam Hussein and the brutality of his regime blinded Bush, Blair and their allies to the political reality of what they were getting into. Bush failed to understand that much of Saddam's behaviour and rhetoric stemmed from a fear of the Shia majority within Iraq and the threat from Iran. In this, Bush and Saddam had common ground, yet Bush continued to associate Saddam Hussein with 9/11 and refused to accept any evidence that contradicted this belief. The more evidence inspectors produced that Saddam had disarmed and posed no threat to the West, the more entrenched Bush became in his belief that Saddam possessed WMDs and was developing nuclear weapons.

In 1998, the inspectors reported that there 'are no indications that there remains in Iraq any physical capability for the production of amounts of weapons-usable nuclear material of any practical significance'. Saddam proved, on multiple occasions, that he wasn't difficult to deter: he dismantled his nuclear weapons programme, he suspended his chemical and biological weapons programme, he allowed intrusive inspections. He showed himself to be cautious in his relationship with the United States and concerned, above all, to preserve his regime and to protect himself against the threat posed by Iran. Yet Bush's default position was to assume the intentions of Saddam Hussein were always malign, that he was supportive of bin Laden and sought to kill Americans in vast numbers at any cost to himself. Colin Powell's notorious speech to the UN in February 2003 claimed Saddam had been 'harbouring' the Jordanian jihadist Abu Musab al-Zarqawi, a 'collaborator of bin Laden' and that Zarqawi had established a 'poison and explosives and training centre'.[8] Both claims were false.

These misperceptions afflicted both sides. When Bush gave a speech at the US Military Academy at West Point in 2002 warning about 'tyrants who solemnly sign non-proliferation treaties and then systematically break them',[9] Saddam assumed Bush was referring to Iran and North Korea. He also overestimated the omniscience of American intelligence. He assumed they knew he had disarmed and that UN inspections were simply a mechanism to keep sanctions in place, rather than a precursor to war.

Eight days before the invasion of Kuwait another misunderstanding occurred. April Glaspie, the American ambassador to Kuwait, said the United States had 'no opinion on Arab-Arab conflicts, like your border disagreement with Kuwait'. Yet, when asked why her attempts at deterring Saddam failed, Glaspie replied that 'we foolishly did not realise that he was stupid, that he did not believe our clear and repeated warnings that we would support our vital interests'.[10] Bush was equally perplexed by Saddam's behaviour: 'How much clearer could I have been?'[11]

There is no doubt that Bush and the neo-conservative backbone of his administration were set on regime change in Iraq at the earliest opportunity. In making the case for war, they displayed single-mindedness and cynicism. However, this should not blind us to the fact they believed the threat from Saddam Hussein was real. There is little doubt that Bush and British Prime Minister Tony Blair convinced themselves of the truth of the claims they made. When that truth was revealed to be a lie, they blamed the intelligence agencies rather than their own interpretation of the information they were given. They heard only what they wanted to hear.

Gathering and interpreting intelligence is imprecise. Information is often incomplete, and operatives are left to fill the gaps. When Bush and Saddam tried to understand each other's motives, they filtered the information they received through a network of beliefs that they were unable to criticise. They saw patterns where they did not exist. The psychologist Michael Shermer claimed 'our perceptions about reality are dependent upon the beliefs we hold about it. Reality exists independent of human minds, but our understanding of it depends upon the beliefs we hold at any given time.'[12] Bush was a believer in the 'evil' of Saddam Hussein and interpreted all information through that lens: he believed it, so he saw it.

Once we classify the world in line with our beliefs, we have a strong compulsion to fit new information into familiar categories. Where there is a conflict between a belief and data that might disprove it, the belief invariably wins. In a study of how readily people believe and how difficult we find it to doubt, the psychologist Daniel Gilbert concluded that we are 'credulous creatures' and that the 'great master fallacy of the human mind is believing too much.'[13]

We default to gullibility because it takes far less cognitive effort than critical thinking. The rush by CNN, along with Bush and Blair, to define the toppling of the statue of Saddam in Firdos Square as a 'seminal moment in a nation's history' is an example of this lack of cognitive restraint. While misplaced moral certainties may give us comfort, they come at a high price. They leave our beliefs emaciated for want of being challenged. They falsify the world by keeping the truth from view and lead us to mistake appearance for truth and fantasy for reality, with catastrophic consequences.

Saddam took his final step on the path to power in July 1979 when he ordered a hasty convention of party leaders in Baghdad. He walked on stage smoking a Cuban cigar and sat behind a desk as Muhyi Adbek Hussein Mashadi, a senior leader in the Ba'ath party, who bore the marks of torture, read out names of alleged conspirators against Saddam's regime. One by one, he named the plotters who were forced to shout the party slogan as security officers marched them out of the hall. Almost seventy men were accused. Those who remained, drenched with relief, began chanting Saddam's name. The one-party state had reached its logical conclusion with absolute power now vested in one man.

The theatricality of the 1979 purge set the stage for the relentless spread of fear into the bones of every Iraqi citizen. People lived in a constant state of dread, where the only certainty was the pervasive threat of random terror. *Whose door would be the next on which the secret police knocked?* To protect themselves against this threat, people became complicit in the fear that threatened them. Some did it while maintaining a private cynicism, others became fervent believers in the Ba'athist cause, investing these beliefs with magical properties to ward off the fate they inflicted on their friends, colleagues, neighbours and families.

In Saddam Hussein's Iraq, fear drove people to police each other. Where everyone was a potential informer, it was necessary to become an informer oneself, especially if you were a small child. In common with Chairman Mao and the United Daughters of the Confederacy, Saddam understood the importance of manipulating young, impressionable minds. Terror began inside the family, at the hands of its youngest members. Saddam wrote that a child should be taught to 'object to his parents if he hears them discussing state secrets and alert them that this is not correct'.[14] He compared the child to 'a piece of raw marble in the hands of a sculptor'. The younger the child, the more important and effective was the work of the sculptor.

For this reason, Saddam sacrificed age to youth and the young to the youngest. Primary school teachers were of utmost importance because they could assure the future of the regime by imprinting its methods on the minds of its children. Saddam believed the 'secret of our success in building the new society' lay in teaching the young 'a love of order'.[15]

Hannah Arendt described the effect of this 'love' on the minds of people living in totalitarian regimes where the masses 'reached the point, where they would at the same time, believe everything and nothing, think that everything was possible and that nothing was true'. In the midst of the psychological disorder of this 'incomprehensible world', the people believed 'the most fantastic statements one day' only, when confronted with the falsehood of these beliefs, to 'admire the leaders for their superior tactical cleverness'.[16]

Even in the cesspit of deception and terror that Saddam created, fear drove people to find meaningful patterns, wisdom even, where there was only the raw exercise of power. Long after dangerous enemies had been purged, the logic of fear demanded an endless supply of enemies, each of whom found their individual differences compressed into a single category: Traitors.

In *The Order of Things*,[17] Michel Foucault attempts to show how classification is a function of power, not truth. He claims the entire book emerged out of a short essay written by Jorge Luis Borges,[18] where Borges describes a Chinese encyclopaedia, the *Heavenly Emporium of Benevolent Knowledge*, in which animals are classified in fourteen extraordinary categories, as '(a) belonging to the Emperor, (b) embalmed, (c) tame, (d) sucking pigs, (e) sirens, (f) fabulous, (g) stray dogs, (h) included in the present classification, (i) frenzied, (j) innumerable, (k) drawn with a very fine camelhair brush, (l) *et cetera*, (m) having just broken the water pitcher, (n) that from a long way off look like flies'. The randomness of the elements brought under a single classification of 'animals' leads Borges to conclude 'there is no classification of the universe that is not arbitrary and speculative'. While science will, rightly, dispute this claim, it does contain a deep psychological truth about how we believe: we make patterns out of information, create order out of fear, regardless of how absurd those patterns and that order turn out to be.

Ultimately, Iraqi society, including Saddam himself, descended into a self-destructive state of unreality. Fear, torture, death became ends in themselves as Saddam watched over his people in art, statues, on television and newspapers, in every office, school and home. With no one able or willing to contradict him, where everyone belonged to lower orders of the social hierarchy and only one man belonged to the highest, Saddam's descent into delusion, megalomania and self-destruction was inevitable.

Buoyed by the success of the 1979 purge, Saddam embarked on a ruinous war with Iran. Calling himself Saddam Qadisiyyah after the Battle of Qadisiyyah fought in 637 in which Arab Muslims defeated the Persians, he imagined himself as the glorious leader of the Arab world. Even after his capture by the Americans, he clung to the narrative he had manufactured in his own mind, making connections as absurd as those found in the confessions extracted under torture by his own secret police. Saddam had lost all contact with reality, except the reality of fear, of which he was himself a victim.

Attempting to justify his actions with reference to historical precedent, Saddam told his interrogator, 'Historians are like people who could see through the dark.'[19] But the light in Iraq had been extinguished. As the Iraqi American writer Kanan Makiya concluded in *Republic of Fear*, 'the ultimate act of degradation, the final human catastrophe' is 'a society held together because it cannot find light in the overthrow of those who plunged it into darkness'.[20]

After a few protestors toppled the statue of Saddam Hussein in Firdos Square, stories soon emerged about what happened to the surviving fragments. His head was wheeled away in a cart. A British soldier returned home with what he claimed was a piece of Saddam's buttock. He tried and failed to sell it on eBay. A US marine came back with one of Saddam's hands, but lost it in the mail. The dictator's left leg found its way to a German man who said he found it in a junk yard in Bremen. After passing through a number of owners, it eventually sold for €99,999.

The fate of the statue, its disintegration into fragments, serves as a metaphor for the break-up of Iraq that led, a few years later, to the rise of ISIS. The body of the dictator was the power that held the pieces of Iraq together. When the body broke apart, the pieces scattered to reveal the truth: the Republic of Fear and the Republic of Iraq that followed its collapse, were illusions of order as absurd (and necessary) as the classification of 'animals' in the *Heavenly Emporium of Benevolent Knowledge*.

B.R. AMBEDKAR

BUILT: *c.*2000

DESTROYED: 25 August 2019

Vanni Arasu, a local leader of the VCK, formerly known as the Dalit Panthers, blamed the violence on the police. 'Hate-politics is growing in India', he lamented. 'A problem between two people has been turned into a caste clash. Since the police didn't do anything to stop the violence, senior officers should be held responsible.'[1]

The incident began at 5 pm the previous day. As a member of a dominant caste drove his SUV through the streets of the small south Indian town of Vedaranyam, he struck and injured a young man. The man belonged to the Dalits or Untouchables. The driver of the vehicle quickly found himself surrounded by a mob. A fierce argument broke out. Fearing for his life, the man abandoned his car and fled. The mob then set fire to the SUV and threw stones at the local police station. As fire consumed the car, the driver returned with a mob of his own. They marched towards the nearby statue of B.R. Ambedkar, the Dalit social reformer who helped frame the Indian constitution in the late 1940s. One of the mob, brandishing a machete, climbed up the pedestal on which the statue stood. He repeatedly hacked at Ambedkar's left hand, which held the constitution. After completing the amputation, the man chopped away at Ambedkar's neck. In seconds, Ambedkar was beheaded. His head fell to the ground and a group of men struck it with shoes and sticks. Some kicked it. Many cheered. Despite the general indifference of the police to the fate of a Dalit, the following day more than 750 officers descended on the town to keep the peace. A well as maintaining order in Vedaranyam, they guarded more than ten statues throughout the southern state of Tamil Nadu to prevent further destruction.

Arasu may have been correct to say that the initial problem was a dispute between two people. However, in a society fractured along caste lines with a long history of inter-caste violence, it is naive to suppose that individual identity can be separated from the caste that defines it. The beheading of Ambedkar and the desecration of his severed head were a dominance display aimed at an entire group of people, as well as the man who championed their cause.

Born in 1891, Ambedkar knew from bitter personal experience what it meant to be a Dalit, to be frozen below even the lowest rung of the caste system. At school, he faced daily humiliations. Teachers prevented him from drinking water from the communal water sources or from sitting alongside his classmates from higher castes. They also forbade him from using the blackboard, since fellow pupils from higher castes would be unable to touch it after him.

Despite the discrimination he faced, Ambedkar, inspired by an activist who gifted him a book on the life of the Buddha, went on to gain two PhDs from Columbia University and the London School of Economics. These achievements were not sufficient to gain him acceptance in India. When he returned, colleagues rolled up office carpets before he entered to prevent themselves from being contaminated and took pleasure in flicking dead flies at him.

Ambedkar, along with almost a fifth of the Indian population, found himself trapped in an ancient prison, whose walls date back to a Vedic text written about 2,000 years ago known as the *Manusmriti* or *The Laws of Manu*. It divided people into *brahmanas* (priests), *kshatriyas* (warriors), *vaishyas* (merchants) and *shudras* (servants), in a complex system broken into as many as 30,000 sub-castes. Beneath the four main castes lay the Dalits, literally the 'crushed' or the 'broken', who formed the wretched ground on which the entire edifice was built.

Anchored in Hinduism, the caste system created a rigid, hierarchical social and spiritual order and the *Manusmriti* states that the place of a Dalit 'should be outside the village ... Their clothing should be the clothes of the dead, and their food should be in broken dishes; their ornaments should be made of black iron, and they should wander constantly'.[2]

Punishments for crossing caste boundaries were severe. If a Dalit 'is so proud as to instruct priests about their duty, the king should have hot oil poured into his mouth and ears'.[3] This enforced inequality persists to this day. In 2015, Sagar Shejwal, a twenty-three-year-old nursing student sat outside a liquor store in the town Shirdi, drinking beer with a few friends when his phone rang. Nearby, a group of men recognised the ringtone as a song in praise of Ambedkar. They shouted at Sagar, demanding he turn his phone off. When Sagar refused, they dragged him along the ground and smashed a beer bottle on his head. Unable to control their rage, they put him on the back of a motorbike, took him outside the city, stripped him naked, beat him and ran over him with their motorbikes until he was dead. When Sagar was first attacked, one of his friends called the police. They didn't respond to the call. The police station was just 250 metres from where the attack took place.

In the months preceding the murder of Sagar, a Dalit family was butchered, a teenage boy killed and hanged from a tree because he fell in love with a woman outside his caste and three villagers were hacked to death, their bodies thrown into a septic tank. A year after Sagar's murder, Rohith Vemula, a Dalit PhD student at the University of Hyderabad, committed suicide after a complaint against him made by the student wing of the ruling BJP party. They managed to get his financial support suspended, accusing him of raising 'issues under the banner of the Ambedkar Students Association'. After being removed from student accommodation, Rohith set up a tent on the campus, which he shared with four friends. They went on hunger strike. Before Rohith killed himself, he wrote a letter, which began, 'I would not be around when you read this letter'. He went on to say that he 'always wanted to be writer. A writer of science, like Carl Sagan' but 'my birth is my fatal accident'. After asking for the remainder of his fellowship to be paid to his family and a debt owed to a friend settled, Rohith apologised to the Ambedkar Students Association, calling them his 'family' and saying he was 'sorry to disappoint you. You loved me very much'. His last words absolved anyone other than himself for his death and he signed off: 'Do not trouble my friends and enemies about this after I am gone.'[4]

For Ambedkar, the caste system kept the Dalits in a state of permanent oppression. In 1935, at a conference of Dalits in Yeola, he said it 'grieves me very much to state how tyrannical caste Hindus thwarted our attempts throughout the country to obtain rights as members of the Hindu community'. He failed to see how 'people divided into several thousand castes can be a nation' and argued that to 'leave inequality … which is the soul of society, untouched … is to make a farce of our constitution and to build a palace on a dung heap'.[5]

In 1927, he led 2,500 Dalit on a march to a water tank in the city of Mahad from which they were forbidden to drink. A rumour spread among upper-caste Hindus that the marchers intended to enter a Hindu temple on their return. After arming themselves with bamboo sticks and other weapons, they beat the protestors and ground their food into the dirt. After the protest was over and the Dalits beaten, a purification ritual using cow urine and cow dung took place at the water tank. When it was over, priests deemed the water fit to drink by high-caste Hindus.

In her book *Caste*, Isabel Wilkerson, compares racial discrimination in the United Sates to the Indian caste system. She, too, tells a story about water. In 1951, a Little League baseball team went to a swimming pool to celebrate winning a city championship. One of the youths was black and not allowed in the pool. He had to watch at a distance from behind a fence while his teammates played in the water. Eventually, the lifeguard let him into the pool on three conditions: that he was the only one in the pool at the time, that the lifeguard pushed him around the pool in a dinghy, and that not even the tips of his fingernails touched the water. If they did, the entire pool would have to be emptied and cleansed. The boy 'was never the same after that'.[6]

Ambedkar, like Wilkerson, wanted to abolish the caste system. After 1935, Ambedkar despaired at the possibility of change coming from within Hinduism, saying, 'Unfortunately I was born a Hindu Untouchable but I will not die a Hindu.'[7] On 14 October 1956, less than two months before his death, Ambedkar converted to Buddhism on the same date that the Indian emperor, Ashoka the Great, became a Buddhist. The following day, Ambedkar stood before a crowd of more than 500,000 followers, most of them Dalit, and asked any who wished to do so to join him and become Buddhists. Almost the entire audience converted.

He saw Buddhism as a 'rational way to eradicate suffering' and at the end of November, Ambedkar gave his last speech on 'Buddha and Karl Marx' to the World Fellowship of Buddhists in Nepal. He clearly marked the difference between the two teachings: where communism saw the means to eradicate the suffering of the proletariat in 'violence and killing ... the Buddha's means of persuading people to adopt the principles is by persuasion, by moral teaching, by love'.[8] It was through love that the caste system with its 'ascending scale of hatred and descending scale of contempt' would be eradicated.

Ambedkar's conversion to Buddhism was not a move away from his commitment to reason and the principles of constitutional democracy. If caste broke apart the unity of people by creating artificial hierarchies of hate, democracy offered the possibility of 'revolutionary changes ... without bloodshed'. It meant discarding superstition and putting in its place a rational awareness of shared suffering, along with the means to overcome it. In a speech delivered at the Bombay Presidency Mahar Conference in 1936, Ambedkar attempted to persuade his audience to abandon Hinduism. Citing the 'slavery' of the Dalit, he believed freedom and Hinduism were incompatible, defining the free person as one who, 'with an awakened consciousness, realises his rights, responsibilities and duties, he is who is not a slave of circumstance ... whose flame of reason is not extinguished'.[9]

Isobel Wilkerson shares a similar hope for the extinction of caste. She writes that in 'America, race is the primary tool and the visible decoy, the front man, for caste'.[10] In a restating of contemporary identity politics, she traces the history of white dominance in the United States and its similarities to the Indian caste system. She summarises the unity of these two systems of dominance in the words of the American lawyer and eugenicist, Maddison Grant, who wrote in 1916 that a 'record of the desperate efforts of the conquering upper classes in India to preserve the purity of their blood persists until this very day in their carefully regulated system of castes. In our Southern States, Jim Crow laws and social discrimination have exactly the same purpose.'[11]

For Wilkerson, the only way out of the prison of caste is for the dominant caste of white people, to 'act when one sees another person treated unfairly. And the least that a person in the dominant caste can do is not make the pain any worse.'[12] The problem with this identitarianism is not its historical analysis, but its failure to grasp the fact that human groups are incapable of not forming dominance hierarchies, regardless of their caste. For Ambedkar, caste was 'a state of the mind' and the world could not be changed 'except by the reformation of the mind of man'.[13] The problem, however, is that changing our mind, navigating our *own* biases, is extremely difficult and compelling another person to change their mind, except under extreme duress, is impossible. We may influence other people, but the decision to accept or reject what we say, to continue along the path they are on or to change course, is theirs and theirs alone.

Ambedkar recognised this. He also saw that every rung on the ladder of caste defended its own privileges. He saw that, while all the lower castes had a grievance against the highest, they also had grievances against each other. This meant the 'low ... would not make common cause with the lower ... Each class being privileged, every class is interested in maintaining the system.'[14] He argued that the religious foundations of the Indian caste system gave everyone a stake in it, since their position was determined by their actions in previous lives. A life well-lived meant a higher caste in the next life. This may have enabled the lower castes to make sense of their suffering and find meaning in it, but it does not explain the mechanism that drives people to create dominance hierarchies. These hierarchies are rooted both in the need to create order and, when that order becomes tyrannical, to inflict pain as a punishment for every transgression against it.

The writer Arundhati Roy tells how a friend called her in extreme distress in February 2002. After taking fifteen minutes to gather herself, she said that one of her friends had been killed by a mob, her stomach ripped open and stuffed with burning rags. After she died, someone carved *Om* on her forehead. Roy's friend was describing one death among the many that occurred during the inter-communal violence between Hindus and Muslims in Gujarat in 2002. These deaths included the Muslim politician Ehsan Jafri, described by his son-in-law Najid Hussain as committed to 'communal harmony, religious tolerance and national pride'.[15] A Hindu mob dragged him out of his house, dismembered him and threw him onto a burning pyre. The police stationed around his house did not intervene. Jafri was a stern critic of the BJP activist, Narendra Modi, now the prime minister of India, a man Roy described as 'a cold-blooded creature'.[16]

During the violence, gang-rapes, killings and all manner of terror were inflicted by mobs armed with guns, knives, petrol bombs and swords. They had computer-generated lists of Muslim homes and businesses and drove trucks loaded with weapons and gas cylinders. The police provided cover for the mob. Dalits and members of indigenous Indian tribes were bused in to participate in the violence, which they did with great enthusiasm. Roy wonders how those who have been 'despised, oppressed and treated worse than refuse by the upper castes for thousands of years, have joined hands with their oppressors, to turn on those who are only marginally less unfortunate'.[17] It takes her less than a few sentences to answer her own question when she says the low will attack the lower, 'the *next* most unfortunate' because their real enemies are inaccessible. However, this misses the point that, to the Dalits who butchered them, the Muslims *were* their real enemy, an Other more degraded than them, upon whose bodies they could demonstrate their dominance.

In the 2019 elections, more than a third of Dalits voted for Modi's BJP, a party predicated on Hindu nationalism and caste hierarchy, and the festival of slaughter, in which each side sought to justify its violence by marking out their differences, only bore witness to the universal human compulsion to create hierarchies. In this, Roy concluded, they all 'worship at the same altar. They're both apostates of the same murderous god, whoever he is.'[18]

In *Hierarchy in the Forest*, the anthropologist Christopher Boehm analysed dominance hierarchies among chimpanzees, human foragers and tribal societies. He concluded that humans always 'live with *some* kind of hierarchy, which suggests that our behaviour is constrained by human nature'.[19] This nature can tend towards what Steven Pinker called its 'better angels'[20] and when this happens, we create what Boehm calls 'reverse dominance hierarchies'. In such societies, of which democracies are the prime example, subordinate groups form coalitions to curb the power of despotic individuals. When this process fails, restoration of the reverse dominance hierarchy can only happen when subordinate castes rise up to curb the power of the dominant caste.

For Wilkerson, America is a dominance hierarchy determined by caste and expressed through racial segregation. She concludes that, if we wish to end this injustice we must be 'pro-African American, pro-woman, pro-Latino, pro-Asian, pro-indigenous, pro-humanity in all its manifestations' and urges us to 'love your neighbour as yourself, not tolerate them'.[21]

But who is my neighbour? And what is love?

For Boehm, the answer to these questions depends on what kind of society we want to create. If our aim is to build an egalitarian society, where there is equality of opportunity, then it must be built on the 'glorification and empowerment of the ordinary individual'.[22] This can be achieved only when individual freedom is balanced with constitutional checks to stop that freedom becoming tyrannical. In other words, we build open societies that have to sustain themselves in a state of perpetual siege, as the despotic demons of our nature attack them on all sides. It is clear, from the wilful participation of Dalits in the Gujarat massacre to the storming of the Capitol building by Trump supporters and the destruction wrought in American cities by Antifa, that democracies are fragile.

In the last line of her book, Wilkerson concludes that a 'world without caste would set everyone free'.[23] The problem with this utopianism is that it breeds impatience and misplaced idealism. It invites us to ignore the progress we have made in extending rights to marginalised groups and inscribing reverse dominance into our laws and institutions. We still live with inequality and injustice, and we always will, but Western democracies have eliminated any legal or religious basis for a state-sanctioned caste system. This has been achieved by taking individual rights and responsibilities, freedoms and obligations as the foundation of our societies. It is these values, anchored in the refusal to extend moral and legal responsibility beyond the individual, that protect us against the temptation of authoritarianism, a temptation to which we have repeatedly succumbed. For much of the twentieth century that temptation was Marxism. It 'captured the hearts of resentful underdogs everywhere' with its promises of an end to caste suffering. Despite its noble ideals, the Marxist experiment morphed into terror. According to Boehm, this was because 'the social engineering was inept: the blueprint was not laid out with an accurate view of human political nature'.[24]

Our great risk is that we repeat this error. This time the temptation is identity politics, which imagines that defining people by the caste to which they belong will lead to a caste-free world. It won't. By highlighting what divides us, principally race and gender, rather than the common humanity that unites us, it will lead to a dystopia of growing mistrust, segregation, violence and terror. It will do this, as all authoritarian hierarchies do, in the name of moral purity and justice. Identitarianism lacks the imagination and the patience to undertake the monotonous labour of reform. It protests about inequality while fighting for caste equity, or equality of outcome, for all identity groups, an aim that is despotic to its core. For those who resist the ideology, moral correction will be required. As Ambedkar said, 'if the mind is not converted, force will be necessary'.[25]

There is, however, another way to move beyond caste, even if we accept the inevitability of dominance hierarchies. Wilkerson tells the story[26] of a man she assumed to be a Trump supporter, who came to repair a water leak at her home. The encounter didn't start well. Wilkerson complained that he 'smelled of beer and tobacco', a familiar trope used by dominant castes when faced with someone from a lower caste. He was equally contemptuous of her, refusing to help as she moved boxes to access the leak. Exasperated, Wilkerson 'threw a Hail Mary at his humanity' and told him her mother died the previous week. She then asked him if his mother was still alive. He said no. She died in 1991. From that simple beginning, they found common ground. They talked about his father, as 'mean as they come', and how he'll 'never get over' losing his mother. Transformed, he helped her move a table. When he found the source of the problem, he was 'jubilant' and fixed it. 'My mother must've been talking to your mother,' Wilkerson said, 'and telling her to get her boy to help her girl down there'. They both smiled. As he left, the man found some old photographs damaged by the water. He handed them to her saying, 'That's memories, right there.'

Wilkerson's courage and intelligence showed how easy it was for both of them to bridge their complex, multi-layered caste differences and find a common humanity, which, shortly after the birth of Ambedkar, the writer Oscar Wilde found in shared suffering. After being convicted for the crime of homosexuality in 1895 and sentenced to two years hard labour, Wilde was held in solitary confinement except for one hour a day, when the prisoners walked in silence around the prison yard. One day, a working-class man who believed Wilde's status and the depth of his fall from grace made his suffering greater, turned to him and whispered, 'I pity you, for you are suffering more than me.'

'No, my friend,' Wilde responded, 'we all suffer alike.'[27]

It is this common humanity that identity politics ruins. We can, and must, acknowledge our differences without repeating the cruelty of the *Manusmriti* by segregating ourselves into fixed castes at birth. It may be, after they found a connection, that the man who came to repair the water leak went back to his habitual resentments and Wilkerson to hers. That is not the point. What matters is they met, even for the briefest moment, on the bridge that divided them. This small, uncertain step towards a world beyond caste was precious and fragile. And we must repeat it, every day, finding unity in difference, where caste demands we see division.

Immediately after the destruction of the statue of Ambedkar, district administrators decided to replace the old statue with a new one. At 5:45 am the following day, the new statue was lowered onto the plinth. An iron cage surrounded it for protection. 'This is us. In India,' wrote Arundhati Roy, 'Heaven help us make it through the night.'[28] In reply to this bleak sentiment, Ambedkar might have repeated the closing words of his speech, delivered in 1936 after his conversion to Buddhism: 'Be a light unto thyself. Believe in Self ... Be your own guide. Take refuge in reason.'[29]

FREDERICK
DOUGLASS

BUILT: 2018

DESTROYED: 5 July 2020

When dawn broke over Maplewood Park in Rochester, New York, the plinth stood empty. Fragments of stone lay scattered on the ground. Nothing of the life-size figure of Frederick Douglass remained. Later that day, the statue was found a short distance away next to a river gorge.

After escaping from slavery, Douglass lived in Rochester for more than twenty years and the date of the destruction of his statue, 5 July, marked the 168th anniversary of Douglass's great speech, 'What to the Slave is the Fourth of July?', which he delivered in Corinthian Hall, a large building located a short distance away from Maplewood Park. From the time of its construction in 1849 to its destruction by fire in 1898, the hall hosted many of America's great orators, writers and activists, including Susan B. Anthony and Ralph Waldo Emerson. The abolitionist William Lloyd Garrison also spoke at the hall. He was a close collaborator of Douglass, before they fell out over whether the American Constitution sanctioned slavery. Garrison believed it did and thought the best route to the abolition of slavery was for free northern states to secede from the Union. While Douglass initially agreed with Garrison, in the 1850s he changed his mind and defended the Constitution.

The destroyed statue of Douglass was one of thirteen erected in 2018 to mark the 200th anniversary of his birth. The statues were the work of the sculptor Olivia Kim, who took the 2.5-metre Frederick Douglass Monument in Memorial Park, Rochester, as her inspiration. She did, however, make one significant modification when she designed her life-sized replicas. She took a cast of the hands of Kenneth B. Morris Jr, the great-great-great-grandson of Frederick Douglass, and incorporated them into the statues, forming a link between the past and the present. The memorial, erected in 1899, was the first statue ever dedicated to a named African American. On the base are several inscriptions. One of them is an extract from a speech Douglass delivered in New York in 1857, which reads: 'I know of no soil better adapted to the growth of reform than American soil. I know of no country where the conditions for effecting great changes in the settled order of things for the development of right ideas of liberty and humanity are more favourable than here in these United States.'[1]

In a country denounced by modern activists as suffering from 'the metastatic cancer' of 'Stage 4' racism, which is 'threatening to kill the American body',[2] it may seem strange that, in the nineteenth century, an escaped slave should stand up for the values of the country that enslaved him. Those values and the journey Douglass took from slavery to the remarkable oration at Corinthian Hall in 1852, is more than a story of our past; it is a story of our present and our future.

Born into slavery in Talbot County, Maryland, in 1818, Douglass, whose slave name was Fred Bailey, wrote three autobiographies detaining the many indignities and acts of violence he witnessed and suffered. In the first of these autobiographies, *Narrative of the Life of Frederick Douglass, an American Slave*, he described the everyday cruelties of slave life. Separated from his mother, who was buried without anyone telling her seven-year-old son that she had died, Douglass was left 'with much the same emotions I should have probably felt at the death of a stranger'.[3] As a small child, he often woke at dawn to the sound of his aunt being beaten by his master, Captain Anthony, who would tie her to a joist and whip her on her naked back until she bled. If she screamed, he whipped her with greater ferocity. He did the same if she remained silent. He stopped only when his exertions left him exhausted. 'It was,' Douglass recalled, 'the blood-stained gate, the entrance to the hell of slavery through which I was about to pass.'[4]

Resistance meant greater violence, even death. Austin Gore, an aptly named slave overseer, whose 'barbarity was equalled by the consummate coolness with which he committed the grossest and most savage deeds', whipped a slave called Demby. Unable to bear the pain and the humiliation, Demby dived into a nearby creek. Gore warned him he would call him to come out three times. If, after the third call, he refused to come out and receive his punishment, he would be shot. Gore did as he promised. He called three times. Demby refused to get out of the water, so Gore shot him. His 'mangled body sank out of sight and blood and brains marked the water where he had stood'.[5]

Throughout his twenty-year enslavement, Douglass had several owners. Of them all, he reserved particulate disgust and hatred for Thomas Auld, whom he described as 'destitute of every element of character commanding respect'.[6] A poor man who became a slave owner by marriage, Thomas was mean, cruel and cowardly. He lacked the strength of character to exhibit any consistency in his behaviour and was unable to hide his sense of his own inferiority. Such was his weakness that he 'was not even a good imitator'. Yet, perhaps because of the flaws in his character, Thomas excelled in cruelty, for which, after his conversion to Methodism, he believed he had found religious justification. Initially, Douglas hoped Auld's conversion would lead him to free his slaves. Instead, he became as fervent in his faith as he was in cruelty, linking physical violence against his slaves to spiritual correction. Douglass gives the example of his cousin Henny, whom Auld beat with particular vindictiveness. She fell into a fire as a child, leaving her scarred, helpless and an expense from which Thomas received no return. As punishment for burdening him with her disability, he often whipped her with a heavy cowskin on her bare shoulders until she bled. He left her tied and bleeding for four or five hours. On occasion, he tied her up and whipped her before breakfast, went about his day's business and returned to whip her again, on the same wounds, before dinner. To justify his cruelty, Auld quoted a passage from the Gospel of St Luke: 'He that knoweth his Master's will and doeth it not, shall be beaten with many stripes.'[7]

Thomas did not spare Douglass. He deprived him of food and flogged him frequently. Despite his power to inflict violence on Douglass, the slave persisted in defying his master. Exasperated and determined to win this battle of wills, on 1 January 1833, when Douglass was fourteen, Thomas sent him to Edward Covey, a poor man who 'had acquired a very high reputation for breaking young slaves'. In the first week, Covey whipped Douglass with such ferocity that it raised ridges as large as a finger on his back. When Douglass dared defy his new master by refusing to strip naked before a beating, Covey lunged at him with 'the fierceness of a tiger', tore off his clothes and thrashed him with lengths of wood, which left deep scars. It was one of many such beatings he received at Covey's hands, yet Douglass persisted in non-compliant behaviour, until 'Mr. Covey succeeded in breaking me ... in body, soul and spirit ... [and] ... the dark night of slavery closed in upon me'.[8]

Douglass was exhausted, and one day he collapsed when carrying wheat to the fan (a tool used to separate the chaff from the grain). Covey rushed from the house and kicked him repeatedly as he lay on the ground. When Douglass refused to get up, Covey split open his head with a hickory slat. When Covey left, Douglass picked himself up and staggered 11 kilometres to Thomas Auld's house to ask for protection, almost bleeding to death on the way. Thomas refused his request and ordered Douglass to return to Covey, which he did the following morning, walking the 11 kilometres back, having been offered neither food to eat nor medicine to soothe his wounds.

One morning, Covey threw a rope around Douglass's legs as he laboured in one of the stables, intending to tie him up and whip him. At that moment, 'from whence came the spirit I don't know – I resolved to fight'. Douglass grabbed Covey by the throat. Covey called other slaves to help him. They refused, leaving the two men to fight. After two ferocious hours, they stopped. Covey had failed to beat Douglass whose 'long-crushed spirit rose, cowardice departed'. In its place came 'bold defiance' and Douglass 'resolved that, however long I might remain a slave in form, the day had passed forever when I could be a slave in fact'.[9]

If the fight with Covey was one moment when Douglass felt his own power, another happened a few years earlier when he was a slave in the Baltimore home of Hugh Auld, Thomas's brother. Sophia, Hugh's wife, encouraged Douglass to learn to read and write. Hugh intervened and stopped it, fearing that it 'would forever unfit him to be a slave'. He was right. The more Douglass read in secret, the more knowledge he acquired 'to torment and sting my soul to unutterable anguish'. It gave Douglass 'a view of my wretched condition, without the remedy'.[10] He read in newspapers about slaves who ran away, set fire to their masters' barns or even killed them. Such acts were described as the 'fruit of abolition'. Douglass had no idea what the phrase meant. He even looked up 'abolition' in a dictionary, but it still made no sense to him. When he eventually learned it meant there were people fighting for the end of slavery, his spirits rose and he resolved to escape from bondage.

In September 1838, Douglass fled and arrived in New York a free man. Ten years later, on the anniversary of his emancipation, he wrote an open letter to Thomas Auld.[11] He began by acknowledging the distance that divided them, 'You, sir, can never know my feelings,' before finding common ground in a shared humanity, 'What you are, I am. You are a man, and so am I ... each equally provided with faculties necessary to our individual existence'. It is on the basis of this shared humanity that Douglass invited Auld to engage in a startling thought experiment. The freed slave asked his former master how he would feel if their roles were reversed, if Douglass in 'some dark night' were to 'seize the person of your own lovely daughter

Amanda ... make her my slave – compel her to work and I take her wages ... feed her coarsely – clothe her scantily, and whip her on the naked back ... leave her unprotected – a degraded victim of the brutal lust of fiendish overseers ... I ask you, how would you regard me, if such were my conduct?'

Having outlined his arguments for the barbarism of slavery, Douglass concluded by saying he will continue to use Auld's name 'as a weapon to assail the system of slavery'. He did this without malice. 'There is,' Douglass affirmed, 'no roof under which you would be more safe than mine' before ending, 'I am your fellow man, but not your slave.'

Douglass's resolve to walk this humanitarian path was tested many times, none more so than by two meetings. The first took place in 1857, a decade after his public letter to Thomas Auld. After delivering a lecture in Philadelphia, a man approached Douglass and told him Auld's daughter, Amanda, had been in the audience that night. Douglass refused to believe him until, the following morning, he received a note from her servant, William Needles, informing him of her husband's business address.

In his letter to Auld, Douglass wrote how he longed to know the fate of his sisters, his brother and his grandmother and he now saw another opportunity to find out what had happened to them. He made his way to the office of Amanda's husband, John Sears, a coal merchant. At first, Sears was loath to talk to Douglass. By this time Douglass was famous, and Sears feared their conversation might find its way into the press. Douglass assured him it would not. After a pause, Sears softened. He remarked how he felt Douglass had been unfair in his treatment of Thomas Auld who 'was really a kind-hearted man and a good master'. Douglass replied that here were two sides to every story and that his experience of Auld was one of unkindness and cruelty. Despite this, he asked Sears if he could speak with Amanda. Reluctantly, Sears agreed, and the following afternoon

Douglass found himself in a large parlour, occupied by thirty people. It had been more than twenty years since he last saw Amanda, yet he recognised her immediately. As he walked towards her, she 'bounded to me with joy in every feature'. The meeting was unconditionally warm. Amanda told Douglass she had freed her slaves and was now an abolitionist. While she knew nothing of the fate of Douglass's family, he was happy to share with her his memories of her mother, Lucretia, who died when Amanda was a small child. He even identified Amanda's own children among the crowd. In his final autobiography, *Life and Times*, written more than twenty years after the meeting, Douglass wrote that the 'interview touched me deeply'.[12] It was, however, not to be his last meeting with the Auld family.

The second meeting,[13] in which his resolve to stay on the path of reconciliation was tested, took place in 1877. Thomas Auld, by then more than eighty years old and close to death, asked Douglass 'to come to the side of his dying bed'. Douglass accepted the invitation. Earlier that year, Douglass had become the first African American to be appointed a marshal by the US Senate. When Auld cast eyes on his former slave, he greeted him as 'Marshal Douglass'; to which Douglass replied, 'not Marshal but Frederick to you as formerly'. They 'shook hands cordially', at which point Auld 'shed tears as men thus afflicted will do when excited by any deep emotion'. In the course of the short time they spent together, Douglass absolved Auld for the cruel treatment of his grandmother. He also asked Auld when he was born. While his former master couldn't remember the exact date, he confirmed the month of Douglass's birth as February 1818. As they conversed, Douglass held Auld's hand. The sight of the frail old man affected him deeply, 'and for a time choked my voice and made me speechless'.

Despite their connection, Douglass began his later account of the meeting with a list of cruelties and indignities inflicted upon him by Auld and a reminder that he had denounced Auld in speeches and writings for more than forty years. Yet, Douglass went on to say that their lives were 'verging towards a point where differences disappear', where 'the slave and his master are reduced to the same level'. From this standpoint, Douglass was able to regard Auld 'as I did myself, a victim of the circumstances of birth, education, law and custom'.

William McFeely, a biographer of Douglass, believed the meeting was more than what Douglass called a 'final settlement of past differences'. He claimed that 'Frederick loved Thomas and that love was returned',[14] but it is doubtful that was how Douglass saw it. He understood what was at stake, as a former slave, a Christian and, by then, a public figure of immense significance. He met Auld from a position of strength. The slave forgave his master on his own terms. In doing so, he bore witness to the brutal truth of slavery and to his own refusal to be a victim of it.

In his great oration delivered on 5 July 1852 at Corinthian Hall, Douglass spent much of it castigating the United States for its support of slavery. To the white people in the audience he said, 'This Fourth of July is *yours*, not *mine*. *You* may rejoice, *I* must mourn ... What to the American slave is your 4th of July? I answer; a day that reveals to him, more than all other days of the year, the gross injustice and cruelty to which he is the constant victim. To him, your celebration is a sham.'[15] He attacked the Church for its inconsistent application of liberty. God 'hath commanded all men, everywhere to love one another; yet you notoriously hate, (and glory in your hatred), all men whose skins are not colored like your own.'[16] But Douglass remained a firm believer that if people interpreted the Constitution of the United States 'as it *ought* to be interpreted', it is a 'GLORIOUS LIBERTY DOCUMENT [sic]' that 'will be found to contain principles and purposes, entirely hostile to the existence of slavery'.[17]

Douglass has been proved right. While racism, like other forms of domination in personal and social relationships, persist, the United

States and other liberal democracies have harnessed their founding principles to progress the cause of racial equality. Yet, today, in universities and cultural organisations in many parts of the Western world, it often seems that no progress has been made. On the contrary, it appears that racism is worse now than ever. In what activists believe is an effort to correct historical injustices and eliminate white supremacy, schools face new forms of segregation as pupils are divided by race to give white pupils the opportunity to make amends for the oppression they perpetuate by virtue of the colour of their skin. A diversity training seminar in San Diego taught that only black people 'know who America really is' and accused schools of the 'spirit murdering of Black children'.[18] At Bryn Mawr College in Pennsylvania, where tuition fees can exceed $70,000 a year, students shut down the college, claiming racism in its classrooms threatened the survival of black students.[19] Brentwood School in California segregated its students, parents and faculty by race and sexual orientation.[20] In an ominous, and by now familiar turn towards authoritarianism, 350 faculty members at Princeton University signed a manifesto that supported the formation of 'a committee composed entirely of faculty that would oversee the investigation and discipline of racist behaviors, incidents, research and publication on the part of faculty'.[21] Ideological conformity, not truth, integrity or scientific fact, is rapidly becoming the determining factor in assessing the value of academic research. It is ironic that voices are being silenced and conformity enforced in the name of diversity.

How is it, when we are more tolerant than we have been, do we appear to be more *intolerant*? This paradox occurs because as we make progress in overcoming discrimination, we expand the concept of discrimination to make it appear as if we are either not making any progress at all, or that things are getting worse. In a landmark series of experiments, psychologists at Harvard University explained this as an example of 'prevalence-induced concept change'.[22] They showed that 'people often respond to the decrease in the prevalence of a stimulus by increasing the concept of it'. In one experiment, participants were shown 800 human faces on a continuum of threatening to non-threatening. When the prevalence of threatening faces was reduced in one group, participants expanded their concept of threat to include faces that they had previously defined as non-threatening.

This psychological bias explains how revolutionary movements consume themselves as the drive towards ideological purity expands the scope of offences and deepens the cycle of punishments. It also explains that, as we become less racist, we appear to be more racist than we ever were. It leads, as we saw with the Princeton manifesto, to an austere scrutiny of our words and actions, in a deepening cycle of struggle sessions, from which, ultimately, no one escapes. An example of this is Ibram X. Kendi's recommendation for the establishment of a Department of Anti-Racism composed of 'formally trained experts on racism ... (which) ... would be empowered with disciplinary tools to wield over and against policymakers and public officials who do not voluntarily change their racist policy and ideas'.[23] They would be tasked with 'investigating' private businesses and 'monitoring' public officials. What happens to those who do not 'voluntarily' conform their behaviour to the demands made by this team of experts is not specified.

Such an ideology can only be sustained when people are defined as representatives of a single identity group (black, white, Asian, Hispanic etc.) and not as individuals who may share beliefs, values and behaviours with multiple identity groups. While there remain serious injustices, principally against the poor, be they black, brown or white, that demand our continual vigilance, there is no equivalence between slavery and micro-aggressions on a university campus. Frederick Douglass knew the horror of legally sanctioned white supremacy, yet he believed in progress, and he was right to so do. The cognitive scientist Steven Pinker analysed data on Americans' opinions on race, gender and sexual orientation since 1985, which demonstrated a '"fundamental shift" toward tolerance and respect of rights, with formerly widespread prejudices sinking into oblivion'.[24] The pluralism and tolerance built into open societies have enabled that progress, imperfect and incomplete as it will always be, and we must ensure those values are harnessed to protect us against illiberalism and the closure of debate. Writing about the case for black optimism, the philosopher Coleman Hughes concluded that the institutions Kendi wants to dismantle are 'the very same institutions [that] have allowed for, if not ushered in, huge amounts of progress for black people...We should not burn the system down. We should reform it one increment at a time'.[25]

In 'Self-made Men', a lecture delivered in 1859, Douglass argued that the engine of that progress was the individual willing to suspend judgement of others and seek greater self-knowledge: 'the best man finds in his breast, the evidence of kinship with the worst, and the worst with the best'.[26] He knew that imprisoning individuals in their racial and social identities led only to endless cycles of violence and retribution. For that reason, Douglass distinguished between individuals and the roles assigned to them. 'I loved all mankind,' he wrote in *My Bondage and My Freedom*, 'slaveholders not excepted; though I abhorred slavery more than ever.'[27] Such love, is perhaps, the most difficult form of love to express. It understands the limitations of our nature and the dangers of exempting from ourselves the judgement we impose on others.

However, Douglass also acknowledged that power 'concedes nothing without a demand' and those who 'deprecate agitation ... want rain without thunder and lightning'.[28] Some commentators, like the philosopher and political activist Cornel West, struggle to reconcile the two sides of Frederick Douglass: the fiery freedom fighter, who sanctioned violence in the struggle against slavery, and the older establishment figure who became the first black

American to be appointed a United States Marshal in 1877. West laments the 'tremendous concessions, compromises' that Douglass made, but he concludes that, while 'it's a beautiful thing to be on fire',[29] Douglass, like the rest of us, was 'shot through with contradictions'.[30]

Maturity is about embracing those contradictions. Douglass was an individualist who also recognised we accomplish nothing alone. Not one among us has more than a partial answer to injustice. Our ignorance demands humility, which should make us tremble when faced with the moral absolutism of men like Kendi, whose moral world is sharply divided into being 'antiracist' or 'racist', Good or Evil, on the side of justice or injustice. The spectre of tyranny haunts these binary distinctions. Kendi's 'formally trained experts in racism' are the mirrored twins of the 'professional revolutionary experts' unleashed during the Cultural Revolution and his moral absolutism will amplify the injustice he seeks to eradicate. As Friedrich Nietzsche warned in *Beyond Good and Evil*, written ten years before Douglass's death in 1895, 'Whoever fights monsters should see to it that in the process he does not become a monster.'[31]

Douglass understood we have to talk to our enemies and see them in ourselves, if we are to tame those monsters. In an age when children are being taught to internalise responsibility for historic injustice and, depending on the identity group to which they are assigned, are ossified as oppressor or oppressed from the moment of birth, we would do well to heed the wisdom of Frederick Douglass when he wrote, 'I have no heart to visit upon children the sins of their fathers.'[32]

We may never know who destroyed the statue of Frederick Douglass in Maplewood Park, Rochester. It may have been a white supremacist who wanted to attack the statue of a black man in retaliation for the destruction of Confederate monuments; or it may have been an antiracist activist who refused to forgive him for soothing the pain of a dying slaveholder or for believing in the potential of the country that enslaved him. Whoever destroyed the statue and whatever they hoped to gain from the destruction, Frederick Douglass towers above them, impervious to their hate.

EPILOGUE

KHALED
AL-ASAAD

BORN: January 1932
EXECUTED: 18 August 2015

In 2015, ISIS occupied the ancient city of Palmyra. As they entered the Syrian city from one side, the archaeologist Khaled al-Asaad was frantically loading artefacts from the museum onto trucks, which left the city from the other side. Al-Asaad and his colleagues saved what they could. He could have saved himself. He could have travelled to safety alongside the fragments of history he had spent his life preserving. Instead, he decided to stay. He was an old man. His heart belonged in Palmyra. He had named his daughter Zenobia, after the city's third-century queen. His son, Mohammed al-Asaad, said his father 'was innocent, so he never thought ISIS would hurt him'.[1] Within weeks, Khaled al-Asaad was dead.

Al-Asaad's ordeal began when ISIS arrested him and demanded to know what had been done with the missing treasures. He refused to tell them. They tortured him. Still, he said nothing. When they realised al-Asaad would not divulge what he knew, they dragged him into a square, where a large crowd had gathered. As he knelt down, a masked executioner beheaded him. As many as a dozen of his colleagues were also executed. The Islamists took al-Asaad's body and hung it from a Roman column before taking it to the city centre, where they tied it to a traffic light with red twine. In a final act of degradation, they put his head, his glasses still on, on the ground between his legs and hung a plaque from his neck, which read, 'Director of Idolatry'.

At the same time as they tortured al-Asaad, ISIS destroyed statues, decorative art, funerary sculptures, icons of ancient deities and the first-century Temple of Baalshamin. For them, the preservation of antiquities was idolatrous and they wanted to obliterate the cultural triumph of the oasis city over the surrounding desert. According to

Algerian journalist Kamel Daoud, they were possessed by a fervour to 'extend the desert's domain: to replace walls with sand, to flatten out the landscape, to return to a vacuum so as to start history all over again.'[2]

The defiant preservation of that history in the face of fanaticism began immediately. The first refusal to mark the burial of Palmyrene civilisation beneath the 'lone and level sands' came in the celebration of the life of Khaled al-Asaad. Maamoun Abdulkarim, the head of the Antiquities and Museums Department in Damascus, described him as 'one of the most important pioneers in Syrian archaeology in the twentieth century'.[3] Professor Andreas Schmidt-Colinet of the University of Vienna first met Khaled al-Asaad as a young scholar in the 1970s. He fell in love with Palmyra and spent two months a year in the city for thirty years: 'All this was directed and organised by Khaled al-Asaad ... All our research and all our life in Palmyra would have been impossible without him. With him everything was possible, without him nothing was possible.' The two archaeologists became 'highly esteemed colleagues and friends ... almost like brothers. I and my whole family will remember him and keep him and all his family in our grateful hearts.'[4] Professor Kiyohide Saito of the Archaeological Institute of Kashihara, Japan, spent many years working with Khaled al-Asaad on the excavation of an underground tomb. He remembered 'a great historian' with a 'wonderful sense of humour', calling him 'the eternal director of the Palmyra museum'.[5]

Born near the Temple of Bel, Khaled al-Asaad served as the custodian of the ancient city of Palmyra for forty years. Even after his retirement in 2003, he continued to play an active and leading role in the preservation of the site. A self-taught scholar, he published articles and books about Palmyra. In addition to overseeing excavations and the restoration of the site, al-Asaad made his own discoveries. They included a third-century mosaic and 700 silver coins, which dated back to the seventh-century Sassanid Empire. Amr al-Azm, a colleague and friend, said, 'you can't write about Palmyra's history or anything to do with Palmyrian work without mentioning Khaled al-Asaad'.[6]

If the preservation of the memory of Khaled al-Asaad was the first step in the preservation of Palmyra, the second was the restoration of the city. The French historian Paul Veyne, a man a few years older than al-Asaad, took it as his duty to bear witness to the city's magnificence. In a short book published the same year as al-Asaad's beheading, Veyne wrote, 'In spite of my advanced age, it is my duty as a former professor and as a human being to voice my stupefaction before this incomprehensible destruction, and to sketch a portrait of the past splendour of Palmyra, which can now only be known and experienced through books.'[7] He memorialised a city where there were 'statues everywhere'. In the second century CE, 'an average city had one official statue per some thousand inhabitants; in Palmyra it was probably one per one hundred'.[8]

Despite Veyne's focus on recovering the experience of Palmyra through books, the preservation of the cultural heritage of the ancient city was not restricted to the written word. In 2016, the photographer Joseph Eid returned to Palmyra. He brought with him photographs of the city he had taken two years earlier, holding each photo in front of the ruins to show the contrast between its past and its desecrated present.

'Palmyra is a wound,' said Frances Pinnock, leader of an Italian expedition to Palmyra. Her team was one of many that sought to find novel ways to heal Palmyra. Two marble busts were brought to Italy for restoration, travelling along what Francesco Rutelli, a former mayor of Rome, called a 'corridor for culture'. The restoration team baptised them 'the war-wounded of Palmyra'.[9]

Among the most extraordinary acts of preservation was the reconstruction of the Triumphal Arch that stood at the entrance to the Temple of Bel. Using 3D computer modelling and 3D machining in stone, a team from Oxford University's Institute for Digital

Archaeology (IDA), recreated the arch in marble, at two-thirds the height of the original. In April 2016, Boris Johnson, a classicist and then Mayor of London, unveiled the arch on Trafalgar Square 'in defiance of the barbarians who destroyed the original'. Alexy Karenowska, who led the Oxford team, said, 'without reconstructions, destroyed sites will, in time, be swallowed by the sands and forgotten'. Roger Michel, the founder and Executive Director of the IDA, agreed that the preservation of cultural heritage was of the greatest importance: 'Monuments – as embodiments of history, religion, art and science – are significant and complex repositories of cultural narratives. No one should consider for one second giving terrorists the power to delete such objects from our collective cultural record.'[10]

It was to preserve this 'collective cultural record' that Khaled al-Asaad gave his life. Before ISIS, the statues, monuments, art, temples and colonnades that made up the UNESCO World Heritage Site at Palmyra attracted more than 150,000 tourists a year. Paul Veyne described the Temple of Bel as 'the San Marco of this desert port'[11] and the city, with its vast trade network, became known as the 'Venice of the Sands'.[12] Khalil Hariri, al-Asaad's son-in-law, called it 'a treasure for Syria and the world'.[13]

Khaled al-Asaad lived and died for Palmyra because he considered our cultural heritage more important than his own life. He didn't judge the heritage bequeathed to him by the intentions or the beliefs of those who built the statues and monuments he preserved. A postcard dated about 1900 and printed by the French company Neurdein Frères, shows the *Arc de Triomphe* at the entrance to the Temple of Bel, on which a man has scribbled a note to his brother. It reads, 'all of this makes me nostalgic and makes me dream about the boat that will take me away'.[14] That is what preserving the past does. It allows us to move back through time and catch a glimpse of what we once were, without which we could not be what we are today. One of

Khaled al-Asaad's favourite quotes came from the Roman statesman and philosopher Cicero: 'To be ignorant of what occurred before you were born is to remain always a child. For what is the worth of human life, unless it is woven into the life of our ancestors by the records of history?'[15]

For al-Asaad, heritage bound us into a global culture and as a species. The past, for al-Asaad, was an anchor that made sense of the present: without it we drift and sink. The presence of the desert, pressing against the city on all sides, a non-civilisational wilderness out of which ISIS emerged, threatened Palmyra with collapse into chaos and it is only our maturity, our refusal to 'remain always a child', that protects us from real and metaphorical deserts that frame the decisions we make about the creation, preservation and destruction of statues.

In 2003, Nigel Bathurst Hankin, an eccentric Englishman who had spent his life in India, took the historian David Cannadine on a tour of New Delhi. After Cannadine confessed to a fascination with ritual and ceremonial, Hankin brought him to a large, open space on the edge of the city where, in 1877, a grand Imperial Assemblage took place to celebrate the assumption of the title Empress of India by Queen Victoria. The event, engineered by the viceroy Robert Lytton, was an ostentatious ritual symbolising British imperial dominance. In a letter to Lord Salisbury, Lytton reflected this dominance and its paternalistic essence, writing that the Indians love 'a bit of bunting'.[16] The 'bunting' was dominated by symbols of the British Empire with the canopy displaying satin bannerets of the Union Jack. Indian culture was noticeable by its absence except for a lotus flower included in a vast frieze where it was overshadowed by the English rose, the Scottish thistle and the Irish shamrock. The state procession stretched 8 kilometres through the city of New Delhi, and six trumpeters, playing Wagner's *Tannhäuser*, accompanied Lytton's entry into the arena.

By the time David Cannadine visited the site in 2003, all that remained of the Imperial Assemblage were 'weeds and undergrowth'. Hankin took Cannadine to a remote corner of the site, where, to his astonishment, a dozen enormous statues rose up out of the bushes. Among them were viceroys and leading figures of British imperial rule, including King George V. In the past, these statues, placed in prominent positions in New Delhi, affirmed British dominance over India. Now, they lay banished among 'the bushes and the brambles' in 'the final graveyard of the British Empire'. Where once these statues signified the eternal splendour of the empire, they now conveyed 'the opposite message: that earthly power is transient, and the imperial dominion is ephemeral'.[17]

Statues do not teach us history in the way that books do, nor are they simply commemorations of the past. They are symbols of dominance, the rising of a *particular* ephemeral order out of the desert of chaos. From the 'colossal wreck' of Ramesses II to the great figures of the British Empire lying in a statue graveyard in New Delhi, that dominance ebbs and flows over time.

The history we celebrate in bronze, marble and stone, is a choice that engages some and enrages others. To preserve the statue of a slave trader in a public space at public expense is, according to the historian David Olusoga, to validate people who did 'terrible things'.[18] The New Orleans mayor Mitch Landrieu made a similar point about Confederate monuments that were attempts to 'rewrite history to hide the truth [and] purposely celebrate a fictional, sanitized Confederacy; ignoring the death, ignoring the enslavement, and the terror that it actually stood for'.[19] Even the Confederate general Robert E. Lee cautioned against erecting statues and monuments to the Confederacy, saying, 'I think it wiser ... not to keep open the sores of war but to ... commit to oblivion the feelings engendered.'[20]

★

However, our need for status and belonging goes too deep to commit our feelings of love and hate to oblivion. They are the forge in which our identities are cast. In the iconoclastic mania that spread through the West after the murder of George Floyd, police stood back as mobs took to the streets and toppled 'racist' statues. Claudine van Hensbergen, an associate professor at the University of Northumbria, saw in this moment an opportunity to redress the historical balance, saying statues 'have historically been raised by those in a position of power. So actually, they just speak to who those people are and they can never be really inclusive of everybody. They're political acts, really, and we need a political act now that speaks for the people that didn't have the power. That is the new type of sculpture.'[21] This is a view shared by Reverend Al Sharpton who saw the public funding of statues linked to the Confederacy as subsidising 'the insult of my family ... an open display of bigotry announced over and over again'.[22]

But if all statues reflect the dominance of a particular religion, political or cultural perspective, it is impossible to erect statues 'inclusive of everybody'.[23] The consequences of this necessary lack of inclusion, and how it has found expression throughout history, is one of the central themes of this book. The most benign cultural figures for one identity group will be seen as malevolent by another. And, since the idea of cohesive identity groups is a psychological and cultural myth that serves its own ideological ends, divisions within identity groups about the fate of statues will be as ferocious as the divisions between them.

In a 1994 article published in *The New York Times*, Isobel Wilkerson framed this dilemma in the context of the removal of statues in post-apartheid South Africa. Nelson Mandela, fearing the effect of black triumphalism on the process of reconciliation, said, 'We must be able to channel our anger without doing injustices to other communities. Some of their heroes may be villains to us. And some of our heroes may be villains to them.'[24] Other members of the African National

Congress were not as conciliatory. Peter Mokaba, a member of parliament said, the 'apartheid statues... must all go. In a revolution, you have won when you have taken the capital. And this is what we are doing.'[25] Kobie Gouws, a white legislator, replied, 'You don't heal an old wound by making a new one'.[26] The 1999 National Heritage Resources Act found a compromise by removing a few of the most offensive statues and by reframing existing statues or adding new ones to reflect the changing cultural and political landscape.

However, as we regress into hyper-tribalism, the battle over statues will reflect growing intolerance on all sides. Graffiti cementing racial division, such as 'Die Whites Die', was repeatedly sprayed on the Confederate statues in New Orleans. In 2017, Heather Heyer went to Charlottesville to make a stand against a Unite the Right rally, organised to protest the removal of Confederate monuments. A white supremacist, James Alex Fields Jr, drove his car into the crowd of anti-Confederate protestors and killed her.

The temptation to sink into the comfort and certainty of an identity group is wired into our biology. It is up to us whether we ignite or dampen that wiring. If moral perfection is to be the standard we use to determine which statues stand and which statues fall, then none will stand. The failure of Julius Nyerere to exhibit sufficient moral purity to be worthy of usurping the tarnished Enlightenment philosopher David Hume, is just one example. That Frederick Douglass could enrage all sides of the moral debate is another. Yet the demands for cultural purity and the triumphalism that accompanies them, persist. The political commentator Angela Rye said in an interview, 'My ancestors weren't deemed human beings to [George Washington]. So to me, I don't care if it's a George Washington statue, or a Thomas Jefferson statue, or a Robert E. Lee statue, they all need to come down.'[27]

The problem with this position is that it reduces historical figures to one dimension. It also demonises people who believe that, for example, George Washington's contribution to ideas that resulted in giving a voice to the voiceless, is worthy of commemoration. It's easy to judge the past from the perspective of the present. We know with certainty that our own moral compass would have pointed us in a virtuous direction, regardless of the time and place of our birth. Everything is crisp and clear. As Milan Kundera wrote, 'Man proceeds in the fog. But when he looks back to judge people of the past, he sees no fog on their path. From his present, which was their faraway future, their path looks perfectly clear to him, good visibility all the way. Looking back, he sees the path, he sees the people proceeding, he sees their mistakes, but not the fog.'[28]

We cannot surrender to tribalism and ideological conformity if the foundations of our open societies are to remain intact. Whether we like it or not, sustaining the fragile democracies in which we live means embracing the fog, accepting pluralism, allowing those who disagree with us to have a voice, talking to the Other. All statues fall: what matters is *how* they fall. If we are to remove or reinterpret old statues and erect new ones to reflect who we are now, let it be as a result of a process of deliberation and negotiation, not the frenzied certainty of the mob.

Statues stand as markers of our collective memory. They connect our past to our present by signifying something beyond themselves. That 'something' is meaning and a sense of belonging. In 1943, as Europe lay in ruins, a Spanish architect, a Swiss historian and a French artist, collaborated on a short essay, *Nine Points on Monumentality*.[29] They concluded that monuments 'are the expression of man's highest cultural needs' and are 'only possible where a unifying consciousness and a unifying culture exists'. When a culture fractures into warring tribes, there is no 'unifying consciousness' because we sever the link between our past and our future. When this separation is extreme, we convince ourselves that history can be split into what came before a Great Awakening and what will come after. A necessary prelude to this disaster is the belief that the past is irredeemably evil. When this idea gains ascendancy, anyone who holds a more nuanced view, anyone who sees the fog, becomes, at best, an outcast. In such a world, guilt for past injustice is transferred onto those seen as beneficiaries of that injustice, who must repent or be punished.

So, we tear our statues down, forgetting that new statues we erect stand on the shoulders of the ones we destroyed. Today, in the West, warring groups fight, with escalating love and hate, to preserve or destroy statues in our towns and cities. They do so because statues are proxies for our struggle for individual and collective dignity. But as tolerance collapses, extremes on either side of the cultural divide compel those in the centre to take sides. Without compromise and a commitment to affirm the dignity of those we oppose, this conflict will not end well.

None of us are sufficiently pure to stand in absolute judgement on another human being nor will any society or culture withstand incessant moral scrutiny. In *Empireland*, Sathnam Sanghera writes that 'it is hard to function if you walk around with full knowledge of every terrible thing that has ever happened'.[30] This knowledge is what we bury about those we love so we can unearth it in those we hate. Whenever we are asked to make a choice between two alternatives, whenever we are told we are either for the past or the future, a class enemy or a loyal revolutionary, a racist or an antiracist, a believer or an infidel, we know enough from the horrors of history, to understand the path we are on.

The Jewish philosopher Walter Benjamin described this path in haunting detail. Fearing persecution, Benjamin fled Nazi Germany and took refuge in France. The day before the Nazis entered Paris in June 1940, Benjamin fled to Spain. Facing deportation back to France and certain capture, he killed himself. In an essay[31] written shortly before his death, Benjamin imagined the Angel of History facing the past: 'His eyes are staring, his mouth is open, his wings are spread.'

He sees a 'single catastrophe' piling 'wreckage upon wreckage' at his feet. He wants to 'awaken the dead and make whole what has been smashed' but 'a storm is blowing from Paradise'. It prevents him from closing his wings and 'propels him into the future, to which his back is turned, while the pile of debris before him grows skyward'. The storm, Benjamin concludes, 'is what we call progress'.

If we persist in talking only to ourselves, if we elevate ourselves above those with whom we disagree and bask in moral superiority and virtuous victimhood, Benjamin's vision will become our reality. When we segregate ourselves into identity groups that define us by our differences, we will lose the ability to speak to each other, understand each other and tolerate each other. Paul Veyne concludes his book on Palmyra by observing that 'without a doubt, knowing, wanting to know, only one culture, one's own, is to be condemned to a life of suffocating sameness'.[32] To speak only to oneself is to sanction the terror that inevitably follows our solipsistic folly. Our intentions may be good, but, as Nietzsche knew, 'blood and cruelty lie at the bottom of all "good things"'.[33]

If we are to survive the witch-hunts, the punitive introspection and the demands for purity of thought and deed, we would do well to remember the 'Venice of the Sands' and a Syrian archaeologist who gave his life to preserve the 'multicultural' heritage that is our collective birthright. Khaled al-Asaad's life and death mark the thin wire, bound on all sides by the seductions of tyranny, that we must walk if we are to survive. His devotion to Palmyra, the city where there were 'statues everywhere', was a devotion to a shared humanity and his sacrifice was a gift of love.

ACKNOWLEDGEMENTS

I've known people, some of them friends, whose lives fell apart quite suddenly. Those who gathered around the wreckage, wondered how such a thing could come 'from nowhere'. Except it didn't: the crack-up is a 'blow that comes from within,' wrote F. Scott Fitzgerald in 1936, 'that you don't feel until it's too late to do anything about it'. It isn't the preserve of individuals. It happens to cities, countries, empires. And it's happened to us.

Some of the people I knew put themselves back together again. It took time and love. But they picked up the pieces and moved on with their lives. We can, too. It's why I wrote this book. If I thought the crack-up was terminal, I would have checked out.

So, special thanks to Katie Bond at Aurum and Carrie Kania at Conville and Walsh for making this book possible and to Philip Parker for his meticulous advice.

Thanks also to Margaret and Aureliana for their support.

With gratitude to Jane, my eyes in the dark, and to my parents, Meurig and Grace, who knew how to love.

NOTES

LONE AND LEVEL SANDS

1 Fr Thaddeus. *Life of Blessed Father John Forest*, (London: Burns & Oates Limited, 1888).

2 Griffiths, J. Gwyn. 'Shelley's "Ozymandias" and Diodorus Siculus', *The Modern Language Review* 43, no. 1, 1948, p.81.

3 Parr, Johnstone. 'Shelley's "Ozymandias"', *Keats-Shelley Journal* 6, 1957, p.31.

4 Gormley, Antony & Gayford, Martin. *Shaping the World: Sculpture from Prehistory to Now*, (Thames & Hudson, 2020), p.231.

5 The quote is from the Nobel Lecture given by Czesław Miłosz in December 1980, the year he won the Nobel Prize for Literature. You can read it here: www.nobelprize.org/prizes/literature/1980/milosz/lecture/

6 www.youtube.com/watch?v=SoC2ioaQUQU

7 Baudelaire, Charles. *Les Fleurs du Mal*, (Librarie Générale Française, 1972), p.177.

8 Kapuściński, Ryszard. *The Other*, tr. Antonia Lloyd-Jones, (Verso, 2018), p.44.

9 Dostoyevsky, Fyodor. *Crime and Punishment*, tr. Oliver Ready, (Penguin, 2014), p.653.

10 Kapuściński, 2018, p.23.

11 Kollwitz, Kaethe. *The Diary and Letters of Kaethe Kollwitz*, tr. Richard and Clara Winston, (Northwestern University Press, 1988), p.144.

12 The title of the poem is *Absence*.

13 Younge, Gary. 'Why every single statue should come down', *The Guardian*, 1 June 2021.

14 Jacobs, Julia. 'Philip Guston Blockbuster Show Postponed by Four Museums,' *The New York Times*, 24 September, 2020: www.nytimes.com/2020/09/24/arts/design/philip-guston-postponed-museums-klan.html

15 Boucher, Brian. 'A Museum Canceled a Show About Police Brutality. Here's the Art', *The New York Times*, 9 June 2020.

16 Meredith, Martin. *The State of Africa*, (Simon & Schuster, 2013), p.255.

17 Nietzsche, Friedrich. *Twilight of the Idols*, tr. R. J. Hollingdale, (Penguin, 1986), p.51.

18 Woolf, Virginia. *To the Lighthouse*, (Penguin, 2000), p.69.

Notes

19 Beck, Aaron T. *Prisoners of Hate*, (HarperCollins, 1999), p.31.
20 Nietzsche. 1986, p.51.

HATSHEPSUT

1 Wilkinson, Toby. *The Rise and Fall of Ancient Egypt*, (Bloomsbury, 2010), p.225.
2 *The Egyptian Book of the Dead*. tr. E.A. Wallis Budge, (Penguin, 2008), p.184.
3 Cooney, Kara. *The Woman Who Would Be God*, (Oneworld, 2014), p.165.
4 Wilkinson. 2010, p.232.
5 Bleiberg, Edward and Weissberg, Stephanie. *Striking Power: Iconoclasm in Ancient Egypt*, (Pulitzer Arts Foundation, 2019), pp.27–8.
6 Goldstein, Pavel, Weissman-Fogel, Irit, Shamay-Tsoory, Simone G. 'The role of touch in regulating inter-partner physiological coupling during empathy for pain', *Scientific Reports*, 2017; 7 (1).
7 Bataille, Georges. *On Nietzsche*, tr. Bruce Boone, (Continuum, 2004), p.25.

NERO

1 Russell, Miles and Manley, Harry. 'A Case of Mistaken Identity? Laser-scanning the bronze "Claudius" from near Saxmundham', *Journal of Roman Archaeology* 26, 2013, p.403.
2 Tacitus. *The Annals of Imperial Rome*, tr. Michael Grant, (Penguin, 1996), p.330.
3 Adler, Eric. 'Boudica's Speeches in Tacitus and Dio', *The Classical World*, Winter 2008, p.187.
4 Ibid., p.189.
5 Tacitus. 1996, p.329.
6 Seneca. 'On Anger', *Moral Essays Volume I*, tr. John W. Basore, (Loeb Classical Library, 1928), p.119.
7 Tacitus. 1996, p.265.
8 Suetonius. *The Twelve Caesars*, tr. Robert Graves, (Penguin, 2007), p.212.
9 Seneca. 'On Mercy', *Moral Essays Volume I*, tr. John W. Basore, (Loeb Classical Library, 1928), p.373.
10 Ibid., p.379.
11 In a letter to Lucilius, Seneca defined love as the deepest form of friendship, quoting the Stoic philosopher Hecato of Rhodes, who said, 'I shall show you a love potion compounded without drug or herb or witch's spell. It is this: if you wish to be loved, love'.

12 Seneca. 'Consolation to Helvia', *Dialogues and Letters*, tr. C.D.N. Costa, (Penguin, 2005), p.22.
13 Tacitus. 1996, p.376.

ATHENA

1 Nixey, Catherine. *The Darkening Age*, (Macmillan, 2017), p.xix.
2 Aeschylus. 'The Eumenides', *Aeschylus II*, tr. Richmond Lattimore, (University of Chicago Press, 2013), p.134.
3 Ibid., p.142.
4 Ibid., p.150.
5 Ibid., p.155.
6 Ibid., p.160.
7 Gaskill, Malcolm. *Witchfinders*, (John Murray Publishers, 2005), p.97.
8 Gibbon, Edward. *The History of the Decline and Fall of the Roman Empire*, (Penguin, 2000), pp.145–6.
9 Borges, Jorge Luis. 'The Duration of Hell', *The Total Library*, tr. Esther Allen, Jill Levine and Eliot Weinberger, (Penguin, 1999), p.48.
10 Tsongas, Galen. 'Iconoclasm: ISIS and Cultural Destruction', *Global Societies Journal* 6, 2018, p.23.

THE BUDDHAS OF BAMIYAN

1 Morgan, Llewelyn. *The Buddhas of Bamiyan*, (Harvard University Press, 2015), pp.11–12.
2 Ibid., p.122.
3 Ibid., p.123.
4 Ibid., p.55.
5 Lawler, Andrew. 'Destroyed Buddhas Reveal Their True Colours', *Science*, 1 March 2011: www.sciencemag.org/news/2011/03/destroyed-buddhas-reveal-their-true-colors
6 Behzad, Nasir and Qarizadah, Daud. 'The man who helped blow up the Bamiyan Buddhas', *BBC News*, 12 March 2015: www.bbc.co.uk/news/world-asia-31813681
7 Naderi, Abbas and Najibullah, Farangis. 'Haunted by the Bamiyan Buddhas', Radio Free Europe, Radio Liberty, 12 March 2015: www.rferl.org/a/afghanistan-bamiyan-statues-destroyed/26896782.html
8 'Conclusions on the Future of the Bamiyan Buddha Statues: Technical

Considerations and Potential Effects on Authenticity and Outstanding Universal Value', UNESCO, 29 September, 2017: www.unesco.org/new/fileadmin/MULTIMEDIA/FIELD/Kabul/pdf/TokyoConclusions.pdf

9   Halbwachs, Maurice. *On Collective Memory*, tr. Lewis A. Coser, (University of Chicago Press, 1992), p.43.

10 Harding, Luke. 'How the Buddha got his wounds', *The Guardian*, 3 March 2001: www.theguardian.com/books/2001/mar/03/books.guardianreview2

11 Flood, Finbarr Barry. 'Between Cult and Culture: Bamiyan, Islamic Iconoclasm, and the Museum', *The Art Bulletin* 84, no. 4, 2002, p.655.

12 'The Afghan Iconoclasts', *The Economist*, 10 March 2001: www.economist.com/leaders/2001/03/08/the-afghan-iconoclasts

13 Foucault, Michel. *Discipline and Punish*, tr. Alan Sheridan, (Peregrine Books, 1979), p.44.

14 Ibid., p.46.

15 'Obituary: Osama bin Laden, a soft-spoken millionaire mass murderer', *News24*, 2 May 2011: www.news24.com/news24/Archives/City-Press/Obituary-Osama-bin-Laden-a-soft-spoken-millionaire-mass-murderer-20150430

16 'Bamiyan Buddhas', Khan Academy: www.khanacademy.org/humanities/ap-art-history/west-and-central-asia-apahh/central-asia/a/bamiyan-buddhas?modal=1

17 Sangharakshita. *A Survey of Buddhism*, (Shambala, 1980), p.247.

18 'The Third Patriarch of Zen Verses on the Faith Mind', Age of the Sage: www.age-of-the-sage.org/buddhism/third_patriarch_zen.html

19 Morgan. 2018, p.7.

HECATE

1   Simeonova, Liliana V. 'The Statuary-Art-Gathering Policy of the Early Byzantine Emperors, 4th–5th Centuries', *Actes du Symposium International le Livre*, La Romanie, L'Europe, Sinaia, 2012, p.5.

2   Ibid., p.9.

3   Ibid., p.15.

4   Brubaker, Leslie. *Inventing Byzantine Iconoclasm*, (Bristol Classical Press, 2012), p.14.

5   Ibid., pp.10–11.

6   'The Quinisext Council (or the Council in Trullo) 692', Fordham University: sourcebooks.fordham.edu/basis/trullo.asp

7   The synod concluded that the 'only admissible figure of the humanity of Christ … is bread and wine in the holy Supper. This and no other form, this and no other type, has he chosen to represent his incarnation'.

8   O'Hagan, Sean. 'Interview: Marina Abramovic', *The Guardian*, 3 October 2010: www.theguardian.com/artanddesign/2010/oct/03/interview-marina-abramovic-performance-artist

9   Karahan, Anne. 'Byzantine Iconoclasm: Ideology and Quest for Power' in Kolrud, Kristine and Prusac, Marina (eds.), *Iconoclasm from Antiquity to Modernity*, (Routledge, 2014), p.87.

10 Miller, James. *The Passion of Michel Foucault*, (Flamingo, 1993), p.205.

OUR LADY OF CAVERSHAM

1   Ridgway, Claire. '14 September 1538 – The Destruction of the Shrine of Our Lady of Caversham', The Tudor Society: www.tudorsociety.com/14-september-1538-destruction-shrine-lady-caversham/

2   Ibid.

3   Bridgen, Susan. *New Worlds, Lost Worlds*, (Penguin, 2000), p.115.

4   'Path to St. Peter ad Vincula: Part VIII-B, Elizregina', 14 June 2015: elizregina.com/tag/eustace-chapuys/

5   Ibid., p.120.

6   See: Stride, P. & Floro, K. Lopes. 'Henry VIII, McLeod syndrome and Jacquetta's curse', *Journal of the Royal College of Physicians of Edinburgh*', 43(4), 2013, p.353–360; see also: thecrownchronicles.co.uk/history/history-posts/what-caused-henry-viiis-personality-change-head-injury-or-leg-pain/

7   Lipscomb, Suzannah. 'Henry VIII and Anne Boleyn', History Extra, February 2014: www.historyextra.com/period/tudor/henry-viii-and-anne-boleyn-suzannah-lipscomb-dispels-myths-about-the-lovers-who-changed-history/. See also: Weir, Alison. *King Henry VIII and Court*, (Vintage, 2020), p.276.

8   Weir, 2020, pp.361–2.

9   Ibid., p.356.

10 Bridgen, 2000, p.122.

11 Ibid., p.135.

12 Ibid., p.109.

13 Gregory, Philippa. 'The Psychology of Henry VIII': www.hrp.org.uk/media/1107/philippa-gregoryfinal.pdf

14 Nietzsche, Friedrich. *The Gay Science*, tr. Walter Kaufmann, (Vintage, 1974), pp.88–9.

15 Weir. 2020, p.347.

16 Bridgen. 2000, p.139.

17 Ibid. p.103.

18 Weir, Alison. *The Six Wives of Henry VIII*, (Vintage, 2007), p.470.

19 Eliot, George. *Middlemarch*, (Penguin, 1994), p.15.

HUITZILOPOCHTLI

1   The term Aztec, as the historian Matthew Restall pointed out, is 'familiar shorthand for a complex identity history'. For an overview of that history and the relationship between the terms Aztec, Mexica, Nahuas and Mesoamerican, see Restell, Matthew. *When Montezuma Met Cortés*, (Ecco, 2018), pp.359–60.

2   Díaz del Castillo, Bernal. *The Conquest of New Spain*, tr. J.M. Cohen, (Penguin, 1963), p.214.

3   Boone, Elizabeth H. 'Incarnations of the Aztec Supernatural: The Image of Huitzilopochtli in Mexico and Europe', *Transactions of the American Philosophical Society* 79, no. 2 (1989), p.50.

4   Ibid., p.43

5   Cortés, Hernán. *Letters from Mexico*, tr. Anthony Pagden, (Yale University Press, 1986), pp.106–7.

6   Restall. 2018, pp.82–3.

7   Thomas, Hugh. *Conquest*, (Simon & Schuster, 2005), p.512.

8   Otto, Rudolf. *The Idea of the Holy*, tr. John W. Harvey, (Martino Publishing, 2010), pp.20–1.

9   Quoted in Restall. 2018, p.321.

10 Ibid., p.320.

11 Thomas. *Conquest*, 2005, p.528.

12 Ibid., p.503.

13 Otto. 2010, p.18.

14 Wood, Michael. *Conquistadors*, (BBC Books, 2010), p.11

15 Restall. 2018, p.237.

16 Ibid., p.271.

17 Ibid., p.323.

18 Thomas. *Conquest*, 2005, p.529.

CONFUCIUS

1   Ye, Sang and Barmé, Geremie R. 'The Fate of the Confucius Temple, the Kong Mansion and Kong Cemetery', *China Heritage Quarterly*, 20 December 2009: www.chinaheritagequarterly.org/scholarship.php?searchterm=020_confucius. inc&issue=020

2   In *Iphigenia in Aulis*, a Greek tragedy, written not long after the death of Confucius, the great hero Achilles is threatened by a mob. They demand the sacrifice of Iphigenia, daughter of Agamemnon and Clytemnestra, to appease the Greek goddess Artemis who refuses to let the Greek ships sail to Troy. Achilles attempts to reason with them but is unable to restrain the mob and barely escapes with his life. Hearing of this, Clytemnestra wails, 'Oh, the mob – what a terror and an evil!' See: Euripides. 'Iphigenia in Aulis', *Euripides V*, tr. Charles R. Walker, (University of Chicago Press, 2013).

3   Ye and Barmé. 2009.

4   Yang, Rae. *Spider Eaters*, (University of California Press, 1997), p.92.

5   Dikötter, Frank. *The Cultural Revolution*, (Bloomsbury, 2017), p.54.

6   Yang. 1997, p.125.

7   Mittler, Barbara. '"Enjoying the Four Olds!" Oral; Histories form a "Cultural Desert"', University of Heidelberg: heiup.uni-heidelberg.de/journals/index. php/transcultural/article/view/10798/4665

8   Buckley, Chris, Tatlow, Didi Kirsten, Perlez, Jane and Qin, Amy. 'Voices from China's Cultural Revolution', *The New York Times*, 16 May 2016: www.nytimes. com/interactive/2016/05/16/world/asia/17china-cultural-revolution-voices. html

9   Wood, Michael. *The Story of China*, (Simon & Schuster, 2020), p.468.

10 Chang, Jung and Halliday, Jon. *Mao: The Unknown Story*, (Vintage, 2007), p.661.

11 *Quotations from Chairman Mao Tse-Tung*, p.5.

12 Ibid., p.6.

13 Confucius. *The Analects*, tr. D.C. Lau, (Penguin, 1979), p.59.

14 In the *Book of Questions*, the French poet Edmond Jabès quotes Rabbi Reb Zale, 'You think that it is the bird who is free. You are deceived; it is the flower'. Commenting on this passage, Jacques Derrida writes that 'freedom allies itself with that which restrains it, with everything it receives from a buried origin'. See: Derrida, Jacques. 'Edmond Jabès and the Question of the Book,' *Writing and Difference*, tr. Alan Bass, (University of Chicago Press, 1978), p.80.

15 Ibid., p.120.

16 Ibid., p.103.

17 The Gospel of John, 8:7.
18 Becker, Jasper. *City of Heavenly Tranquility*, (Oxford University Press, 2008), p.177.
19 Yang. 1997, p.100.
20 Jacobs, Rabbi Andrew. 'It is Easy to Hate and it is Difficult to Love', 7 August 2015: rabbiandrewjacobs.org/2015/08/07/it-is-easy-to-hate-and-it-is-difficult-to-love/
21 Yang. 1997, p.151.
22 Dikötter. 2017, p.198.
23 Yang. 1997, p.131.
24 Yang. 1997, pp.165–6.
25 Bowles, Nellie. 'Learning How To (and How Not To) Kill', 4 February 2021: chosenbychoice.substack.com/p/learning-how-to-and-how-not-to-kill
26 'CACAGNY Denounces Critical Race Theory as Hateful Fraud', 23 February 2021: nebula.wsimg.com/9499c73d959b9f49be9689476a990776?AccessKeyId=45A6F09DA41DB93D9538&disposition=0&alloworigin=1
27 Confucius. 1979, p.69.

LOUIS XV

1   'Paris walks: The path to purgatory', *Time Out*: www.timeout.com/paris/en/things-to-do/paris-walks-the-path-to-purgatory
2   Desmas, Anne-Lise. 'The Hand of Louis XV', Getty, 31 March 2017: blogs.getty.edu/iris/the-hand-of-louis-xv/
3   McClellan, Andrew. 'The Life and Death of a Royal Monument: Bouchardon's Louis XV', *Oxford Art Journal* 23, no. 2, 2000, p.16.
4   Ibid., p.21.
5   Ibid., p.22.
6   Foucault. 1979, p.28.
7   McClellan. 2000, p.24.
8   Ibid., p.8.
9   Clay, Richard. *Signs of Power: Iconoclasm in Paris, 1789–1795*, (University of London – Doctoral Thesis), 1999, p.152.
10 Schama, Simon. *Citizens*, (Penguin, 1989), p.534.
11 Ibid., p.725.
12 Žižek, Slavoj. *Robespierre*, (Verso, 2017), p.vii.
13 Bataille, Georges. *Eroticism*, tr. Mary Dalwood, (Marion Boyars, 1987), p.65.
14 Ibid., p.67.

15 Schama. 1989, p.587.

16 Ibid., p.532.

17 Ibid., p.38.

18 Ibid., p.457.

19 Ibid., p.273.

20 Robespierre, Maximilien. 'On the Principles of Political Morality that Should Guide the National Convention in the Domestic Administration of the Republic', Žižek, 2017, p.109.

21 Robespierre, Maximilien. 'Extracts From Speech of 8 Thermidor Year II', Žižek, 2017, p.129.

22 Schama. 1989, p.537.

23 Thomas, Donald. *The Marquis de Sade*, (Allison & Busby, 1992), p.210.

24 Ibid., p.212.

25 De Sade, Marquis. *Philosophy in the Boudoir*, tr. Joachim Neugroschel, (Penguin, 2006), p.141.

26 Schama. 1989, p.369.

27 Bataille. 1987, p.196.

28 Paglia, Camille. *Sexual Personae: Art and Decadence from Nefertiti to Emily Dickinson*, (Vintage, 1991), p.265.

29 De Sade, Marquis. *Justine or the Misfortunes of Virtue*, tr. John Phillips, (Oxford University Press, 2012), p.6.

30 Clay. 1999, p.145.

31 McClellan. 2000, p.25.

32 Robespierre. Žižek, 2017, pp.129–30.

FELIX MENDELSSOHN

1 Barlow, Keith. 'Cultural Liquidation in the Third Reich', 9 November 2016: rtuc. wordpress.com/2016/11/09/demolition-of-the-monument-to-mendelssohn-in-leipzig-under-the-nazis/

2 Wagner, Richard. *Judaism in Music*, tr. William Ashton Ellis, p.5. The essay can be found here: users.skynet.be/johndeere/wlpdf/wlpr0066.pdf

3 Ibid., p.7.

4 Ibid., pp.12–13.

5 Loeffler, James. 'Richard Wagner's "Jewish Music": Antisemitism and Aesthetics in Modern Jewish Culture', *Jewish Social Studies: History, Culture, Society* n.s.15, no. 2, Winter 2009, p. 21.

Notes

6   Browning, Christopher R. *Ordinary Men*, (Penguin, 2001), p.12.

7   www.marcuse.org/herbert/people/adorno/AdornoPoetryAuschwitzQuote.htm

8   Fackenheim, Emil L. *To Mend the World*, (Indiana University Press), 1994, p.299.

9   The quote is amended slightly from the original in Nietzsche, 1986, p.23.

10 Kushner, Harold S. *When Bad Things Happen to Good People*, (Pan, 1981), p.3.

11 Ibid., p.130.

12 Ibid., p.98.

13 Fackenheim. 1994, p.299.

14 Ibid., p.153.

15 Fackenheim. 1994, p.267.

16 Havel, Václav. *Letters to Olga*, tr. Paul Wilson, (Faber and Faber, 1990), p.369.

17 Levinas, Emmanuel. *Existence and Existents*, tr. Alphonso Lingis, (Martinus Nijhoff, 1978), p.58.

18 Levinas, Emmanuel. 'The Name of a Dog, or Natural Rights', *Difficult Freedom*, tr. Seán Hand, (Johns Hopkins University Press, 1997), p.153.

19 Mendelssohn, Moses. 'On the question: what does to enlighten mean?', *Philosophical Writings*, tr. Daniel O. Dahlstrom, (Cambridge University Press, 1997), p.316.

20 Carpenter, Bernard. *Mendelssohn in the Condemned Cell*, 5 October 2020: www.conservativewoman.co.uk/mendelssohn-in-the-condemned-cell/

THE CONFEDERATE MONUMENT

1   Vincent, Tom. 'Evidence of Womans Loyalty, Perseverance, and Fidelity: Confederate Soldiers' Monuments in North Carolina, 1865–1914', *The North Carolina Historical Review* 83, no. 1, 2006, p.74.

2   McPherson, James M. *Battle Cry of Freedom*, (Penguin, 1990), p.849.

3   Ibid., p.849–50.

4   Janney, Caroline E. *Remembering the Civil War*, (University of North Carolina Press, 2013), p.20.

5   Watkins, Sam R. *Company Aytch*, (Turner Publishing Company, 2011), p.6.

6   Ibid., p.274.

7   'Governor Aycock on "The Negro Problem"', Anchor: www.ncpedia.org/anchor/governor-aycock-negro

8   Vincent. 2006, p.78.

9   *Southern Historical Society Papers*, Volume 26: www.perseus.tufts.edu/hopper/text?doc=Perseus%3Atext%3A2001.05.0284%3Achapter%3D1.11&force=y

10   Cox, Karen L. *No Common Ground*, (University of North Carolina Press, 2021), p.29.

11   www.ncpedia.org/anchor/governor-aycock-negro

12   Cox, Karen L. 2021, p.23.

13   Quoted in West, Cornel. *Black Prophetic Fire*, (Beacon Press, 2014), p.213.

14   Wells, Ida B. 'A Red Record', *The Light of Truth*, (Penguin, 2014), p.268.

15   Ibid., p.311.

16   Ibid., p.243.

17   Hale, F. Sheffield. 'Finding Meaning in Monuments: Atlanta History Center Enters Dialogue on Confederate Symbols', *History News* 71, no. 4, 2016, p.21.

18   Lopez, German. 'New Orleans mayor: we can't ignore the death, enslavement, and terror the Confederacy stood for,' *Vox*, 23 May 2017: www.vox.com/policy-and-politics/2017/5/23/15680472/new-orleans-mayor-confederate-monuments

19   Christian, Warren, and Christian, Jack. 'The Monuments Must Go: Reflecting on Opportunities for Campus Conversations'. *South: A Scholarly Journal* 50, no. 1. 2017, p.48.

20   Quoted in Horwitz, Tony. 'A Death for Dixie', *The New Yorker Magazine*, March 18, 1996.

21   'The Inaugural address of President Abraham Lincoln, delivered at the National Capitol, March 4th, 1865': www.gilderlehrman.org/sites/default/files/inline-pdfs/t-06044.pdf

22   King Jr., The Reverend Dr. Martin Luther. *A Gift of Love*, (Beacon Press, 2012), pp.45–6.

23   Ibid., p.47.

24   Ibid., p.47.

25   Ibid., p.42.

26   Wells, Ida B. 2014, p.307.

27   Ibid., p.309.

28   Faust, Drew Gilpin. *The Republic of Suffering*, (Vintage Civil War Library, 2008), p.xi.

29   Ibid., p.55.

30   Ibid., p.192–3.

31   Ibid., p.194.

32   McPherson, James M. 1990, p.238.

33   Ibid., p.413.

34   Ibid., p.477.

35   Watkins, Sam R. 2011, p.128.

Notes

36 Cox, Karen L. 2021, p.67.
37 Hale, F. Sheffield. 2016, p.21.

SIR JOHN A. MACDONALD

1 'Wilfrid Laurier's Speech to the House of Commons, June 8, 1891': www.
macdonaldproject.com/wp-content/uploads/2015/11/House-of-Commons-
Full-Transcript-of-Wilfrid-Lauriers-Speech-June-8–1891.pdf
2 Ibid.
3 'Canada statue of John A Macdonald toppled by activists in Montreal', BBC
News, 30 August 2020: www.bbc.co.uk/news/world-us-canada-53963665
4 Gebhard, Amanda. 'Reconciliation or Racialization?: Contemporary Discourses
about Residential Schools in the Canadian Prairies', Canadian Journal of Education
/ Revue Canadienne de L'éducation 40, no. 1, 2017, pp.4–5.
5 Ibid., p.4.
6 MacDonald, David B., and Graham Hudson. 'The Genocide Question and
Indian Residential Schools in Canada', Canadian Journal of Political Science /
Revue Canadienne de Science Politique 45, no. 2, 2012, p.432.
7 Woods, Eric Taylor. 'A Cultural Approach to a Canadian Tragedy: The Indian
Residential Schools as a Sacred Enterprise', International Journal of Politics,
Culture, and Society 26, no. 2, 2013, p.182.
8 Young, Bryanne. '"Killing the Indian in the Child": Death, Cruelty, and Subject-
formation in the Canadian Indian Residential School System', Mosaic: An
Interdisciplinary Critical Journal 48, no. 4, 2015, p67.
9 www.theguardian.com/world/2015/jun/06/canada-dark-of-history-
residential-schools
10 Adams, Ian. 'The lonely death of Chanie Wenjack,' Macleans, 1 February 1967:
www.macleans.ca/society/the-lonely-death-of-chanie-wenjack/
11 The bodies of children are still being found. In May 2021, the remains of 215
children were found in the grounds of the Kamloops Indian Residential School
in British Columbia, which closed in 1978. The Canadian Prime Minister Justin
Trudeau said the discovery 'breaks my heart'. See: www.bbc.co.uk/news/
world-us-canada-57291530
12 Gualtieri, Claudia. 'The Release of the Truth and Reconciliation Commission
Findings on Indian Residential Schools in Canada, 2 June 2015', in Bait, Miriam;
Brambilla Marina and Crestani, Valentina (eds). Utopian Discourses Across
Cultures, (Peter Lang, 2016), p.197.

13 Masco, Joseph. '"It Is a Strict Law That Bids Us Dance": Cosmologies, Colonialism, Death, and Ritual Authority in the Kwakwaka'wakw Potlatch, 1849 to 1922', *Comparative Studies in Society and History 37*, no. 1, 1995, p.65.

14 Mauss, Marcel. *The Gift*, tr. W.D. Halls, (Routledge, 2002), p.59.

15 Mauss. 2002, p.98.

16 Bataille, Georges. 'The Notion of Expenditure', *Visions of Excess: Selected Writings 1927–1939*, tr. Allan Stoekl, (University of Minnesota Press, 1985), p.128.

17 Ibid., p.120. The nineteenth-century economist Thorstein Veblen made a similar point in *The Theory of the Leisure Class* (Oxford University Press, 2007), when he observed that 'not even the most abjectly poor, forgoes conspicuous consumption ... except under the stress of the direst necessity'.

18 Ibid., p.129.

19 Levell, Nicola. 'Reconciliation Pole' in Tortell, Philippe, Turin, Mark and Young Margot, *Memory*, (Peter Wall Institute for Advanced Studies, 2018), p.74.

20 Preece, Rod. 'The Political Wisdom of Sir John A. Macdonald', *Canadian Journal of Political Science / Revue Canadienne De Science Politique 17*, no. 3, 1984, p.465.

EDWARD COLSTON

1 Humphries, Will. 'Edward Colston statue: Bristol faces up to legacy of the man who helped build it', *The Times*, 9 June 2020: www.thetimes.co.uk/article/edward-colston-statue-bristol-faces-up-to-legacy-of-the-man-who-helped-build-it-zndzrdcg3

2 Coward, Teddy. 'Demands grow for removal of Edward Colston statue from Bristol City Centre', *Epigram*, 6 June 2020: epigram.org.uk/2020/06/06/removal-edward-colston-statue-from-bristol-city-centre-online-petition/

3 Grimshaw, Emma. 'David Olusoga says Edward Colston was "a slave trader and murderer" as he defends Bristol protest', *Chronicle Live*, 8 June 2020: www.chroniclelive.co.uk/news/uk-news/david-olusoga-says-edward-colston-18380761

4 Horton, Helena. 'Edward Colston plaque listing his links to slavery scrapped after mayor says wording isn't harsh enough', *The Telegraph*, 25 March 2019: www.telegraph.co.uk/news/2019/03/25/plaque-acknowledging-slave-owning-history-edward-colston-scrapped/

5 Miller, Naomi. 'Vanessa Kisuule, Hollow,' Bristol Festival of Ideas, 9 June 2020: www.ideasfestival.co.uk/blog/bristol-city-poet/vanessa-kisuule-hollow/

6   Eliot, T.S. 'The Hollow Men', *Collected Poems 1909–1962*, (Faber and Faber, 2002), p.79–82.

7   'In Eliot's Own Words: "The Hollow Men"': tseliot.com/editorials/in-eliots-own-words-the-hollow-men

8   Achebe, Chinua. 'An Image of Africa: Racism in Conrad's Heart of Darkness', *Massachusetts Review*, 18, 1977.

9   Hochschild, Adam. *King Leopold's Ghost*, (Pan, 2012), p.149.

10 Meredith, Martin. *The State of Africa*, (Simon & Schuster, 2005), p.96

11 Ibid., p.98.

12 Kenyon, Paul. *Dictatorland*, (Head of Zeus, 2018), p.4.

13 Hochschild. 2012, p.166.

14 Conrad, Joseph. *Heart of Darkness*, (Penguin, 2007), p.62.

15 Lindqvist, Sven. *Exterminate All the Brutes*, (Granta, 2018), p.62.

16 Ibid., p.130.

17 Conrad. 2007, p.7.

18 Ibid., p.72.

19 Meredith. 2005, p.539.

20 Stearns, Jason K. *Dancing in the Glory of Monsters*, (Public Affairs, 2012), p.10.

21 Hochschild. 2012, p.321.

22 Conrad. 2007, p.86.

23 Ibid., p.85.

24 Ibid., p.69.

25 Ibid., p.96.

26 Lindqvist. 2018, p.172.

27 Ibid., p.79.

28 Furedi, Frank. 'Why did the protests over George Floyd turn into mass hysteria?', *Spiked*, 9 June 2020: www.spiked-online.com/2020/06/09/why-did-the-protests-over-george-floyd-turn-into-mass-hysteria/

CHRISTOPHER COLUMBUS

1   This is the Taíno name for the island Columbus re-named San Salvador, although some historians maintain Guanahaní may refer to another island in the Bahamas.

2   Urooba, Jamal. 'The Chavistas Who Toppled Columbus: Venezuela's Fight Against Colonialism', Venezuela Analysis, 13 October, 2017: venezuelanalysis.com/analysis/13435

3 'Christopher Columbus in the Golfo Triste': statues.vanderkrogt.net/object.
   php?webpage=ST&record=ve003
4 Carroll, Rory. 'Columbus toppled as indigenous people rise up after five
   centuries', *The Guardian*, 12 October 2007: www.theguardian.com/world/2007/
   oct/12/spain.venezuela
5 Masakatsu, Miyazaki. 'The Legend of "Zipangu", the Land of Gold', *Nipponia*,
   15 June 2008: web-japan.org/nipponia/nipponia45/en/feature/feature01.html
6 Fernández-Armesto, Felipe. *Columbus*, (Oxford University Press, 1991), p.174.
7 The value of a maravedi is difficult to quantify. However, Harry L. Shipman
   in *Humans in Space: 21ˢᵗ Century Frontiers* (Plenum, 1989) pp.333–4, suggests 'the
   purchasing power of a maravedi' is 'roughly 50 cents and the salary equivalent
   being about $1'.
8 Fernández-Armesto. 1991, p.129.
9 Delaney, Carol. 'Columbus's Ultimate Goal: Jerusalem', *Comparative Studies in
   Society and History* 48, no. 02 2006, p.270.
10 Hubers, John. 'It is a Strange Thing: The Millennial Blindness of Christopher
   Columbus', *Missology*, 37:3, July 2009, pp.333–353.
11 Fernández-Armesto. 1991, p.109.
12 De Las Casas, Bartolomé. *A Short Account of the Destruction of the Indies*, tr.
   Anthony Pagden, (Penguin, 2004), p.11.
13 Given the impossibility of exactitude, Las Casas' numbers can only be estimates.
   However, his assessment of the decline in indigenous populations through
   diseases like smallpox and mass killing is accepted by historians as broadly
   accurate.
14 De Las Casas. 2004, p.13.
15 Ibid., p.22.
16 'All the World is Human': www.pbs.org/conquistadors/devaca/lascasas_01.
   html
17 O'Driscoll, Mary T. 'St. Catherine of Siena: Life and Spirituality', *Angelicum* 57,
   no. 3 1980, p.317.
18 De Las Casas. 2004, p.127.
19 Gutiérrez, Gustavo and Müller, Cardinal Gerhard Ludwig. *On The Side of the
   Poor*, tr. Robert A. Krieg and James B. Nickoloff, (Orbis Books, 2015), p.101.
20 Ibid., p.88.
21 Ibid., p.119.
22 Løland, Ole Jakob. 'Hugo Chavez's Appropriation of the Liberationist Legacy
   in Latin America', *Relegere: Studies in Religion and Reception* 6, no. 2, 2016, p.136.

23 Løland. 2016, pp.159–60.

24 Ibid., p.133

25 Ibid., p.139.

26 Zúquete, José Pedro. 'The Missionary Politics of Hugo Chávez', *Latin American Politics and Society* 50, no. 1, 2008, p.104.

27 Løland. 2016, p.152.

28 Ibid., p.155.

29 Gutiérrez. 2015, p.119.

30 Carroll. 2007.

31 Gutiérrez. 2015, p.123.

CECIL RHODES

1   Maylam, Paul. 'Monuments, Memorials and the Mystique of Empire: The Immortalisation of Cecil Rhodes in the Twentieth Century: The Rhodes Commemoration Lecture Delivered on the Occasion of the Centenary of Rhodes' Death', 26 March 2002, *African Sociological Review / Revue Africaine de Sociologie* 6, no. 1, 2002, p.143.

2   Lowry, Donal. '"The granite of the North": race, nation and empire at Cecil Rhodes's mountain mausoleum and Rhodes House, Oxford' in Wrigley, Richard and Craske, Matthew (eds.), *Pantheons: Transformations of a Monumental Idea*, (Routledge, 2004), p.207.

3   Ibid., pp.194–5

4   Ibid., p.196

5   Ibid., p.213.

6   Ferguson, Niall. *Empire*, (Penguin, 2003), p.223.

7   Arendt, Hannah. *The Origins of Totalitarianism*, (Penguin, 2017), p.160

8   Ibid., p.261.

9   Ibid., p.280.

10 Ziegler, Philip. *Legacy*, (Yale University Press, 2008), p.8

11 From: *1877: Cecil Rhodes, "Confession of Faith,"* which can be found here: pages. uoregon.edu/kimball/Rhodes-Confession.htm

12 Ziegler. 2008, Appendix I, p.5.

13 Arendt. 2017, p.280.

14 Lowry. 2004, p.200.

15 Ziegler. 2008, Appendix I, p.7.

16 Ibid., p.8.

17 Olivarius, Ann. 'Cecil Rhodes' statue will gaze down at another kind of scholar', *Financial Times*, 22 February 2018: www.ft.com/content/137025f0–171a-11e8–9c33–02f893d608c2

18 Fairclough, H. Rushton. 'The Rhodes Scholarships', *The Journal of Education* 64, no. 4 (1589), 1906, pp.112 & 118.

19 Osmer-McQuade, Margaret. 'The Legacy of Rhodes', *The New York Times Magazine*, 20 November 1983: www.nytimes.com/1983/11/20/magazine/the-legacy-of-rhodes.html

20 Ziegler. 2008, p.13.

21 Ziegler. 2008, p.239.

22 Khomami, Nadia. 'Oxford students step up campaign to remove Cecil Rhodes statue', *The Guardian*, 22 December 2015: www.theguardian.com/education/2015/dec/22/oxford-students-campaign-cecil-rhodes-statue-oriel-college

23 'OxHRHub Director Sandy Fredman and other Oxford fellows publish letter on Mandela and Rhodes Must Fall', *The Telegraph*, 17 June 2020: ohrh.law.ox.ac.uk/the-telegraph-letters-the-rhodes-must-fall-campaign-follows-the-ideals-of-nelson-mandela/

24 Lasch, Christopher. *The Revolt of the Elites and the Betrayal of Democracy*, (Norton, 1996), pp.44–5.

25 Ibid., p.177.

26 Ibid., p.185.

27 Ibid., p.28.

28 'NYC protester taunts officer as "Black Judas"', Law Officer, 2 July 2020: www.lawofficer.com/nyc-protester-taunts-officer-as-black-judas/

29 Mulraney, Frances. 'White protester screams at three black cops during D.C. protest telling them "they are part of the problem" and yells that she's "allowed to say this to whoever"', *Daily Mail*, 25 June 2020: www.dailymail.co.uk/news/article-8457467/White-female-protester-tells-black-cops-problem.html. Breonna Taylor was a twenty-six-year-old African American EMT nurse shot and killed by police in Louisville, Kentucky on 13 March 2020.

30 Ok, Ekin, Qian, Yi, Strejcek, Brendan, Aquino, Karl. 'Signalling virtuous victimhood as indicators of Dark Triad personalities', *Journal of Personality and Social Psychology*, Jul 02, 2020: psycnet.apa.org/buy/2020–46166–001

31 Ziegler. 2008, p.325.

32 Gladwell, Malcolm. *Talking to Strangers*, (Penguin, 2020), p.346.

33 Khomami. 2015.

Notes

GEORGE WASHINGTON

1   'From George Washington to Robert Morris, 12 April 1786', Founders Online: founders.archives.gov/documents/Washington/04–04–02–0019

2   Morgan, Philip D. '"To Get Quit of Negroes": George Washington and Slavery', *Journal of American Studies* 39, no. 3, 2005, p.425.

3   Chernow, Ron. *Washington: A Life*, (Penguin, 2011), p.800.

4   Ibid.

5   Ibid., p.801.

6   Ibid., p.802.

7   Morgan. 2005, p.415.

8   Bell, David A. *Men on Horseback*, (Farrar, Strauss and Giroux, 2020), p.58.

9   Dunlap, David W. 'Long-Toppled Statue of King George III to Ride Again, From a Brooklyn Studio', *The New York Times*, 20 October 2016: www.nytimes.com/2016/10/21/nyregion/toppled-statue-of-king-george-iii-to-ride-again.html

10 Chernow. 2011, p.726.

11 Plato, *The Republic*, tr. R.E. Allen, (Yale University Press, 2006), p.286.

12 Ibid., p.287.

13 Ibid., p.292.

14 Bell. 2020, p.60.

15 Restuccia, Andrew. 'The Sanctification of Donald Trump', *Politico Magazine*, 30 April 2019: www.politico.com/story/2019/04/30/donald-trump-evangelicals-god-1294578

16 LaFrance, Adrienne. 'The Prophecies of Q', *The Atlantic*, June 2020: www.theatlantic.com/magazine/archive/2020/06/qanon-nothing-can-stop-what-is-coming/610567/

17 Kant, Immanuel. 'An Answer to the Question: What is Enlightenment?', *Perpetual Peace and Other Essays*, (Hackett, 1983), p.41.

18 Ibid., p.42.

19 Ibid.

20 De Tocqueville, Alexis. *Democracy in America and Two Essays on America*, (Penguin, 2003), p.642.

21 Luce, Edward. *The Retreat of Western Liberalism*, (Abacus, 2018), p.35.

22 As Shoshana Zuboff points out in *The Age of Surveillance Capitalism* (Profile Books, 2019), General Motors 'employed more people during the height of the Great Depression than either Google or Facebook employs at their heights of market capitalisation'.

23 Cohn, Norman. *The Pursuit of the Millennium*, (Pimlico, 2004), p.21.
24 LaFrance. 2020.
25 Miłosz, Czesław, *The Captive Mind*, tr. Jane Zielonko, (Penguin, 2001), p.29.
26 Miłosz. 2001, p.26.

JOSEPH STALIN

1 Sebestyen, Victor. *Twelve Days: Revolution 1956*, (Phoenix, 2006), p.25.
2 The AVO became the AVH in 1948, although Hungarians continued to call it the AVO. See Sebestyen, 2006, p.28 fn.
3 Ibid., p.31.
4 Ibid., p.36.
5 Ibid., p.119.
6 Khrushchev's Secret Speech, 'On the Cult of Personality and Its Consequences', delivered at the Twentieth Congress of the Communist Party of the Soviet Union, 25 February 1956, History and Public Policy Program Digital Archive, From the Congressional Record: Proceedings and Debates of the 84th Congress, 2nd Session, (22 May 1956–11 June 1956), 1956, CII, Part 7 (4 June 1956), pp.9389–9403. digitalarchive.wilsoncenter.org/document/115995.pdf?v=3c22b71b65b cbbe9fdfadead9419c995
7 Griffith, William E. 'The Petöfi Circle: Forum for Ferment in the Hungarian Thaw', p.20: www.rev.hu/rev/images/content/kiadvanyok/petofikor/ petofikor_griffith.pdf
8 Ibid., p.22.
9 Arendt, Hannah. 'Totalitarian Imperialism: Reflections on the Hungarian Revolution'. *The Journal of Politics* 20, no. 1, 1958, p.23.
10 Sebestyen. 2006, p.31.
11 Paloczi-Horvath, George. *The Undefeated*, (Eland, 1993), p.147.
12 Ibid., p.154.
13 Ibid., pp.231–2.
14 Vajda, Julia. 'The Hungarian Revolution of 1956 as Narrated by Shoah Survivors', in Adam, Christopher, Egervari, Tibor, Laczko, Leslie and Young, Judy, *The 1956 Hungarian Revolution: Hungarian and Canadian Perspectives*, (University of Ottawa Press, 2010), p.128.
15 Paloczi-Horvath. 1993, p.164.
16 At the height of Stalinist terror in the Soviet Union, the prominent politicians Grigory Zinoviev and Lev Kamenev were sentenced to be executed on the

same day. Zinoviev begged his executioner, the merciless V.M. Blockhin, known to wear a butcher's apron during executions to protect his uniform, for mercy. When Zinoviev's pleas for the executioner to call Stalin failed, he went down on his knees and licked Blockhin's boots. Kamenev, on the other hand, appalled by Zinoviev's snivelling pleas, simply said, 'we deserved this because of our unworthy attitude'. They were both shot through the back of the head. The bullets were pulled out of their skulls, cleaned up and sent as relics to Genrikh Yagoda, head of the Secret Police. Two years later, Yagoda himself was purged and shot. Stalin delighted in hearing about the degradation of his enemies and when his head of security, Karl Pauker, re-enacted Zinoviev's futile pleading, Stalin almost passed out from laughter. The following August, Pauker became the first of Stalin's courtiers to be executed. He, too, was shot. (See Simon Sebag Montefiore. *Stalin*, Weidenfeld & Nicolson, 2003, pp.201–2 and 224–5).

17 Kołakowski, Leszek. 'The Death of Gods', in *Is God Happy?*, (Penguin, 2012), p.6.
18 Ibid., p.16.
19 Paloczi-Horvath. 1993, p.178.
20 Ibid., p.195.
21 Kołakowski. 2012, p.18.
22 Nietzsche, Friedrich. *The Gay Science*, tr, Walter Kaufmann, (Vintage, 1974), p.181.
23 Ibid., p.280.
24 Kołakowski. 2012, p.19.
25 Griffith. p.24.
26 Sebestyen. 2006, p.265.
27 Ibid., p.269.
28 Polanyi, Michael. 'The Message of the Hungarian Revolution', *The American Scholar* 35, no. 4, 1966, p.676.
29 Paloczi-Horvath. 1993, p.251.
30 Arendt. 1958, p.21.
31 Orwell, George. *Nineteen Eighty-Four*, (Penguin, 2013), p.60.

YAGAN

1 McGlade, H. 'The repatriation of Yagan: a story of manufacturing dissent', *Law Text Culture*, 4, 1998, p.245.

2   Reece, R.H.W. 'Yagan (1795–1833)', *Australian Dictionary of Biography*: adb.anu. edu.au/biography/yagan-2826

3   'Yagan, The Black Napoleon and Other Aboriginal Warriors. Exciting Incidents of the Old Days,' *Call*, 14 December 1923: trove.nla.gov.au/newspaper/article /210904557?searchTerm=Yagan

4   Ibid.

5   'Yagan, "Wallace" of the Aborigines: A Stirring Epic of Swan River Conflict With Colonists', *The Daily News*, 23 December 1933: trove.nla.gov.au/newspaper/ar ticle/82915936?searchTerm=Yagan

6   Pascoe, Bruce. *Dark Emu*, (Scribe, 2018), p.179.

7   Broome, Richard. *Aboriginal Australians*, (Allen & Unwin, 2019), p.40.

8   Dawson, Barbara. *In the Eye of the Beholder*, (ANU Press, 2015), p.17.

9   Ibid., pp.22–3.

10 Ibid., p.21.

11 Madley. 2008, pp.77–8.

12 Madley, Benjamin. 'From Terror to Genocide: Britain's Tasmanian Penal Colony and Australia's History Wars', *Journal of British Studies* 47, no. 1, 2008, p.92.

13 Ibid., p.95.

14 'The Abandonment of Gilberton', *The Queenslander*, 4 April 1874: trove.nla. gov.au/newspaper/article/18330241

15 'Destructive Fire At Perth', *The Perth Gazette and Western Australian Journal*, 16 March 1833: trove.nla.gov.au/newspaper/article/642175?browse=ndp%3Abr owse%2Ftitle%2FP%2Ftitle%2F6%2F1833%2F03%2F16%2Fpage%2F44%2F article%2F642175

16 'The Revenge Of Yagan', *Clare's Weekly*, 27 August 1897: trove.nla.gov.au/ newspaper/article/256022519?searchTerm=Yagan

17 'Yagan of Mount Eliza. Prince and Outlaw. A Tale of Perth in 1833,' *Western Mail*, 16 July 1915: trove.nla.gov.au/newspaper/article/37428750?searchTerm =Yagan

18 'Yagan, "Wallace" of the Aborigines: A Stirring Epic of Swan River Conflict With Colonists', *The Daily News*, 23 September 1933: trove.nla.gov.au/newspaper/ article/82915936?searchTerm=Yagan

19 'Death Of Yagan', *Truth*, 24 March 1929: trove.nla.gov.au/newspaper/article /208718425?searchTerm=Yagan

20 'Murder of Thomas and John Velvick by a Party of Natives,' *The Perth Gazette and Western Australian Journal*, 4 May 1833: trove.nla.gov.au/newspaper/article

/642096?browse=ndp%3Abrowse%2Ftitle%2FP%2Ftitle%2F6%2F1833%2F0
5%2F04%2Fpage%2F73%2Farticle%2F642096

21 Battye, R.J.S. 'Yagan The Incorrigible', *Truth*, 10 March 1929: trove.nla.gov.au/
newspaper/article/208718064?searchTerm=Yagan

22 'Yagan and Heegan, Two Natives Shot. William Keats, a Youth Speared', *The
Perth Gazette and Western Australian Journal,*' 13 July 1833: trove.nla.gov.au/
newspaper/article/641988?searchTerm=Yagan

23 'Yagan's Head', *The Perth Gazette and Western Australian* Journal, 13 December
1834: trove.nla.gov.au/newspaper/article/641141?searchTerm=Yagan

24 Ackland, Richard. 'Where to next for 18C, and why the pub test won't work',
The Guardian, 12 March 2017: www.theguardian.com/commentisfree/2017/
mar/13/where-to-next-for-18c-and-why-the-pub-test-wont-work

25 Daley, Paul. 'The story of Yagan's head is a shameful reminder of colonialism's
legacy', *The Guardian*, 31 August 2017: www.theguardian.com/australia-news/
postcolonial-blog/2017/aug/31/the-story-of-yagans-head-is-a-shameful-
reminder-of-colonialisms-legacy

26 Mantel, Hilary. 'The princess myth', *The Guardian*, 26 August 2017: www.
theguardian.com/books/2017/aug/26/the-princess-myth-hilary-mantel-on-
diana

27 Lewis, C.S. *A Grief Observed*, (Faber and Faber, 1961).

28 Derrida, Jacques. *Adieu to Emmanuel Levinas*, tr. Pascale-Anne Brault and Michael
Nass, (Stanford University Press, 1999), p.6

SADDAM HUSSEIN

1 Maass, Peter. 'The Toppling: How the Media Inflated the Fall of Saddam's
Statue in Firdos Square', ProPublica, 3 January 2011: www.propublica.org/
article/the-toppling-saddam-statue-firdos-square-baghdad

2 Ibid.

3 Fahmy, Shahira. '"They Took it Down": Exploring Determinants of Visual
Reporting in the Toppling of the Saddam Statue in National and International
Newspapers', *Mass Communication and Society*, 10(2), 2007, pp.143–170.

4 Nixon, John. *Debriefing the President*, (Corgi, 2017), p.30.

5 Kaufmann, Chaim. 'Threat Inflation and the Failure of the Marketplace of
Ideas: The Selling of the Iraq War', *International Security* 29, no. 1, 2004, p.19.

6 Nixon. 2017, pp.51–2.

7 Marozzi, Justin. *Baghdad*, (Penguin, 2015), p.352.

8   Kaufmann. 2004, p.18.
9   Duelfer, Charles A., and Stephen Benedict Dyson. 'Chronic Misperception and International Conflict: The U.S.-Iraq Experience', *International Security* 36, no. 1, 2011, p.91.
10 Ibid., p.86.
11 Ibid., p.92.
12 Shermer, Michael. *The Believing Brain*, (Robinson, 2011), p.6.
13 Gilbert, D.T. 'How Mental Systems Believe', *American Psychologist*, 46(2), 1991, p.116.
14 Makiya, Kanan. *Republic of Fear*, (University of California Press, 1998), p.78.
15 Ibid., p.81.
16 Ibid., p.115.
17 Foucault, Michel. *The Order of Things*, (Tavistock Publications, 1970), pp.xv–xxiv.
18 Borges, Jorge Luis. 'John Wilkins' Analytical Language', *The Total Library*, tr. Esther Allen, Suzanne Jill Levine and Eliot Weinberger, (Penguin, 2001), pp.229–232.
19 Nixon. 2017, p.86.
20 Makiya, 1998, p.276.

B.R. AMBEDKAR

1   Koushik, Janardhan. '28 arrested after Ambedkar statue vandalised in Tamil Nadu's Vedaranyam', *The Indian Express*, 26 August 2019: indianexpress.com/article/india/28-arrested-after-ambedkar-statue-vandalised-in-tamil-nadus-vedaranyam-town/
2   *The Laws of Manu*, tr. Wendy Doniger and Brian K. Smith, (Penguin, 1991), p.242.
3   Ibid., p.182.
4   'My Birth is My Fatal Accident: Ronith Vemula's Searing Letter is an Indictment of Social Prejudices', *The Wire*, 17 January 2019: thewire.in/caste/rohith-vemula-letter-a-powerful-indictment-of-social-prejudices
5   Khilnani, Sunil. *Incarnations*, (Penguin, 2017), p.344.
6   Wilkerson, Isobel. *Caste*, (Allen Lane, 2020), p.121.
7   Stroud, Scott R. 'The Rhetoric of Conversion as Emancipatory Strategy in India: Bhimrao Ambedkar, Pragmatism, and the Turn to Buddhism', *Rhetorica: A Journal of the History of Rhetoric*, 35 (3), 2017, p.315.
8   Ibid. p.340.

9   The full speech, 'What Path to Salvation?', can be found here: www.columbia. edu/itc/mealac/pritchett/00ambedkar/txt_ambedkar_salvation.html#22

10 Wilkerson. 2020, p.18.

11 Ibid., p.25.

12 Ibid., p.386.

13 Stroud. 2017, p.343.

14 Jaffrelot, Christophe. *India's Silent Revolution*, (C. Hurst & Co., 2003), p.21.

15 'Interview: "Ahsan Jafri Was Not a Muslim Fanatic"', *Outlook*, 28 April 2002: www. outlookindia.com/website/story/ahsan-jafri-was-not-a-muslim-fanatic/215350

16 Roy, Arundhati. 'Democracy', *The Algebra of Infinite Justice*, (Flamingo, 2002), p.243.

17 Ibid., pp.257–8.

18 Ibid., p.236.

19 Boehm, Christopher. *Hierarchy in the Forest*, (Harvard University Press, 2001), p.237.

20 Pinker, Steven. *The Better Angels of Our Nature*, (Penguin, 2011).

21 Wilkerson. 2020, p.387.

22 Boehm. 2001, p.254.

23 Wilkerson. 2020, p.388.

24 Boehm. 2001, pp.256–7.

25 Stroud. 2017, p.343.

26 Wilkerson. 2020, pp.370–5.

27 Sturgis, Matthew. *Oscar*, (Head of Zeus, 2018), p.612.

28 Roy. 2002, p.260.

29 These are the closing lines to 'What Path to Salvation?', the speech delivered at the Bombay Presidency Mahar Conference in 1936: www.columbia.edu/ itc/mealac/pritchett/00ambedkar/txt_ambedkar_salvation.html#22

FREDERICK DOUGLASS

1   'The Dred Scott Decision', speech delivered before American Anti-Slavery Society, New York, 14 May 1857. The full text can be found in Douglass, Frederick, *Selected Speeches and Writings*, (Lawrence Hill Books, 1999), p.350. Dred Scott was a Black slave who, in 1857, sued for his freedom in Missouri. He lost the case, a defeat that increased tensions between North and South and pushed the country closer towards Civil War.

2   Kendi, Ibram X. *How To Be An Antiracist*, (Bodley Head, 2019), p.234.

3 Douglass, Frederick. *Narrative of the Life of Frederick Douglass, an American Slave*, (Penguin, 2014), p.18.

4 Ibid., pp.20–1.

5 Ibid., pp.34–5.

6 Ibid., p.58.

7 Ibid., p.60.

8 Ibid., p.67.

9 Ibid., p.73.

10 Ibid., p.48.

11 Douglass. 1999, pp.111–117.

12 Douglass, Frederick. *Life and Times of Frederick Douglass*, (independently published, 2019), p.332.

13 For a full account of the meeting see Douglass. 2019, pp.372–5

14 Levine, Robert S. 'Frederick Douglass and Thomas Auld: Reconsidering the Reunion Narrative', *The Journal of African American History* 99, nos. 1–2, 2014, p.34

15 Douglass, Frederick. 'What to the Slave is the Fourth of July?' Douglass, 2014, p.128.

16 Ibid., p.142.

17 Ibid., pp.144–5.

18 Rufo, Christopher F. 'Radicals in the Classroom', *City Journal*, 5 January 2021: www.city-journal.org/radicalism-in-san-diego-schools

19 Doe, Minnie. 'A Student Mob Took Over Bryn Mawr. The College Said Thank You', *Quillette*, 27 December 2020: quillette.com/2020/12/27/a-student-mob-took-over-bryn-mawr-the-college-said-thank-you/

20 Sanzi, Erika, 'Segregation and Sorting as Community Building?' 28 January 2021: sanzi.substack.com/p/segregation-and-sorting-as-community

21 docs.google.com/forms/d/e/1FAIpQLSfPmfeDKBi25_7rUTKkhZ3cyMICQ icp05ReVaeBpEdYUCkyIA/viewform

22 Levari D.E., Gilbert D.T., Wilson T.D., Sievers B., Amodio D.M., Wheatley T. 'Prevalence-induced concept change in human judgment', *Science*, 29 June 2018; 360(6396):1465–1467: wjh-www.harvard.edu/~dtg/LEVARI2018COMPLETE. pdf

23 Kendi, Ibram X. 'Pass an Anti-Racist Constitutional Amendment,' *Politico Magazine*: www.politico.com/interactives/2019/how-to-fix-politics-in-america/inequality/pass-an-anti-racist-constitutional-amendment/

24 Pinker, Steven. *Enlightenment Now*, (Allen Lane, 2018) pp.215–19. Increased intolerance and respect has led to increased opportunity. For instance: Ruiz-

Notes

Grossman, Sarah. *Record Number of Women of Color Running for Congress in 2020*, (*Huffington Post*, 11 August 2020).

25 Hughes, Coleman. 'The Case for Black Optimism', *Quillette*, 28 September 2019: quillette.com/2019/09/28/the-case-for-black-optimism/

26 Douglass, Frederick. 'Self-made Men', 1872. The complete lecture is here: monadnock.net/douglass/self-made-men.html

27 Douglass, Frederick. *My Bondage and My Freedom*, (Penguin, 2003), pp.122–3.

28 'West India Emancipation', speech delivered at Canandaigua, New York, 3 August 1857 in Douglass, Frederick, 1999, p.367.

29 West, Cornel. *Black Prophetic Fire*, (Beacon Press, 2014), p.38.

30 West. 2014, p.31.

31 Nietzsche, Friedrich. *Beyond Good and Evil*, tr. Walter Kaufmann, (Vintage, 1966), p.89.

32 Douglass. 2019, p.332.

EPILOGUE

1 Hubbard, Ben. 'Syrian Expert Who Shielded Palmyra Antiquities Meets a Grisly Death at ISIS' Hands', *The New York Times*, 19 August 2015: www.nytimes.com/2015/08/20/world/middleeast/isis-palmyra-syria-antiquities-scholar-beheaded.html

2 Daoud, Kamel. 'ISIS' War on Christmas', *The New York Times*, 1 January 2016: www.nytimes.com/2016/01/02/opinion/isis-war-on-christmas.html

3 'Syrian archaeologist "killed in palmyra" by IS militants', *BBC News*, 19 August 2015: www.bbc.co.uk/news/world-middle-east-33984006

4 'The Martyr of Palmyra – Khaled Al Asaad': www.icomos.org/images/DOCUMENTS/Secretariat/2016/Memoire_Khaled_al_Asaad_18082016/Khaled_al_Asaad_Booklet_DGAM_2016.pdf

5 Ibid.

6 Shaheen, Kareem and Black, Ian. 'Beheaded Syrian scholar refused to lead Isis to hidden Palmyra antiquities', *The Guardian*, 19 August 2019: www.theguardian.com/world/2015/aug/18/isis-beheads-archaeologist-syria

7 Veyne, Paul. *Palmyra*, tr. Teresa Lavender Fagan, (University of Chicago Press, 2017), p.2.

8 Ibid. p.25.

9 Francesco Rutelli, a former mayor of Rome, called a 'corridor for culture'. The restoration team baptised them 'the war-wounded of Palmyra'.

299

10 Brown, Mark. 'Palmyra's Arch of Triumph recreated in Trafalgar Square', *The Guardian*, 19 April 2016: www.theguardian.com/culture/2016/apr/19/palmyras-triumphal-arch-recreated-in-trafalgar-square

11 Veyne. 2017, p.8.

12 Butcher, Prof. Kevin. 'Palmyra: IS threat to "Venice of the Sands"', *The Guardian*, 15 May 2015: www.bbc.co.uk/news/world-middle-east-32748392

13 Davies, Caroline and Shaheen, Kareem. 'Khaled al-Asaad profile: the Howard Carter of Palmyra', *The Guardian*, 19 August 2015: www.theguardian.com/world/2015/aug/19/khaled-al-asaad-profile-syria-isis-howard-carter-palmyra-archaeology

14 Mary Bergstein. 'Palmyra and Palmyra: Look On These Stones, Ye Mighty, And Despair', *Arion: A Journal of Humanities and the Classics* 24, no. 2, 2016, p.28.

15 Cicero, Marcus Tullius. *Cicero: Brutus, Orator,* tr. G.L. Hendrickson and H.M. Hubbell, (Loeb, 1971), Chapter 34, Section 120.

16 Trevithick, Alan. 'Some Structural and Sequential Aspects of the British Imperial Assemblages at Delhi: 1877–1911', *Modern Asian Studies* 24, no. 3, 1990, p.577.

17 Cannadine, David. 'Where statues go to die', *BBC News*, 21 January 2008: news.bbc.co.uk/1/hi/magazine/7196530.stm

18 Coughlan, Sean. 'TV historian rejects "nonsense" over keeping statues', *BBC News*, 2 February 2021: www.bbc.co.uk/news/education-55893706

19 'Mitch Landrieu's Speech on the Removal of Confederate Monuments in New Orleans', *The New York Times*, 23 May 2017: www.nytimes.com/2017/05/23/opinion/mitch-landrieus-speech-transcript.html

20 Cox, Karen L. 2021, p.39.

21 Weiss, Sabrina. 'When we tear down racist statues, what should replace them?', *Wired*, 12 June 2020: www.wired.co.uk/article/topple-racist-statues-uk

22 Kass, John. 'While we're toppling offensive symbols, what about the Democratic Party?', *Chicago Tribune*, 18 August 2017: www.chicagotribune.com/columns/john-kass/ct-statues-democrats-kass-0820-20170818-column.html

23 This is, of course, also true of people from historically marginalised groups who, when they become a dominant cultural power, demand statues in public spaces. See, Bellafante, Ginia, 'Where Are the Statues of L.G.B.T.Q. Pioneers? Here Are 11 Worthy New Yorkers,' *The New York Times*, 17 May 2019: www.nytimes.com/2019/05/17/nyregion/lgbtq-statues-new-york.html

24 Wilkerson, Isobel. 'Apartheid Is Demolished. Must Its Monuments Be?' *The New York Times*, 25 September 1994: www.nytimes.com/1994/09/25/world/apartheid-is-demolished-must-its-monuments-be.html

25 Ibid.

26 Ibid.

27 Kenton, Luke. 'CNN analyst suggests tearing down all George Washington and Thomas Jefferson statues because they were slave owners as protesters deface more memorials and call for the "Spokesman of the South" Henry Grady to be removed from Atlanta', *Mail Online*, 12 June 2020: www.dailymail. co.uk/news/article-8413185/CNN-analyst-calls-remove-George-Washington-Thomas-Jefferson-statues-owned-slaves.html

28 Kundera, Milan. 'Part Eight: Paths in the Fog', *Testaments Betrayed: an Essay in Nine Parts*, tr. Linda Asher, (Faber and Faber, 1995) p.238.

29 Sert, J.L., Léger, F., and Giedion, S. *Nine Points on Monumentality*. You can read the essay here: monoskop.org/images/7/72/Sert_Leger_Giedion_1943_1958_Nine_Points_on_Monumentality.pdf

30 Sanghera, Sathnam. *Empireland*, (Viking, 2021), p.200.

31 Benjamin, Walter. 'Theses on the Philosophy of History', *Illuminations*, tr. Harry Zorn, (Bodley Head, 2015), p.249.

32 Veyne. 2017, p.85.

33 Nietzsche, Friedrich. *The Genealogy of Morals*, tr. Walter Kaufmann, (Vintage, 1989), p.62.

BIBLIOGRAPHY

Adam, Christopher, Egervari, Tibor, Laczko, Leslie and Young, Judy. *The 1956 Hungarian Revolution: Hungarian and Canadian Perspectives*, (University of Ottawa Press, 2010).

Aeschylus. *Aeschylus II*, tr. Richmond Lattimore, (University of Chicago Press, 2013).

Ali, Ayaan Hirsi. *Prey*, (HarperCollins 2021).

Almond, Philip C. *Heaven & Hell in Enlightenment England*, (Cambridge University Press, 1984).

Ambedkar, B.R. *Annihilation of Caste*, (Verso, 2016).

Anderson, Jon Lee. *The Fall of Baghdad*, (Abacus, 2005).

Arendt, Hannah. *Eichmann in Jerusalem*, (Penguin, 2006).

Arendt, Hannah. *The Human Condition*, (University of Chicago Press, 2018).

Arendt, Hannah. *The Origins of Totalitarianism*, (Penguin, 2017).

Augustine of Hippo. *City of God*, tr. Henry Bettenson, (Penguin, 1984).

Augustine of Hippo. *Confessions*, tr. R.S. Pine-Coffin, (Penguin, 1961).

Aurelius, Marcus. *Meditations*, tr. Martin Hammond, (Penguin, 2006).

Bataille, Georges. *Eroticism*, tr. Mary Dalwood, (Marion Boyars, 1987).

Bataille, Georges. *On Nietzsche*, tr. Bruce Boone, (Continuum, 2004).

Bataille, Georges. *The Accursed Share Volume I*, tr. Robert Hurley, (Zone Books, 1988).

Bataille, Georges. *Visions of Excess: Selected Writings 1927–1939*, tr. Allan Stoekl, (University of Minnesota Press, 1985).

Baudelaire, Charles. *Les Fleurs du Mal*, (Libraire Générale Française, 1972).

Beck, Aaron T. *Prisoners of Hate*, (HarperCollins, 1999).

Becker, Jasper. *City of Heavenly Tranquility*, (Oxford University Press, 2008).

Behrendt, Larissa. *Finding Eliza*, (University of Queensland Press, 2016).

Bell, David A. *Men on Horseback*, (Farrar, Strauss and Giroux, 2020).

Benjamin, Walter. *Illuminations*, tr. Harry Zorn, (Bodley Head, 2015).

Besançon, Alain. *The Forbidden Image*, tr. Jane Marie Todd, (University of Chicago Press, 2009).

Bleiberg, Edward and Weissberg, Stephanie. *Striking Power: Iconoclasm in Ancient Egypt*, (Pulitzer Arts Foundation, 2019).

Blight, David W. *Frederick Douglass*, (Simon & Schuster, 2018).

Bo, Ma. *Blood Red Sunset*, tr. Howard Goldbaltt, (Penguin, 1996).

Bibliography

Boehm, Christopher. *Hierarchy in the Forest*, (Harvard University Press, 2001).

Boym, Svetlana. *The Future of Nostalgia*, (Basic Books, 2001).

Braudel, Fernand. *A History of Civilisations*, tr. Richard Mayne, (Penguin, 1993).

Bridgen, Susan. *New Worlds, Lost Worlds*, (Penguin, 2000).

Borges, Jorge Luis. *The Total Library*, tr. Esther Allen, Jill Levine and Eliot Weinberger, (Penguin, 1999).

Broome, Richard. *Aboriginal Australians*, (Allen & Unwin, 2019).

Browning, Christopher R. *Ordinary Men*, (Penguin, 2001).

Brubaker, Leslie. *Inventing Byzantine Iconoclasm*, (Bristol Classical Press, 2012).

Buber, Martin. *Between Man and Man*, tr. Ronald Gregor Smith, (T & T Clark, 1984).

Buber, Martin. *I and Thou*, tr. Ronald Gregor Smith, (Routledge, 2002).

Budge, Wallis, E.A. (tr.). *The Egyptian Book of the Dead*. (Penguin, 2008).

Burke, Edmund. *Reflections on the Revolution in France*, (Penguin, 2004).

Butler, Judith. *Precarious Life*, (Verso, 2006).

Campbell, Bradley & Manning, Jason. *The Rise of Victimhood Culture*, (Palgrave, 2018).

Carlin, Dan. *The End Is Always Near*, (William Collins, 2019).

Carroll, Rory. *Commandante*, (Canongate, 2013).

Case, Anne and Deaton, Angus. *Deaths of Despair*, (Princeton University Press, 2020).

Catton, Bruce. *A Stillness at Appomattox*, (Anchor Books, 1990).

Cervantes, Fernando. *Conquistadores*, (Allen Lane, 2020).

Chang, Jung and Halliday, Jon. *Mao: The Unknown Story*, (Vintage, 2007).

Chernow, Ron. *Washington: A Life*, (Penguin, 2011).

Cicero, Marcus Tullius. *Cicero: Brutus, Orator*, tr. G.L. Hendrickson and H.M. Hubbell, (Loeb, 1971).

Cicero, Marcus Tullius. *On The Good Life*, tr. Michael Grant, (Penguin, 1971).

Cohn, Norman. *Europe's Inner Demons*, (Pimlico, 2005).

Cohn, Norman. *The Pursuit of the Millennium*, (Pimlico, 2004).

Confucius. *The Analects*, tr. D.C. Lau, (Penguin, 1979).

Conrad, Joseph. *Heart of Darkness*, (Penguin, 2007).

Cook, Deborah. *Adorno, Foucault and the Critique of the West*, (Verso, 2018).

Cooney, Kara. *The Woman Who Would Be God*, (Oneworld, 2014).

Cortés, Hernán. *Letters from Mexico*, tr. Anthony Pagden, (Yale University Press, 1986).

Cox, Karen L. *No Common Ground*, (University of North Carolina Press, 2021).

Crenshaw, Kimberlé, Gotanda, Neil, Peller, Gary and Thomas, Kendall (eds.). *Critical Race Theory*, (The New Press, 1995).

Crosby, Alfred W. *Ecological Imperialism*, (Cambridge University Press, 1986).

Curtis, John. *Shipwreck of the Stirling Castle*, (independently published, 2011).

Dalley, Stephanie (tr.). *Myths from Mesopotamia*, (Oxford University Press, 2008).

Dan, Yu. *Confucius From the Heart*, tr. Esther Tyldesley, (Pan, 2009).

Dawson, Barbara. *In the Eye of the Beholder*, (ANU Press, 2015).

De Las Casas, Bartolomé. *A Short Account of the Destruction of the Indies*, tr. Anthony Pagden, (Penguin, 2004).

Deleuze, Gilles and Guattari, Félix. *Anti-Oedipus*, tr. Robert Hurley, Mark Seem and Helen R. Lane, (University of Minnesota Press, 1983).

Derrida, Jacques. *Adieu to Emmanuel Levinas*, tr. Pascale-Anne Brault and Michael Nass, (Stanford University Press, 1999).

Derrida, Jacques. *Margins of Philosophy*, tr. Alan Bass, (University of Chicago Press, 1982).

Derrida, Jacques. *Writing and Difference*, tr. Alan Bass, (University of Chicago Press, 1978).

De Sade, Marquis. *Justine or the Misfortunes of Virtue*, tr. John Phillips, (Oxford University Press, 2012).

De Sade, Marquis. *Philosophy in the Boudoir*, tr. Joachim Neugroschel, (Penguin, 2006).

De Sade, Marquis. *Selected Letters*, tr. W.J. Strachan, (Peter Owen, 1992).

De Tocqueville, Alexis. *Democracy in America and Two Essays on America*, (Penguin, 2003).

Díaz del Castillo, Bernal. *The Conquest of New Spain*, tr. J.M. Cohen, (Penguin, 1963).

Dikötter, Frank. *Mao's Great Famine*, (Bloomsbury, 2010).

Dikötter, Frank. *The Cultural Revolution*, (Bloomsbury, 2017).

Djilas, Milovan. *Conversations with Stalin*, tr. Michael B. Petrovich, (Penguin, 2014).

Doniger, Wendy and Smith, Brian K. (trs.). *The Laws of Manu*, (Penguin, 1991).

Dostoyevsky, Fyodor. *Crime and Punishment*, tr. Oliver Ready, (Penguin, 2014).

Douglass, Frederick. *Life and Times of Frederick Douglass*, (independently published, 2019).

Douglass, Frederick. *My Bondage and My Freedom*, (Penguin, 2003).

Douglass, Frederick. *Narrative of the Life of Frederick Douglass, an American Slave*, (Penguin, 2014).

Douglass, Frederick. *Selected Speeches and Writings*, (Lawrence Hill Books, 1999).

Du Bois, W.E.B. *The Souls of Black Folk*, (Clydesdale Press, 2019).

Duncan, Mike. *The Storm Before the Storm*, (Public Affairs, 2017).

Eliade, Mircea. *A History of Religious Ideas Volume 1*, tr. Willard R. Trask, (University of Chicago Press, 1981).

Eliade, Mircea. *A History of Religious Ideas Volume 2*, tr. Willard R. Trask, (University of Chicago Press, 1984).

Eliade, Mircea. *A History of Religious Ideas Volume 3*, tr. Alf Hiltebeitel and Diane Apostolos-Cappadona, (University of Chicago Press, 1988).

Eliot, George. *Middlemarch*, (Penguin, 1994).

Eliot, T.S. *Collected Poems 1909–1962*, (Faber and Faber, 2002).

Elkin, A.P. *Aboriginal Men of High Degree*, (University of Queensland Press, 1994).

Ellenberger, Henri F. *The Discovery of the Unconscious*, (Basic Books, 1970).

Equiano, Olaudah. *The Interesting Narrative and Other Narratives*, (Penguin, 2003).

Euripides. *Euripides V*, tr. Charles R. Walker, (University of Chicago Press, 2013).

Fox, Robin Lane. *Augustine*, (Penguin, 2016).

Girard, René. *The Scapegoat*, tr, Yvonne Freccero, (Johns Hopkins University Press, 1986).

Girard, René. *Violence and the Sacred*, tr. Patrick Gregory, (Bloomsbury, 2013).

Gladwell, Malcolm. *Talking to Strangers*, (Penguin, 2020).

Gormley, Antony & Gayford, Martin. *Shaping the World: Sculpture from Prehistory to Now*, (Thames & Hudson, 2020).

Gourevitch, Philip. *We Wish to Inform You That Tomorrow We Will Be Killed with Our Families*, (Picador, 2000).

Fackenheim, Emil L. *To Mend the World*, (Indiana University Press, 1994).

Faust, Drew Gilpin. *The Republic of Suffering*, (Vintage Civil War Library, 2008).

Ferguson, Niall. *Empire*, (Penguin, 2003).

Ferguson, Niall. *The Square and the Tower*, (Penguin, 2018).

Fernández-Armesto, Felipe. *Columbus*, (Oxford University Press, 1991).

Fields, Karen E. and Fields, Barbara J. *Racecraft*, (Verso, 2014).

Fitzgerald, F. Scott. *The Crack-Up*, (New Directions, 1993).

Foucault, Michel. *Discipline and Punish*, tr. Alan Sheridan, (Peregrine Books, 1979).

Foucault, Michel. *History of Madness*, tr. Jonathan Murphy and Jean Khalfa, (Routledge, 2009).

Foucault, Michel. *Power/Knowledge*, tr. Colin Gordon, Leo Marshall, John Mepham and Kate Soper, (The Harvester Press, 1980).

Foucault, Michel. *The Archaeology of Knowledge*, tr. A.M. Sheridan Smith, (Tavistock, 1972).

Foucault, Michel. *The Order of Things*, (Tavistock Publications, 1970).

Fr Thaddeus. *Life of Blessed Father John Forest*, (London: Burns & Oates Limited, 1888).

Frankl, Viktor E. *Man's Search for Meaning*, tr, Isle Lasch, (Rider, 2004).

Freud, Sigmund. *Volume 11: On Metapsychology*, tr. James Strachey, (Pelican, 1984).

Freud, Sigmund. *Volume 12: Civilisation, Society and Religion*, tr. James Strachey, (Pelican, 1985).

Furedi, Frank. *How Fear Works*, (Bloomsbury, 2019).

Gaskill, Malcolm. *Witchfinders*, (John Murray Publishers, 2005).

Gibbon, Edward. *The History of the Decline and Fall of the Roman Empire*, (Penguin, 2000).

Gretton, Dan, *I You We Them*, (William Heinemann, 2019).

Gryn, Hugo with Gryn, Naomi. *Chasing Shadows*, (Penguin, 2000).

Gutiérrez, Gustavo and Müller, Cardinal Gerhard Ludwig. *On the Side of the Poor*, tr. Robert A. Krieg and James B. Nickoloff, (Orbis Books, 2015).

Hadot, Pierre. *The Inner Citadel*, tr. Michael Chase, (Harvard University Press, 2001).

Hadot, Pierre. *What is Philosophy?* tr. Michael Chase, (Harvard University Press, 2002).

Haidt, Jonathan. *The Righteous Mind*, (Penguin, 2012).

Halbwachs, Maurice. *On Collective Memory*, tr. Lewis A. Coser, (University of Chicago Press, 1992).

Hall, Edith. *The Ancient Greeks*, (Vintage, 2015).

Havel, Václav. *Letters to Olga*, tr. Paul Wilson, (Faber and Faber, 1990).

Herrin, Judith. *Byzantium*, (Penguin, 2007).

Hesiod. *Theogony and Works and Days*, tr. Dorothea Wender, (Penguin, 1973).

Hinton, Devon E. and Hinton Alexander L. (eds.). *Genocide and Mass Violence*, (Cambridge University Press, 2015).

Hobbes, Thomas. *Leviathan*, (Dent, 1973).

Hochschild, Adam. *Bury the Chains*, (Pan, 2005).

Hochschild, Adam. *King Leopold's Ghost*, (Pan, 2012).

Hollander, Paul. *From Benito Mussolini to Hugo Chavez*, (Cambridge University Press, 2016).

Hooks, Bell. *All About Love*, (Morrow, 2001).

Horkeheimer, Max and Adorno, Theodor W. *Dialectic of Enlightenment*, tr. Edmund Jephcott, (Stanford University Press, 2002).

Horwitz, Tony. *Midnight Rising*, (Picador, 2011).

Horwitz, Tony. *Spying on the South*, (Penguin, 2019).

Hume, David. *A Treatise of Human Nature*, (Penguin, 1985).

Ignotus, Paul. *Political Prisoners*, (Routledge & Keegan Paul, 1959).

Isenberg, Nancy. *White Trash*, (Atlantic Books, 2017).

Jabès, Edmond. *The Book of Questions Volume I*, tr. Rosmarie Waldrop, (Wesleyan University Press, 1991).

Jabès, Edmond. *The Book of Questions Volume II*, tr. Rosmarie Waldrop, (Wesleyan University Press, 1991).

Jaffrelot, Christophe. *India's Silent Revolution*, (C. Hurst & Co., 2003).

Janney, Caroline E. *Remembering the Civil War*, (University of North Carolina Press, 2013).

Jicai, Feng. *Ten Years of Madness*, tr. Jane Y. Burk, (China Books, 1996).

Jisheng, Yang. *Tombstone*, tr. Stacy Mosher and Guo Jian, (Penguin, 2012).

Jung, C.G. *Archetypes and the Collective Unconscious*, tr. R.F.C. Hull, (Princeton University Press, 1980).

Kakutani, Michiko. *The Denial of Truth*, (William Collins, 2018).

Kant, Immanuel. *Critique of Pure Reason*, tr. Werner S. Puhar, (Hackett, 1996).

Kant, Immanuel. *Groundwork of the Metaphysic of Morals*, tr. H.J. Paton, (Harper Torchbooks, 1956).

Kant, Immanuel. *Lectures on Ethics*, tr. Louis Infield, (Methuen, 1979).

Kant, Immanuel. *Perpetual Peace and Other Essays*, (Hackett, 1983).

Kantorowicz, Ernst H. *The King's Two Bodies*, (Princeton University Press, 2016).

Kapuściński, Ryszard. *The Other*, tr. Antonia Lloyd-Jones, (Verso, 2018).

Kendi, Ibram X. and Blain, Keisha N. (eds.). *Four Hundred Souls*, (Bodley Head, 2021).

Kendi, Ibram X. *How To Be An Antiracist*, (Bodley Head, 2019).

Kenyon, Paul. *Dictatorland*, (Head of Zeus, 2018).

Kettler, Andrew. *The Smell of Slavery*, (Cambridge University Press, 2020).

Khilnani, Sunil. *Incarnations*, (Penguin, 2017).

Kierkegaard, Søren. *Either/Or Volume I*, tr. David F. Swenson and Lillian Marvin Swenson, (Princeton University Press, 1971).

Kierkegaard, Søren. *Either/Or Volume II*, tr. Walter Lowrie, (Princeton University Press, 1971).

Kierkegaard, Søren. *Fear and Trembling. Repetition*, tr. Howard V. Hong and Edna H. Hong, (Princeton University Press, 1983).

Kierkegaard, Søren. *Works of Love*, tr. Howard V. Hong and Edna H. Hong, (Harper Perennial, 2009).

King Jr., The Reverend Dr. Martin Luther. *A Gift of Love*, (Beacon Press, 2012).

Kitto, H.D.F. *Greek Tragedy*, (Routledge, 2011).

Kołakowski, Leszek. *Is God Happy?*, (Penguin, 2012).

Kollwitz, Kaethe. *The Diary and Letters of Kaethe Kollwitz*, tr. Richard and Clara Winston, (Northwestern University Press, 1988).

Kolrud, Kristine and Prusac, Marina (eds.). *Iconoclasm from Antiquity to Modernity*, (Routledge, 2014).

Kundera, Milan. *Testaments Betrayed: An Essay in Nine Parts*, tr. Linda Asher, (Faber and Faber, 1995).

Kushner, Harold S. *When Bad Things Happen to Good People*, (Pan, 1981).

Lambert, Johanna. *Wise Women of the Dreamtime*, (Inner Traditions International, 1993).

Lasch, Christopher. *The Culture of Narcissism*, (Norton, 2018).

Lasch, Christopher. *The Revolt of the Elites and the Betrayal of Democracy*, (Norton, 1996).

Lefebvre, Georges. *The Coming of the French Revolution*, tr. R.R. Palmer, (Princeton University Press, 2005).

Lefebvre, Georges. *The Great Fear of 1789*, tr. Joan White, (NLB, 1973).

Levinas, Emmanuel. *Difficult Freedom*, tr. Seán Hand, (Johns Hopkins University Press, 1997).

Levinas, Emmanuel. *Existence and Existents*, tr. Alphonso Lingis, (Martinus Nijhoff, 1978).

Levinas, Emmanuel. *Nine Talmudic Readings*, tr. Annette Aronowicz, (Indiana University Press, 2019).

Levitsky, Steven and Ziblatt, Daniel. *How Democracies Die*, (Penguin, 2018).

Lewis, C.S. *A Grief Observed*, (Faber and Faber, 1961).

Lindqvist, Sven. *Exterminate All the Brutes*, (Granta, 2018).

Locke, John. *Political Writings*, (Penguin, 1993).

Luce, Edward. *The Retreat of Western Liberalism*, (Abacus, 2018).

Lukianoff, Greg and Haidt, Jonathan. *The Coddling of the American Mind*, (Allen Lane, 2018).

Lyotard, Jean-François. *The Postmodern Condition*, tr. Geoff Bennington and Brian Massumi, (Manchester University Press, 2019).

Machiavelli, Niccoló. *The Prince*, tr. Russell Price, (Cambridge University Press, 2016).

Makiya, Kanan. *Republic of Fear*, (University of California Press, 1998).

Makiya, Kanan. *The Monument*, (University of California Press, 2004).

Mao Tse-Tung. *Quotations from Chairman Mao Tse-Tung*.

Marcuse, Herbert. *The Essential Marcuse*, (Beacon Press, 2007).

Marcuse, Herbert. *One-Dimensional Man*, (Routledge, 2002).

Marozzi, Justin. *Baghdad*, (Penguin, 2015).

Marshall, Peter. *Heretics and Believers*, (Yale University Press, 2017).

Bibliography

Mauss, Marcel. *The Gift*, tr. W.D. Halls, (Routledge, 2002).

May, Simon. *Love*, (Oxford University Press, 2019).

Mayer, Arno J. *The Furies*, (Princeton University Press, 2002).

McMahon, Darrion. *Enemies of the Enlightenment*, (Oxford University Press, 2001).

McPherson, James M. *Battle Cry of Freedom*, (Penguin, 1990).

Mendelssohn, Moses. *Philosophical Writings*, tr. Daniel O. Dahlstrom, (Cambridge University Press, 1997).

Meredith, Martin. *The State of Africa*, (Simon & Schuster, 2013).

Mill, John Stuart. *On Liberty*, (Penguin, 1987).

Miller, Alice. *The Drama of Being a Child*, tr. Ruth Ward, (Virago Press, 1987).

Miller, James. *The Passion of Michel Foucault*, (Flamingo, 1993).

Miłosz, Czesław, *The Captive Mind*, tr. Jane Zielonko, (Penguin, 2001).

Montaigne, Michel de. *The Complete Works*, tr. Donald M. Frame, (Alfred A. Knopf, 2003).

Morgan, Llewelyn. *The Buddhas of Bamiyan*, (Harvard University Press, 2015).

Murphy, Cullen. *Are We Rome?* (Mariner Books, 2008).

Murray, Douglas. *The Madness of Crowds*, (Bloomsbury, 2019).

Neumann, Erich. *The Origins and History of Consciousness*, tr. R.F.C. Hull, (Princeton University Press, 1970).

Nietzsche, Friedrich. *Beyond Good and Evil*, tr. Walter Kaufmann, (Vintage, 1966).

Nietzsche, Friedrich. *The Birth of Tragedy*, tr. Walter Kaufmann, (Vintage, 1967).

Nietzsche, Friedrich. *The Gay Science*, tr. Walter Kaufmann, (Vintage, 1974).

Nietzsche, Friedrich. *The Genealogy of Morals*, tr. Walter Kaufmann, (Vintage, 1989).

Nietzsche, Friedrich. *The Will to Power*, tr. Walter Kaufmann and R.J. Hollingdale, (Vintage, 1989).

Nietzsche, Friedrich. *Twilight of the Idols*, tr. R.J. Hollingdale, (Penguin, 1986).

Nixey, Catherine. *The Darkening Age*, (Macmillan, 2017).

Nixon, John. *Debriefing the President*, (Corgi, 2017).

North, Douglas C. & Thomas, Robert Paul. *The Rise of the Western World*, (Cambridge University Press, 1973).

Norwich, John Julius. *A Short History of Byzantium*, (Penguin, 2013).

Noyes, James. *The Politics of Iconoclasm*, (I.B. Tauris, 2016).

Olusoga, David. *Black and British*, (Macmillan, 2016).

Orwell, George. *Nineteen Eighty-Four*, (Penguin, 2013).

Otto, Rudolf. *The Idea of the Holy*, tr. John W. Harvey, (Martino Publishing, 2010).

Otto, Walter F. *Dionysus*, tr. Robert B. Palmer, (Indiana University Press, 1965).

Pagden, Anthony. *The Enlightenment*, (Oxford University Press, 2013).

Paglia, Camille. *Sexual Personae: Art and Decadence from Nefertiti to Emily Dickinson*, (Vintage, 1991).

Paine. Thomas. *Rights of Man, Common Sense and Other Political Writings*, (Oxford University Press Classics, 1995).

Paine. Thomas. *The Age of Reason*, (Citadel Press, 1997).

Paloczi-Horvath, George. *Mao Tse-Tung*, (Secker & Warburg, 1962).

Paloczi-Horvath, George. *The Undefeated*, (Eland, 1993).

Pascal, Blaise. *Pensées*, tr. A.J. Krailsheimer, (Penguin, 1995).

Pascoe, Bruce. *Dark Emu*, (Scribe, 2018).

Patterson, Orlando. *Freedom in the Making of Western Culture*, (Basic Books, 1991).

Patterson, Orlando. *Slavery and Social Death*, (Harvard University Press, 2018).

Peterson, Jordan. *12 Rules for Life*, (Allen Lane, 2018).

Peterson, Jordan. *Beyond Order*, (Allen Lane, 2021).

Peterson, Jordan. *Maps of Meaning*, (Routledge, 1999).

Pingh, Geraldine. *Egyptian Mythology*, (Oxford University Press, 2004).

Pinker, Steven. *Enlightenment Now*, (Allen Lane, 2018).

Pinker, Steven. *The Better Angels of Our Nature*, (Penguin, 2011).

Pinker, Steven. *The Blank Slate*, (Penguin, 2003).

Plato. *The Last Days of Socrates*, tr. Christopher Rowe, (Penguin, 2010).

Plato. *The Republic*, tr. R.E. Allen, (Yale University Press, 2006).

Polo, Marco. *The Travels*, tr. Ronald Latham, (Penguin, 1958).

Popper, Karl. *The Open Society and Its Enemies*, (Routledge, 2011).

Puett, Michael and Gross-Loh, Christine. *The Path*, (Viking, 2016).

Rawls, John. *Lectures on the History of Moral Philosophy*, (Harvard University Press, 2000)

Restell, Matthew. *When Montezuma Met Cortés*, (Ecco, 2018).

Rogers, Carl R. *On Becoming a Person*, (Constable, 2004).

Roper, Lyndal. *Witchcraze*, (Yale University Press, 2004).

Rosenblatt, Helena. *The Lost History of Liberalism*, (Princeton University Press, 2018).

Roy, Arundhati. *The Algebra of Infinite Justice*, (Flamingo, 2002).

Rufus, Musonius. *Lectures & Sayings*, tr. Cynthia King, (William B. Irvine, 2011).

Russell, Bertrand. *Power*, (Routledge, 2004).

Sangharakshita. *A Survey of Buddhism*, (Shambala, 1980).

Sanghera, Sathnam. *Empireland*, (Viking, 2021).

Schama, Simon. *Citizens*, (Penguin, 1989).

Schama, Simon. *Rough Crossings*, (Vintage, 2009).

Scheidel, Walter. *The Great Leveler*, (Princeton University Press, 2017).

Bibliography

Scurr, Ruth. *Fatal Purity*, (Vintage, 2007).

Sebag, Simon. *Stalin*, (Weidenfeld & Nicolson, 2003).

Sebestyen, Victor. *Twelve Days: Revolution 1956*, (Phoenix, 2006).

Seneca. *Dialogues and Letters*, tr. C.D.N. Costa, (Penguin, 2005).

Seneca. *Moral Essays Volume I*, tr. John W. Basore, (Loeb Classical Library, 1928).

Sheehan, Bernard W. *Seeds of Extinction*, (University of North Carolina Press, 1973).

Shermer, Michael. *The Believing Brain*, (Robinson, 2011).

Shipman, Harry L. *Humans in Space: 21st Century Frontiers*, (Plenum, 1989).

Siedentrop, Larry. *Inventing the Individual*, (Penguin, 2014).

Snyder, Timothy. *On Tyranny*, (Bodley Head, 2017).

Sowell, Thomas. *Intellectuals and Race*, (Basic Books, 2013).

Sowell, Thomas. *Race and Culture*, (Basic Books, 1994).

Sowell, Thomas. *The Vision of the Anointed*, (Basic Books, 1995).

Spinoza, Benedict de. *On the Improvement of the Understanding. The Ethics. Correspondence*, tr. R.H.M. Elwes, (Dover Publications, 2003).

Stanley, Jason. *How Fascism Works*, (Random House, 2018).

Stearns, Jason K. *Dancing in the Glory of Monsters*, (Public Affairs, 2012).

Sturgis, Matthew. *Oscar*, (Head of Zeus, 2018).

Suetonius. *The Twelve Caesars*, tr. Robert Graves, (Penguin, 2007).

Tacitus. *The Annals of Imperial Rome*, tr. Michael Grant, (Penguin, 1996).

Thomas, Donald. *The Marquis de Sade*, (Allison & Busby, 1992).

Thomas, Hugh. *Conquest*, (Simon & Schuster, 2005).

Tuchman, Barbara W. *The March of Folly*, (Abacus, 1984).

Turchin, Peter. *Ages of Discord*, (Beresta Books, 2016).

Turchin, Peter. *War and Peace and War*, (Plume, 2007).

Vance, J.D. *Hillbilly Elegy*, (William Collins, 2016).

Veblen, Thorstein. *The Theory of the Leisure Class*, (Oxford University Press, 2007).

Venter, Sahm (ed.). *The Prison Letters of Nelson Mandela*, (Liveright, 2018).

Veyne, Paul. *Palmyra*, tr. Teresa Lavender Fagan, (University of Chicago Press, 2017).

Veyne, Paul. *The Roman Empire*, (Belknap, 1997).

Walvin, James. *A Short History of Slavery*, (Penguin, 2007).

Walvin, James. *Resistance, Rebellion & Revolt*, (Robinson, 2019).

Watkins, Sam R. *Company Aytch*, (Turner Publishing Company, 2011).

Weir, Alison. *The Six Wives of Henry VIII*, (Vintage, 2007).

Wells, Ida B. *The Light of Truth*, (Penguin, 2014).

West, Cornel. *Black Prophetic Fire*, (Beacon Press, 2014).

West, Cornel. *Race Matters*, (Beacon Press, 2017).

Westad, Odd Arne. *The Cold War*, (Penguin, 2017).
Wilkerson, Isobel. *Caste*, (Allen Lane, 2020).
Wilkinson, Toby. *The Rise and Fall of Ancient Egypt*, (Bloomsbury, 2010).
Williams, Eric. *Capitalism and Slavery*, (Franklin Classics, 2018).
Wood, Michael. *Conquistadors*, (BBC Books, 2010).
Wood, Michael. *The Story of China*, (Simon & Schuster, 2020).
Woolf, Virginia. *To the Lighthouse*, (Penguin, 2000).
Wrigley, Richard and Craske, Matthew (eds.). *Pantheons: Transformations of a Monumental Idea*, (Routledge, 2004).
Yang, Rae. *Spider Eaters*, (University of California Press, 1997).
Yi, Zheng. *Scarlet Memorial*, tr. T.P. Sym, (Westview Press, 1996).
Ziegler, Philip. *Legacy*, (Yale University Press, 2008).
Žižek, Slavoj. *Robespierre*, (Verso, 2017).
Žižek, Slavoj. *The Sublime Object of Ideology*, (Verso, 2008).
Zuboff, Shoshana. *The Age of Surveillance Capitalism*, (Profile Books, 2019).

INDEX

Abdulkarim, Maamoun 263
Abel 39–40
Aborigines 212–21
Abramovic, Marina 60
Achebe, Chinua 154
Acropolis 36
Adorno, Theodor W. 117
Aegisthus 37
Aelius Herodianus 61–2
Aeschylus 37–8
Afghanistan 48
African National Congress 268–9
Agamemnon, King 37–8
Agrippina 26, 27
Aguirre, Lope de 83–4
Ahmes 15
Ahuitzotl 80
Al-Lat, Temple of 35–6
al-Qaeda 46, 48, 49, 226
Alamán, Lucas 85
Alde, River 23
Alexander VI, Pope 167
Allah 34, 49
Alport, Lord 177
Ambedkar, B. R. 234–46
Amenhotep, Prince 17
American Civil War 127–31, 135–6
Ames, Fisher 192
Amun, Temple of 16, 17
Amun-Ra 14–16
Anacaona, Queen 168
Anastasios 58–9

Anastasios of Sinai 60
Anaximander 18
Anderson, James 189
Anthony, Captain 249
Anthony, Susan B. 248
Anubis 16
Apollo 25, 38, 56
Arasu, Vanni 235, 236
Arculf 57–8
Ardaburius 61–2
Arendt, Hannah 177, 204, 209–10, 231
Ares 36
Arnold, Matthew 7
Artabasdos 58
Arthur, King 1
al-Asaad, Khaled 261–7, 272
al-Asaad, Mohammed 262
al-Asaad, Zenobia 262
Ashoka the Great 239
al-Assad, Bashar 34, 49
Athena 33–42, 44
Auld, Hugh 252
Auld, Lucretia 254
Auld, Sophia 252
Auld, Thomas 250–1, 252–3, 254–5
Aurelian, Emperor 35
AVO 200, 204
Aycock, Charles Bradley 129–30, 131
al-Azm, Amr 263–4
Aztec 77–83, 84–6